D0731463

IMAGE AND PILGRIMAGE IN CHRISTIAN CULTURE

Anthropological Perspectives

VICTOR TURNER AND EDITH TURNER

NEW YORK   COLUMBIA UNIVERSITY PRESS

LIBRARY OF CONGRESS CATALOGING-IN-PUBLICATION DATA

Turner, Victor Witter.
    Image and pilgrimage in Christian culture.

    (Lectures on the history of religions; new ser.,
no. 11)
    Bibliography: p.
    Includes index.
    1. Christian pilgrims and pilgrimages.   I. Turner,
Edith, 1921–   II. Title.   III. Series.
BX2323.T87   248'.29   77-25442
ISBN 0-231-04286-8
ISBN 0-231-04287-6 (pb.)

COLUMBIA UNIVERSITY PRESS   NEW YORK

COPYRIGHT © 1978 COLUMBIA UNIVERSITY PRESS
ALL RIGHTS RESERVED
PRINTED IN THE UNITED STATES OF AMERICA

p 10 9 8 7 6 5 4 3

In memory of Max Gluckman
1910–1975
teacher and friend
who died in Jerusalem

THIS VOLUME is the eleventh to be published in the series of Lectures on the History of Religions for which the American Council of Learned Societies, through its Committee on the History of Religions, assumed responsibility in 1936.

Under the program the Committee from time to time enlists the services of scholars to lecture in colleges, universities, and seminaries on topics in need of expert elucidation. Subsequently, when possible and appropriate, the Committee arranges for the publication of the lectures. Other volumes in the series are Martin P. Nilsson, *Greek Popular Religion* (1940), Henri Frankfort, *Ancient Egyptian Religion* (1948), Wing-tsit Chan, *Religious Trends in Modern China* (1953), Joachim Wach, *The Comparative Study of Religions*, edited by Joseph M. Kitagawa (1958), R. M. Grant, *Gnosticism and Early Christianity* (1959), Robert Lawson Slater, *World Religions and World Community* (1963), Joseph M. Kitagawa, *Religion in Japanese History* (1966), Joseph L. Blau, *Modern Varieties of Judaism* (1966), Morton Smith, *Palestinian Parties and Politics That Shaped the Old Testament* (1971), and Philip H. Ashby, *Modern Trends in Hinduism* (1974). Annmarie Schimmel, *As Through a Veil: Mystical Poetry in Islam* (1982); Peter Brown, *The Body and Society: Men, Women, and Sexual Renunciation in Early Christianity* (1988); and W. H. McLeod, *The Sikhs: History, Religion, and Society* (1989).

Contents

Illustrations

Maps

Preface to the Paperback Edition

Edith Turner

> *Pilgrimage may be thought of as extroverted mysticism, just as mysticism is introverted pilgrimage. The pilgrim physically traverses a mystical way; the mystic sets forth on an interior spiritual pilgrimage.*
>
> (page 33 this volume)

AT THE HEART of pilgrimage is the folk, the ordinary people who choose a "materialist" expression of their religion. In other words, pilgrimage as a religious act is a kinetic ritual, replete with actual objects, "sacra," and is often held to have material results, such as healing.

Victor Turner and I took up the research for *Image and Pilgrimage in Christian Culture* in 1969, which, the reader will remember, was during the hippie era; and it was also around this time that he completed *The Ritual Process* (1969)—a book that became underground reading for the counterculture because of its "antistructural" bent. Pilgrimage is also antistructural and liberating, in much the same way that the mysteries within the liminal period of rites of passage are.

The Weltgeist of *Image and Pilgrimage* was indeed that of the common folk, and it is clearly anticlerical. Pilgrimage is not an intellectual activity but rather a religious one. Many middle-class people also undertake it, not because they are doing something "in" or touristy, but because they too have felt the call to do so. Although *Image and Pilgrimage* is an intellectual book and the result of deep thought—certainly not a book for the public at large nor for any of those remaining in the counterculture—it is very much on the defensive for the people's religion. The heart of the book lies in the translation of the story of Juan Diego, "the little Indian" visionary who saw the lady of Guadalupe, as recounted in the chapter "Mexican Pilgrimages: Myth and History." Here is a Victor Turner–type hero, an anxious little man who is deceitful and, at heart, innocent. All these "mortal men," in Victor Turner's writings and treasured in my own memory, appear in the book in their ordinary humanness: Bernadette, somewhat sharp; the nasty controversialists of the iconoclasm era; Melanie and Maximin, the horrid children who saw the lady of Salette, starting a big pilgrimage, again on the word of people who were no better than they ought to be. These paradoxes of inexplicable incoming power and the research that shows the Toynbee-esque embeddedness of the events in their times together compose a slice of reality, the dimensions of which go off the edge of our limited graph paper.

Image and Pilgrimage is antistructural. It jives perhaps with the artists of our present time and with those anthropologists who read their peoples' cultures as one reads poetry. A great deal of history appears in the book, but it is included to satisfy the appetite for "chapter and verse," that is, the facts. The book does not argue a theory of history—it feels out the threads of cultural borrowings and shows, for instance, how a transplanted religion takes on vitality in Mexico and then flowers into many visionary occasions, accompanied by the welcoming and multitudinous response of the Indian people. The people are the heroes, not the thinkers laboring to set it all on paper. Victor Turner and I were originally left-wing radicals, yet what we learned was to show not how exploited and helpless "the people" always were, but how their weakness made it possible for them to be open to clues that other ways of answering political questions always closed off. This may not have been the right sort of Marxism. It was anticlerical, antistructural, of the party of Bakhtin, "agin the heiheedjuns," as Victor Turner the Scotsman called the "high head ones." This is an underground form of Marxism that

xiv

looks fondly at the religious foibles of the people. Now, when anthropology has spent some time being scared into superintellectualism and is just showing signs of wanting to come out of it, is the occasion when the ordinary people and what they say about their deepest impulses might at last be honored and trusted.

In the original preface Victor Turner explains the advantages of advocacy, and deals gracefully with an anthropological problem that besets us today. He is probing the difficulty of the Catholic affiliation of the two researchers, the two of us.

How could we approach the data without partisanship? . . . We also hold that in studies of human culture and behavior the tension between motivation and scientific objectivity can sometimes prove fruitful. When the deeper levels of the self, deeply tinctured by culture, are reflexively engaged, the knowledge brought back from the encounter between self as subject and self as object may be just as valid as knowledge acquired by "neutral" observation of others. (p. xv)

Each of the chapters may now be seen in a different light, and in this new preface I lay out what these additional perspectives are. In the introduction liminality appears not as transition, but as potentiality, "what may be." The pilgrim is on an adventure, a quest. Her enlightenment is in the lap of the gods. She is not bound to make the passage to membership in some religious community. Optation—individualism—reigns. What draws her is perhaps some message from the holy spheres, not the dictates of biology and the community, as with puberty initiation. She embarks on an adventure, drawn by a kind of magic, the call of the saint. It is like a spiritual work of archeology, delving in the ancient past for the renewal of the original experience, where that which is timeless folds back upon itself. The search for *illud tempus* is not a search for a fusty, dead past, or nostalgia: in pilgrimage it is the journey to the actual place containing the actual objects of the past, whose very stones seem to emit the never-obliterated power of the first event—a certain shadowy aura. Pilgrims almost invariably *touch* the sacred object and then touch themselves. This is the "archeology of experience"—to paraphrase Turner's concept of the anthropology of experience (the anthropology of actual effectiveness and of the body).

Turner and I listed four different types of pilgrimage: the prototypical, those established by the founder or great saint of a religion;
the archaic, deriving from an earlier devotion and with syncretic features; the medieval, from A.D. 500–1400, set in a broad era of theolo-
gizing, and with all the faults and virtues of the vigorous and venal
popular world of the time; and the relatively modern, appearing to
be concerned with the abuses of industrialization and strongly female in character.

About modern Mexican pilgrimages (chapter 2), the question of
the connection between an apparition and the colonization and later
independence of Mexico has become even more interesting since the
book was first written. The Catholic Church, even after forty years,
has remained obdurately political, always translating the reports of
visionaries into its own idiom: "he saw the Holy Virgin Mary, the
Mother of God"—this was not the Aztec goddess Tonanzin sending
commands to Archbishop Zumarraga. This persistent line tempts
one to infer that "apparitions" are a trick of the colonizers' "hegemony" (a word rarely used when *Image and Pilgrimage* was written).
But curious universal threads connect apparitions: conversations
with spiritual entities, walking images, the importance of animals or
plants. A true Native American interpretation might look quite different from that of the Church.

In Mexico there are an astonishing number of substitution shrines,
that is, pilgrimage shrines that are located on ancient Native American sites. A new argument might run that the Mexican natives'
sense of the presence of their gods was extraordinarily accurate, so
much so that it was imperative to continue to make use of the place
as a center of worship, even if the newcomers denied the previous
gods. This is rather a different viewpoint from that of "baptizing the
customs"—the Christians' paternalistic phrase for syncretism. It has
only recently become possible for anthropologists to attempt different and non-ethnocentric evaluations.

St. Patrick's Purgatory in Ireland (chapter 3), listed as an archaic
pilgrimage, now seems revealed as a place for the testing of a truly
strong pilgrim, of strong nerve, almost of machismo. One goes today, as in the sixth century, to seek an experience of awesome hor-
ror which transmutes to total bliss—a sensational flip-flop effect.

xvi

Maybe the methanelike gases found in the original cave on Saint's Island affected those who stayed overnight in this strange place. Spirituality can be learned from hallucinogens, as we have seen in anthropology. Blockages getting in the way of experience are sometimes broken by hallucinogens and usually do not need a repeat. Only in the hands of greedy people are hallucinogens addictive and dangerous. The pilgrims then could see what was real, as Eliade used to call it: hell and, afterward, heaven. The focus of the pilgrimage has long since been changed to another island, Station Island, and it is now asceticism that has the seesawing effect on the pilgrim—also with that extraordinary gain in spirituality. These added views of St. Patrick's Purgatory need mentioning, because time has passed and the anthropology of ritual has shifted a good deal.

Chapter 4, on iconophily and iconoclasm, also needs comment. "Iconoclasm" looks at first glance to be a matter of the furious destruction of "graven images"—Moses' assault on the golden calf, for instance, done in the name of the true God, against idolaters. This is the deepest essence of moralism and exclusivism. How does this look in the light of a luminous passage by Victor Turner in the conclusion of *Image and Pilgrimage*? He is referring to the creation of sacred objects in animist religions followed by their ritual destruction:

The guiding notion here seems to be that the cosmos can be seen and ritually represented as plural and complex it is also very simple and deep, nondualistic perhaps, and always exceeds any representation of it. Its secret powers are, moreover, invisible. By destroying the elaborate signifiers made to represent the plural nature of things, one indicates "there is that of which we cannot speak," a pure nonduality. (p. 235)

The "exclusive God" meaning fades from this interpretation. We see and welcome this point. Even we ourselves, as anthropologists, do not have to adopt the Archbishop Latimer kind of iconoclasm referred to in this chapter, deconstructing all images to nothing or to some venal explanation. We can look forward to the unsayable, not back to just dirt. Times have changed.

In this chapter the problem of the iconicity—that is, the ever-present imaging—of the Virgin Mary is faced. Her iconicity is largely

no longer "exclusive—God"

of manipulation of religions of figures

Mary and women enslaved

what divides the Christian Church into Protestants and Catholics. She has been made over by clerics as the image of the woman who is obedient to the male, and so this image has rightly been repudiated by the women's movement. Yet when we look at her pilgrimages we see her as "a personification of the Church in its nonlegalistic aspect, a collective mother in the order of freedom . . . [and of] global communitas" (p. 171). If she is "captured" and enslaved by the Church, her global communitas aspect goes out the window. Until this is seen by the Church, feminists will continue to repudiate her false image and we will continue to experience political iconoclasm—or deconstructionism. A later chapter illustrates the tremendous success of Mary as the most sought-after pilgrimage goal in all Christendom, including God.

In the chapter on medieval pilgrimages a great scene is revealed—of fervent and numerous pilgrimages all over Europe with an accompanying development of communications and cosmopolitan experience for many classes. These varied classes (numerically, mostly peasant) met at pilgrimage centers and sometimes hatched out a peasant's revolt, as at Canterbury in England in 1381. Communitas was strong, as was the idea of the Virgin and saints as protectors of the poor and unfortunate. At the threat of revolt, structures of state and church began to be enforced, such as passports and the institution of penitential pilgrimage as a punishment for criminals. Alongside these misuses of religious power grew the Church-promoted indulgences system, commoditizing the whole universe of the "symbolic object." Communitas still endured, somehow part and parcel of the place of pilgrimage itself, but during the Reformation and Enlightenment pilgrimages fell into decay, with the shrines often razed to the ground. Then in the nineteenth century (along with the Romantic movement) these selfsame sites began to revive, and apparitions of the Virgin in new places, often in sensationally beautiful, wild spots such as Lourdes, began again. I have often asked myself whether the lady of Lourdes was a very important nature spirit, whose message has not yet been understood. For the original adolescent-girl-to-adolescent-girl communion of the vision speaks something relevant to us that is hard to put into words.

Thus in medieval pilgrimage, as Victor Turner puts it,

xviii

communitas persists through religious and theological change. . . . While one religion prevails, social and cultural structures seem immutable. But structures, and the symbols which manifest them, do break up and crumble. What often persists is communitas, no longer normative or ideological, but waiting to be given new form by a new religion. (p. 202)

Finally, regarding the chapter on modern Marian pilgrimage, I now find myself interested in tracing how the revival of the Catholic pilgrimage system paralleled the revivalist movements in Protestantism—only concretized, spatialized, and materialized in the form of the always difficult journey to an impelling center, literally "out there." In the Victorian era and up to the present, both systems urged the world to convert and to reform its evil ways. Pilgrimage became a type of revivalism, full of emotion. However as time went on a large new body of the public, the intelligentsia, developed—scientists, avant-garde artists, the political left—and to them pilgrimage represented the acme of ignorance corresponding to superstitious fakirs on beds of nails. This section of the public began to pour scorn—with the intention of bringing the light of truth—on the candle-lighting and peregrinating Catholics and on the born-agains. The research for *Image and Pilgrimage* took place right in the middle of that era. In these circles it was almost embarrassing to say one had gone to Lourdes unless one was doing research. To understand something of how a saint like Thérèse de Lisieux became totally certain of the closeness of God to her, one would need a religious sense. It so happened that Victor Turner and I had been converted prior to our research. At the present time the phenomenon of apodicticity, the religious sense of absolute certainty, is being brought forward in the work of Charles Laughlin as worthy of interest to anthropologists. He, like others who have experienced the nonordinary in their fieldwork, argues that the full impact of religious material cannot be understood by an anthropologist without some kind of plunge into the experience of it.

One more comment from the mid-nineties on Marian pilgrimage—the obvious one concerning feminism. The map on page 5 shows eighteen shrines to Mary, four to other saints, and none to Christ or the cross. The numbers visiting Marian shrines are astronomical.

xix

PREFACE TO THE PAPERBACK EDITION

What is going to be the future of Marian pilgrimage? The masses are still thrilled by her recent apparitions at Medjugorje in Yugoslavia. Has feminist disapproval of Mary's motherhood and of the Church's insistence on her "obedience" had no effect? Or maybe the female-ness of the most revered figure in Christendom is imperceptibly merging into the gender consciousness of Catholic women. (Possibly half of these in the United States would like to see female priests. Countless nuns feel the same.) If Jesus was both human and divine, was not Mary also? How could she have been somehow lesser than that? Theological hairsplitting is no longer likely to be heeded. Nevertheless it should be stated that old-guard Catholics are still the ones who seem to receive a call to go on pilgrimage and revere the Virgin in the traditional way. Their reverence shows their own kind of unshakable feminism, which is not the kind we usually see. More research is certainly needed. One more thing: the loathing with which a great number of feminists view men, and their perhaps unconscious longings for a baby born without the necessity of a male, are curiously consonant with the idea of the Virgin birth. But these extremes never touch.

Where are pilgrimage studies at the moment? In 1992 Alan Morinis published *Sacred Journeys*, originally inspired by *Image and Pilgrimage*. His book includes sociological analyses of many world pilgrimage systems, and there is a number of other sociologically oriented books. In addition a flood of works has appeared in the field of religion. A new sympathetic cultural study, *Pilgrimages in Popular Culture* (Walter, ed., 1993), includes pioneering works on such pilgrimage centers as Elvis Presley's Graceland—studies that make a refreshing change from the purely religious examples. Modern pilgrimages can include the New Age pilgrimages to Glastonbury and to Stonehenge at dawn on Midsummer day. Political pilgrimages abound: the Dallas Book Repository, the Washington shrines and monuments. Civil War reenactments have become a kind of pilgrimage draw, as was the celebration of the fiftieth anniversary of D-Day in Normandy.

Anthropology now has better tools for studying all contemporary pilgrimages. It looks deeply into the ritualization of the body and the emotions and experiences that this ritualization gives. Pilgrimage is a lengthy, laborious bodily act, involving some idea of a connection with a long-dead spiritual figure at the end of it. The oxymoron "the body of the spirit" is what the pilgrims are looking for: palpable experience, the "where-she-actually-appeared" sense. The deeper anthropology of this kind of quest has not yet been done, and I am greatly looking forward to the attempt.

REFERENCES

Morinis, Alan, ed. 1992. *Sacred Journeys.* New York: Greenwood.
Walter, J. A., ed. 1993. *Pilgrimage in Popular Culture.* Houndsmills, Basing-stoke, U.K.: Macmillan.

Preface

THIS BOOK began as a set of six lectures, "The Pilgrimage Process," sponsored by the American Council of Learned Societies, Committee on the History of Religion, in the series entitled "The American Lectures in the History of Religion." Though the lectures were delivered by Victor Turner, they were the product of joint authorship by Victor and Edith Turner at every stage, from field and library research to completed manuscript.

The book differs from the lectures in the emphasis it lays on cul ture rather than behavior. The lectures focused on social structures and processes associated with pilgrimages; the book examines in more detail the theological doctrines and popular notions which promote and sustain Christian pilgrimage, and the symbols and images which embody them. Not that we consider the ideas, norms, values, symbols, and other constructs, which constitute the "coherent system of symbols and meanings" (Schneider 1968:8) of Catholic pilgrimage, to be fully independent of pilgrim behavior. Rather do we regard such "cultural units" (to use Schneider's term) as "expressed in" (see Hanson 1975:102) actual pilgrim behavior. Thus we find that the doctrine of the Assumption of the Blessed Virgin Mary, for example, is intrinsically involved with several con- crete aspects of Marian pilgrimage, from the origin of many Marian pilgrimages in "apparitions" of the Virgin, perceived in her bodily form, to the mass movement of pilgrims seeking cures at the shrines commemorating such appearances. Thus, too, the verbal and physical clashes between iconophiles and iconoclasts are behavioral expressions of doctrinal difference, iconophiles affirming, iconoclasts denying the need for a visible embodiment of religious values. In other words, we find that behavior is informed by culture at every point. Discrepant norms are just as much a part of culture as consistently arrayed subsystems of norms. But we have tried, in this volume, to uncover the institutional structures and "implicational meanings" (Hanson 1975:10) of pilgrimage behavior, rather than to analyze (as Victor Turner has done in most of his earlier publications) the relations and processes in a single circumscribed social field. The "extended-case method" has been temporarily set aside, the "social drama" abandoned, in order to expound the interrelations of symbols and meanings framing and motivating pilgrim behavior in a major world religion. This seemed to us to be a necessary prelude to more detailed studies, by anthropologists and historians, of concrete behavior related to specific shrines.

On the other hand, no attempt has here been made to write a comprehensive history of Christian pilgrimage. That task is better left to professional historians. Our intent has been to ask what Hanson calls "institutional questions," rather than "individual questions," about the pilgrimage data. As Hanson argues (pp. 3–7), these two types should not be arranged in "levels" or "layers" (the Comtian position). It is a matter of perspective that determines the kind of questions one asks. "Individual questions" inquire into "the nature of the drives, reasons, intentions, needs that people manifest in their behavior." If we had examined pilgrimages from this perspective, we would have become heavily involved with medical and psychological anthropology, with the structures of guilt, anxiety, and stress which impelled pilgrims to undertake penitential pilgrimages, and with examining the evidence of reputedly miraculous cures at major pilgrim centers. Or we might have tried to isolate social psychological factors to account for changes in the popularity of a given pilgrimage under varying historical circumstances. "Institutional questions" inquire into "the structure of the values, norms, symbols, customs, roles, relationships" manifested in the same behavior about which it is legitimate to ask individual questions. We chose to follow this procedure, since inquiry into a relatively unresearched realm of data requires some preliminary "mapping," and institutional questions elicit the objective coordinates of cultural fields better than individual ones. We are also in agreement with Hanson's argument that institutional analyses "are not abstracted from individual analyses and hence are not reducible to them"; the two perspectives are "not arranged one above the other but side by side." Yet, in our view, it is convenient to regard the institutional analysis as a set of framing devices within which individual questions may be asked. This book is, in effect, an attempt to map and frame some of the institutional "territories" within which pilgrimage processes circulate, and to suggest how institutional changes within pilgrimage may be linked to changes outside it. We hope that other scholars will ask individual questions, and that psychologists, historians, and psychological anthropologists, each from his own perspective, will find in pilgrimage a realm worthy of their skills.

Our original intention was to compare the pilgrimage systems of several major historical religions, but it soon became apparent that the study of Christian pilgrimage alone is an awesome task, made all the more awesome by our own Catholic affiliation. How could we approach the data without partisanship? Our hope is that our anthropological "pilgrimages" to, and sojourn among, African societies have given us a vantage point from which to view our personally cherished values with some objectivity. The reader will be the best judge of our success or failure in this. We also hold that in studies of human culture and behavior the tension between motivation and scientific objectivity can sometimes prove fruitful. When the deeper levels of the self, deeply tinctured by culture, are reflexively engaged, the knowledge brought back from the encounter between self as subject and self as object may be just as valid as knowledge acquired by "neutral" observation of others.

Our thanks are due to many individuals and institutions whose aid made this intellectual pilgrimage possible. Fr. Jorge Serrano-Moreno, S. J. (whose research with us was supported by a grant from the Wenner-Gren Foundation), was our guide and interpreter on many Mexican pilgrim journeys, while L. Plascensia, of the University of Chicago Graduate School of Anthropology, gave us invaluable help in uncovering and appraising a voluminous literature on Marian pilgrimage in Mexico. In Ireland we were indebted for aid and advice to the Most Reverend Dr. Joseph Cunnane, archbishop of Tuam; Fr. Michael Walsh, principal of St. Jarlath's College, Tuam; and especially to Mrs. Coyne, who has contributed, with her late husband William Coyne, so much to the development and spiritual life of the Knock pilgrimage. Our two visits to Mexico and two visits to Ireland were made possible by grants from the Lichstern Fund of the Department of Anthropology, and from the Division of Social Sciences—of the University of Chicago. The recasting of the lectures into book form was completed at the Institute for Advanced Study, Princeton. We are most grateful to all these sources of assistance.

Many colleagues have discussed this book or parts of it with us. Particular mention is due to David Grene (who with his wife Ethel offered us hospitality on his Irish farm, as well as rich intellectual stimulation in Chicago), Roger Abrahams, Barbara Babcock, Dario Zadra, John MacAloon, Luther Harshbarger, James Redfield, Greg Stanton, Patricia Pessar, Anne Betteridge, and Barbara Myerhoff, and members of the Comparative Symbology seminar at the University of Chicago. Saul Bellow, then chairman of the Committee on Social Thought, provided encouragement and support throughout the long haul from lecture tour to completed manuscript. During that tour, the Departments of Anthropology, Religion, History, English, Folklore, and Latin American Studies at Stanford University, Columbia University, the University of Texas at Austin, Pennsylvania State University, Swarthmore College, Yale University, Wesleyan University, the University of Connecticut, the University of Southern California, the University of California at San Diego, and Rice University all lavished hospitality (far greater than the pilgrim's traditional crust of bread and cup of water!) on the lecturer.

Finally, we thank Robina Armour and Christine Kondracyk, of the University of Chicago, and Amy Jackson, Jamesina Edwards, and Rebecca Szurovy, of the Institute for Advanced Study at Princeton, for splendid secretarial help and meticulous typing.

Victor Turner
Center for Advanced Study and
Department of Anthropology
University of Virginia, Charlottesville

Edith Turner
Charlottesville

If I did not somewhat fear the reproach of exaggeration, I would say that in the twentieth century ethnography will be the foundation on which a new philosophical conception of humanity will be built.

—Arnold van Gennep

CHAPTER ONE [※

Introduction:
Pilgrimage as a Liminoid Phenomenon

pilqrams = tribal, rural

PILGRIMAGES are probably of ancient origin and can, indeed, be found among peoples classed by some anthropologists as "tribal," peoples such as the Huichol, the Lunda, and the Shona. But pilgrimage as an institutional form does not attain real prominence until the emergence of the major historical religions—Hinduism, Buddhism, Judaism, Christianity, and Islam. In view of its importance in the actual functioning of these religions, both quantitatively and qualitatively, pilgrimage has been surprisingly neglected by historians and social scientists. But perhaps it has merely shared in the general disregard of the liminal[1] and marginal phenomena of social process and cultural dynamics by those intent either upon the description and classification of orderly institutionalized "facts" or upon the establishment of the "historicity" of prestigious, unrepeated events.

[1] We refer here and throughout this work to a number of concepts formulated in earlier books and articles on ritual and its symbolism. Readers not familiar with the earlier work are referred to Appendix A for a summary.

1

INTRODUCTION

It was Arnold van Gennep (1908; 1960), the French folklorist and ethnographer neglected by the pundits, savants, and mandarins of the French school of sociology in his own time, who gave us the first clues about how ancient and tribal societies conceptualized and symbolized the transitions men have to make between well-defined states and statuses, if they are to grow up to accommodate themselves to unprecedented, even antithetical conditions. He showed us that all *rites de passage* (rites of transition) are marked by three phases: separation, limen or margin, and aggregation. The first phase comprises symbolic behavior signifying the detachment of the individual or group, either from an earlier fixed point in the social structure or from a relatively stable set of cultural conditions (a cultural "state"); during the intervening liminal phase, the state of the ritual subject (the "passenger" or "liminar") becomes ambiguous, he passes through a realm or dimension that has few or none of the attributes of the past or coming state, he is betwixt and between all familiar lines of classification; in the third phase the passage is consummated, and the subject returns to classified secular or mundane social life. The ritual subject, individual or corporate (groups, age-sets, and social categories can also undergo transition), is again in a stable state, has rights and obligations of a clearly defined structural type, and is expected to behave in accordance with the customary norms and ethical standards appropriate to his new settled state.

By identifying liminality Van Gennep discovered a major innovative, transformative dimension of the social. He paved the way for future studies of all processes of spatiotemporal social or individual change. For liminality cannot be confined to the processual form of the traditional rites of passage in which he first identified it. Nor can it be dismissed as an undesirable (and certainly uncomfortable) movement of variable duration between successive conservatively secure states of being, cognition, or status-role incumbency. Liminality is now seen to apply to all phases of decisive cultural change, in which previous orderings of thought and behavior are subject to revision and criticism, when hitherto unprecedented modes of ordering relations between ideas and people become possible and desirable. Van Gennep made his discovery in relatively conservative societies, but its implications are truly revolutionary. In the liminality of tribal societies, traditional authority nips radical deviation in the bud. We find there symbolic inversion of social roles, the mirror-imaging of normative secular paradigms; we do not find open-endedness, the possibility that the freedom of thought inherent in the very principle of liminality could lead to major reformulation of the social structure and the paradigms which program it. But in the limina throughout actual history, when sharp divisions begin to appear between the root paradigms which have guided social action over long tracts of time and the antiparadigmatic behavior of multitudes responding to totally new pressures and incentives, we tend to find the prolific generation of new experimental models—utopias, new philosophical systems, scientific hypotheses, political programs, art forms, and the like—among which reality-testing will result in the cultural "natural selection" of those best fitted to make intelligible, and give form to, the new contents of social relations.

It has become clear to us that liminality is not only *transition* but also *potentiality*, not only "going to be" but also "what may be," a formulable domain in which all that is not manifest in the normal day-to-day operation of social structures (whether on account of social repression or because it is rendered cognitively "invisible" by prestigious paradigmatic denial) can be studied objectively, despite the often bizarre and metaphorical character of its contents. In *The Ritual Process* (V. Turner 1969), certain modes of liminality in preindustrial society were examined, and further studies in more developed cultures were suggested. The present book is an attempt to examine in some detail what we consider to be one characteristic type of liminality in cultures ideologically dominated by the "historical," or "salvation," religions.

When we first began to look for ritual analogues between "archaic," or "tribal," and "historical" religious liminality, beginning with the Catholic Christian tradition which we know best, we turned, naturally enough, to the ceremonies of the Roman rite. But in the liturgical ceremonies of the Mass, baptism, female purification, confirmation, nuptials, ordination, extreme unction, and funerary rituals, though it was possible to discern somewhat truncated

3

liminal phases, we found nothing that replicated the scale and complexity of liminality in the major initiation rituals of the tribal societies with which we were familiar. One obvious difference was seen in the spatial location of liminality. In many tribal societies, initiands are secluded in a sacralized enclosure, or *temenos*, clearly set apart from the villages, markets, pastures, and gardens of everyday usage and trafficking (see Junod 1962: vol. 1, pp. 74–94; Wilson 1957:86–129; Richards 1957; Turner 1968:210–39; Barth 1975:47–102). But in the "historical" religions, comparable seclusion has been exemplified only in the total life-style of the specialized religious orders. In other words, the progressive division of labor made of the liminal phase a specialized state, complex and intense enough to involve the entire lives of the deeply devoted. Of course, as the history of monasticism has shown, the orders become decreasingly liminal as they enter into manifold relations with the environing economic and political milieus. That, however, is matter for a different book. But the religious, though relatively numerous in the heyday of the historical religions, were easily outnumbered by the ordinary worshipers, the peasants and the citizens. Where was their liminality? Or was there indeed any liminality for them at all?

In European societies with a rurally based economy and feudal political structures, life for the masses tended to be intimately localized. Indeed, for Christian serfs and villeins the law itself ordained their attachment to particular manors or demesnes. Their religious life was also locally fixated; the parish was their spiritual manor. Yet during its development, Christianity generated its own mode of liminality for the laity. This mode was best represented by the pilgrimage to a sacred site or holy shrine located at some distance away from the pilgrim's place of residence and daily labor. Beginning with the pilgrimage to remote Jerusalem (*Palestine Pilgrims' Text Society*, 1887; 1889; 1891a,b,c; 1893)—made by a few choice, pious, and relatively well-to-do persons—to which was swiftly joined the pilgrimage to the shrines of Peter and Paul in Rome (Jusserand 1891:374–78; Sigal 1974:99–110), the map of Europe, particularly after the Saracenic occupation of the Holy Land and domination of the Mediterranean sea routes thither, came to be crisscrossed with pilgrim ways and trails to the shrines of European

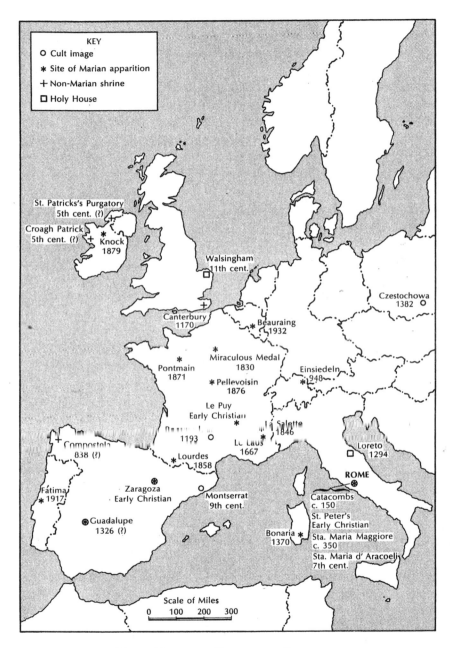

KEY
○ Cult image
✳ Site of Marian apparition
✛ Non-Marian shrine
□ Holy House

St. Patricks's Purgatory
5th cent. (?)
Croagh Patrick
5th cent. (?)
Knock
1879

Walsingham
11th cent.

Czestochowa
1382 ○

Canterbury
1170

Beauraing
1932

Miraculous Medal
1830

Pontmain
1871

Pellevoisin
1876

Einsiedeln
948

Le Puy
Early Christian

La Salette
1846

1193 ○

Le Laus
1667

Loreto
1294

Compostola
838 (?)

Lourdes
1858

ROME

Fátima
1917

Zaragoza
Early Christian

Montserrat
9th cent.

Catacombs
c. 150

St. Peter's
Early Christian

Guadalupe
1326 (?)

Bonaria
1370

Sta. Maria Maggiore
c. 350

Sta. Maria d' Aracoeli
7th cent.

Scale of Miles
0   100   200   300

MAJOR EUROPEAN PILGRIMAGE SHRINES

5

saints and advocations of the Holy Virgin (varieties of mode of address, such as Our Lady of Walsingham) and to churches containing important relics of Christ's ministry and passion (Turner 1974a:224–26). Such pilgrim centers and ways, frequented increasingly by the poor, can be regarded as a complex surrogate for the journey to the source and heartland of the faith.

The pilgrim trails cut across the boundaries of provinces, realms, and even empires (Jusserand 1891:362–71, 393–95). In each nascent nation certain shrines became preeminent centers of legitimate devotion. But since the church laid claim to universality, pilgrims were encouraged to take up staff and scrip to travel to the great shrines in other Christian lands. In time this international religious tourist traffic became organized. (Venice became the model for later secular tourism, as well as for modern agencies of pilgrim travel.)[2] Many Englishmen made the pilgrimage to St. James the Apostle's shrine in Spain, while French and Dutch pilgrims swarmed across the Channel to visit St. Thomas's tomb at Canterbury. Within each country one can detect a loose hierarchy, or at least a rough scale of priorities, among its shrines. In plural societies, each linguistic or ethnic group has its favored pilgrimage places. Provinces, districts, even the shrines themselves, have their focal devotions. All sites of pilgrimage have this in common: they are believed to be places where miracles once happened, still happen, and may happen again. Even where the time of miraculous healings is reluctantly conceded to be past, believers firmly hold that faith is strengthened and salvation better secured by personal exposure to the beneficent unseen presence of the Blessed Virgin or the local saint, mediated through a cherished image or painting. Miracles or the revivification of faith are everywhere regarded as rewards for undertaking long, not infrequently perilous, journeys and for having temporarily given up not only the cares but also the rewards of ordinary life. Behind such journeys in Christendom lies the paradigm of the *via crucis*, with the added purgatorial element appropriate to fallen men. While monastic contemplatives and mystics could daily make

[2] For a first-rate account of the late fifteenth-century Venetian pilgrimage "trade," readers should consult M. Margaret Newett's Introduction to her book *Canon Pietro Casola's Pilgrimage to Jerusalem; in the Year 1494* (1907:1–113).

interior salvific journeys, those in the world had to exteriorize theirs in the infrequent adventure of pilgrimage. For the majority, pilgrimage was the great liminal experience of the religious life. If mysticism is an interior pilgrimage, pilgrimage is exteriorized mysticism.

The point of it all is to get out, go forth, to a far holy place approved by all. In societies with few economic opportunities for movement away from limited circles of friends, neighbors, and local authorities, all rooted alike in the soil, the only journey possible for those not merchants, peddlers, minstrels, jugglers, tumblers, wandering friars, or outlaws, or their modern equivalents, is a holy journey, a pilgrimage or a crusade. On such a journey one gets away from the reiterated "occasions of sin" which make up so much of the human experience of social structure. If one is tied by blood or edict to a given set of people in daily intercourse over the whole gamut of human activities—domestic, economic, jural, ritual, recreational, affinal, neighborly—small grievances over trivial issues tend to accumulate through the years, until they become major disputes over property, office, or prestige which factionalize the group. One piles up a store of nagging guilts, not all of which can be relieved in the parish confessional, especially when the priest himself may be party to some of the conflicts. When such a load can no longer be borne, it is time to take the road as a pilgrim.

For many pilgrims the journey itself is something of a penance. Not only may the way be long, it is also hazardous, beset by robbers, thieves, and confidence men aplenty (as many pilgrim records attest), as well as by natural dangers and epidemics. But these fresh and unpredictable troubles represent, at the same time, a release from the ingrown ills of home. They are not one's own fault, though they may be sent by the Almighty to try one's moral mettle. (There are, of course, legends that very bad sinners will have extra trouble on their pilgrimage. One cycle of stories, for example, recounts the mishaps on the penitential pilgrimage to Jerusalem by the four knights who martyred St. Thomas Becket. Finally, so the tale runs, persistent offshore gales prevented them from setting foot on the Holy Land, and they had to return, as it were, unforgiven.)

Although the pilgrim may take the path because he has made a promise to a saint whose intercession he once sought on his own or a beloved's behalf, nevertheless it is he who decides on the day and hour of his going. This freedom of choice in itself negates the obligatoriness of a life embedded in social structure. In many tribal societies, on the other hand, rituals such as initiation, which contain extended liminal phases, tend to be obligatory. Nearly everyone has to pass through certain main-stem rites. There is some room for choice, certainly, but it is usually confined to such questions as the precise timing and placement of corporate performance rather than to whether an individual is willing to undergo the ritual at all. Often, too, it is left to complex divinatory procedures to determine when and where rites should take place; thus the scope of individual choice is further narrowed. Of course, some religious pilgrimages, like the hajj in Islam, are defined as a duty incumbent on all believers. But in such cases there are so many qualifying clauses and extenuating circumstances that the individual is placed once more in a situation of virtual choice.

Yet there is undoubtedly an initiatory quality in pilgrimage. A pilgrim is an initiand, entering into a new, deeper level of existence than he has known in his accustomed milieu. Homologous with the ordeals of tribal initiation are the trials, tribulations, and even temptations of the pilgrim's way. And at the end the pilgrim, like the novice, is exposed to powerful religious sacra (shrines, images, liturgies, curative waters, ritual circumambulations of holy objects, and so on), the beneficial effect of which depends upon the zeal and pertinacity of his quest. Tribal sacra are secret; Christian sacra are exposed to the view of pilgrims and ordinary believers alike. Again, the mystery of choice resides in the individual, not in the group. What is secret in the Christian pilgrimage, then, is the inward movement of the heart. In tribal rituals, on the other hand, what is concealed from the profane—the sacred objects and teachings—is the possession of an elite group within the community, whether this be, for example, an inner core of initiated men or a nuclear group of mothers and potential mothers. In the pilgrimages of the historical religions the moral unit is the individual, and his goal is salvation or release from the sins and evils of the structural world, in preparation for participation in an afterlife of pure bliss. In tribal

8

initiation the moral unit is the social group or category, and the goal is the attainment of a new sociocultural status and state. While the pilgrim seeks temporary release from the structures that normally bind him, the tribal initiand seeks a deeper commitment to the structural life of his local community, ultimately, in many cases, to the state of being a venerated, legitimate ancestor after death, rather than a homeless ghost. Of course, historically the distinction has not always been so clearcut. Pilgrims sometimes enhance their mundane status through having made the journey. And in tribal religions certain kinds of initiation, notably the shamanic and the priestly, frequently offer a measure of release from the duties and necessities of the structural order, and a measure of participation in the invisible milieu of the gods or ancestors. Robert F. Gray (1963:14) has described how the Khambageu cult among the Sonjo of Tanzania promises salvation for believers who have undergone a specific initiation rite. Jacques Maquet (1954:183–84) mentions a similar cult in Ruanda. We must also face the fact of an opposite tendency in the historical religions, where the community of believers has often acquired something of a tribal character, on a world scale, and where religious wars are, as it were, magnified tribal feuds. While politics and economics become increasingly international and noncorporate as markets, merchants, and cities multiply, salvation religions, though universal in principle, raise corporate walls against outsiders in practice. This exclusiveness is reflected in the pilgrimage systems. With rare and interesting exceptions, the pilgrims of the different historical religions do not visit one another's shrines, and certainly do not find salvation *extra ecclesia*. Pilgrimage, then, offers liberation from profane social structures that are symbiotic with a specific religious system, but they do this only in order to intensify the pilgrim's attachment to his own religion, often in fanatical opposition to other religions. That is why some pilgrimages have become crusades and jihads. Nevertheless, within the institution of pilgrimages, human freedom made a historic advance. Inside the Christian religious frame, pilgrimage may be said to represent the quintessence of voluntary liminality. In this, again, they follow the paradigm of the *via crucis*, in which Jesus Christ voluntarily submitted his will to the will of

9

Pilgramage provides freedom for from society

FREEDOM / Release

God and chose martyrdom rather than mastery over man, death *for* the other, not death *of* the other.

Toward the end of a pilgrimage, the pilgrim's new-found freedom from mundane or profane structures is increasingly circumscribed by symbolic structures: religious buildings, pictorial images, statuary, and sacralized features of the topography, often described and defined in sacred tales and legend. Underlying the sensorily perceptible symbol-vehicles are structures of thought and feeling—ideological forms—which may be truly described as "root paradigms" (see Appendix A for a discussion of this term). These derive from the seminal words and works of the religion's founder, his disciples or companions, and their immediate followers, and constitute the "deposit of faith." Quite often they owe their systematic formulation to the collective deliberations of later dogmatists and theologians, who aimed at giving an institutional shape to the spontaneous insights and inspired actions of the founder. The root paradigms draw upon crises in the founder's life—especially those of his birth, coming of age, and death—to clothe abstract patterns of relationships in vivid forms accessible, through the sympathy of common experience, to all believers. Thus we see images, icons, and paintings of Jesus as infant, child, young preacher, scourged victim, crucified scapegoat, and resurrected God-man. Each of these representations is set, however sketchily in some cases, in the context of images derived from the sacred narrative of the founder's life. In this way, something is shown of his relations with his parents and kinsfolk, with his disciples, with strangers, with his accusers and enemies, with the anonymous people he healed or instructed, and even with supernatural beings, such as the other Persons of the Trinity, angels, and devils. Between founder and setting (those features of the natural and cultural landscape regarded as pertinent to the paradigm being expressed), there exist sets of relationships which together compose a message about the central values of the religious system. The pilgrim, as he is increasingly hemmed in by such sacred symbols, may not consciously grasp more than a fraction of the message, but through the reiteration of its symbolic expressions, and sometimes through their very vividness, he becomes increasingly capable of entering in imagination

The trip/voyage alters the eyes of the pilgrim. He finds new meaning

and with sympathy into the culturally defined experiences of the
founder and of those persons depicted as standing in some close
relationship to him, whether it be of love or hate, loyalty or awe.
The trials of the long route will normally have made the pilgrim
quite vulnerable to such impressions. Religious images strike him,
in these novel circumstances, as perhaps they have never done before, even though he may have seen very similar objects in his
parish church almost every day of his life. The innocence of the eye
is the whole point here, the "cleansing of the doors of perception."
Pilgrims have often written of the "transformative" effect on them
of approaching the final altar or the holy grotto at the end of the
way. Purified from structural sins, they receive the pure imprint of
a paradigmatic structure. This paradigm will give a measure of coherence, direction, and meaning to their action, in proportion to
their identification with the symbolic representation of the
founder's experiences. For them the founder becomes a savior, one
who saves them from themselves, "themselves" both as socially
defined and as personally experienced. The pilgrim "puts on Christ
Jesus" as a paradigmatic mask, or persona, and thus for a while
becomes the redemptive tradition, no longer a biopsychical unit
with a specific history—as in tribal initiations, where the individual
who dons the ceremonial mask becomes for a while the god or
power signified by the mask and the costume linked to it. But since
Christ signifies "the individual" (he represents uniqueness for everyone), a fundamental difference between corporate and singular
initiatory traditions is still discernible.

"mask" connection b/w Tribe and pilgram

But pilgrimages are not merely optational equivalents of obligatory tribal initiations. They also have affinities with what have been
called "rituals of affliction" (see V. Turner 1957:292; 1968:15–16, 22).
In many tribal societies the world over, rituals are performed to
propitiate or exorcize supernatural beings or forces believed to be
the cause of illness, ill luck, or death. Not infrequently, the curative
process is conducted by an association of religious specialists or
"doctors." These doctors are often recruited from former patients,
for it is believed that to personal experience with illness or misfortune, a state liminal both to life and to death, they owe their contact
with, and knowledge of, the invisible entities that shape human

tribal ritual to get rid of something

11

life. Those afflicted are thought to be afflicted for definite reasons. Sometimes, as in many African societies, the agents of affliction are ancestral shades, who punish their living kin either for moral misdemeanors or for breach of ritual prescriptions or prohibitions. But, consonant with the corporate character of morality, it may not be the actual culprit who is afflicted, but another member of his family, lineage, or clan, someone with whom the culprit shares bodily substance or "blood." Since breach of morality is almost identical with breach of social norms, and since the patient is bound by such norms in a complex web of social relationships, the target of ancestral affliction is as much the patient's kin group or residential unit as the patient himself. He may even be said to furnish the pretext or occasion for a revaluation of all its current relationships. In another sense, though, the therapeutic ritual is a rite of passage which transforms the patient into an adept ready to learn the mysteries of the healing cult.

Pilgrimage is both like and unlike affliction ritual. It is similar in that in the feudal and semifeudal societies in which it seems most to flourish there is widespread belief that illness and mischance are punishments for moral transgressions in thought, word, or deed. The agents of punishment are not thought to be ancestral spirits or lesser deities or demons, however, but God himself—though he may be thought to act indirectly, as in the classic affliction of Job, by giving the devil permission to test out a person's spiritual mettle with affliction. Again, since the historical religions stress individual salvation rather than corporate harmony as their supreme goal, the treatment of affliction does not generally proceed within the localized corporate structure of a cult group and a kin group who play important roles in the ritual. The individual person is now the ethical unit, though the misfortune of others may still be thought to be caused by one's own moral failings. For example, we have seen in Mexico, and have read about in the English literature, parents who take the penitential journey to a saint's shrine on the occasion of their child's illness. But it is generally the victim's innocence, rather than the group's turpitude, that is emphasized here. Essentially the individual is regarded as responsible for his acts and thoughts. His will is at the heart of the matter. Thus in many re·

spects a pilgrimage is the converse of a ritual of affliction. An individual pilgrimage often originates in a vow by a supplicant to God or the saints to undertake the arduous pilgrim's way if he or his dear ones are freed from present affliction. Or the afflicted person may choose to travel or be conveyed to a pilgrimage center, there to hope for a miraculous cure, or the equal miracle of the gift of resignation to his painful lot. It may well be that he travels in fellowship with others, either in an organized party or in a Chaucerian company met with by happenstance. Pilgrims have found that there is some safety in numbers, that it decreases their vulnerability to human predators. But the groupings so formed are "associational" rather than "primary" (though nuclear family groups often do travel together); that is, they are based on contract, friendship, voluntary association, and even casual acquaintance, rather than on ties of ascribed status. Again, pilgrims go out to be cured, while tribal patients draw kin and curers to themselves: pilgrims abandon the tight structures of kinship and locality, and voyage far to their font of healing; tribal sufferers remain within the arenas that are believed to provide the conditions of their affliction, while unrelated doctors come in from outside the village to cure them. At the pilgrimage's end—at Guadalupe, Lourdes, and Knock, for example—the pilgrim may find himself a member of a vast throng. But this is a throng of similars, not of structurally interdependent persons. It is only through the power ascribed by all to ritual, particularly to the Eucharistic ritual (which in part commemorates the pilgrim saint), that likeness of lot and intention is converted into commonness of feeling, into "communitas." All religious rituals have a strong affectual aspect, whether this be muted or displaced or given full liturgical expression. Symbols, which originate in elevated feeling as well as cognitive insight, become recharged in ritual contexts with emotions elicited from the assembled congregants. At major pilgrim centers, the quality and degree of the emotional impact of the devotions (which are often continuously performed, night and day), derive from the union of the separate but similar emotional dispositions of the pilgrims converging from all parts of a huge sociogeographical catchment area (see V. Turner 1974a:178–79, 209). It is not merely the troubles of an individual village or villager that induce

13

grouping of pilgrims & their woes makes atmosphere much more powerful

this affectual atmosphere. It is the confluence of innumerable individual woes and hopes: manifold woes engendered by the most various of circumstances; incalculable hopes that the religion's paradigms and symbols will restore order and meaning to a sad and senseless state of personal and interpersonal affairs—and from these hopes derives the pilgrim's proverbial happiness.

There is yet another profound difference between pilgrimage and tribal affliction ritual. The therapeutic action in a ritual of affliction has a systematic and quasi-pragmatic character: the action is normally expected to render the patient whole and healthy, unless he is the victim of the invincible malice of a living person, that is, of witchcraft. A pilgrim, on the other hand, is not supposed to *expect* any corporeal remedy. If a miraculous healing does occur, it is attributed to the grace of God, often through the seemingly capricious mediation of the pilgrimage saint. If magic is, as Sir James Frazer held, "a primitive kind of science," then tribal therapeutic rituals, despite their involvement with "spiritual beings" in the Tylorian sense, must clearly be regarded as "magical," on account of their systematic and causative character, given the cultural context-dependent principles governing therapeutic practice; while pilgrimages must be seen as essentially antimagical, since they are thought to depend upon the exercise of free will on both the human and the superhuman side of the encounter. Of course, in most pilgrimages, magical beliefs do in fact abound: beliefs in the supernatural efficacy of the water from sacred springs, in the contagious beneficent power of relics and images, and in the nonempirical curative virtue of certain formulae—"white magic," as it were. But even in these cases much weight is attached to the moral, as well as the ritual, condition of the subject. The water will not work a cure, nor the litany a benefit, unless the subject's "heart" is penitent, absolved, and therefore cured—all the result of a virtuous inclination of his will.

Thus the curative, charismatic aspect of pilgrimage is not thought of as an end in itself. In the paradigmatic Christian pilgrimage, the initiatory quality of the process is given priority, though it is initiation to, not through, a threshold. Initiation is conceived of as leading not to status elevation (though in practice it may often have that

1° diff. about "Expectation" of being cured

Supernatural

14

effect) but to a deeper level of religious participation. A pilgrim is one who divests himself of the mundane concomitants of religion—which become entangled with its practice in the local situation—to confront, in a special "far" milieu, the basic elements and structures of his faith in their unshielded, virgin radiance. It is true that the pilgrim returns to his former mundane existence, but it is commonly believed that he has made a spiritual step forward. Again in antithesis with the status climbing implicit in both tribal initiation and affliction ritual, the Christian pilgrim experiences no rise in status. His moral standing in the community may be increased, but often at the expense of his economic standing—no great loss in a culture which defines material gain as spiritual retrogression. To become more the Christian, one must be less the successful citizen. (This was at least the formula until the onset of the Protestant ethic, which holds that worldly success may result from the practice of such virtues as thrift, industry, punctuality, temperance, and just dealing—virtues manifesting to the world and to the actor himself that he has been elected by God for salvation.) The fact that the pilgrim's initiation was hidden and symbolic, further safeguarded the role of pilgrimage as something that did not merely subserve the functional requirements of mundane society but was its metaphorical opposite. This was the case in Christendom, at any rate. (In Islam, the pilgrimage to Mecca became, in many instances, a functional component of localized sociopolitical systems. The hajji sometimes attained superior status, or at least standing, after his return.) In medieval Christian countries, the returned pilgrim, though perhaps outwardly acclaimed for his deepened piety, may have actually set back his chances of preferment to positions of higher office or trust, through his long absence. If some form of initiation is involved here, it is a secret, invisible one, not an enhancement of status. Yet there has undoubtedly accrued to the pilgrim a heightened respect and moral standing among the pious in the local community, as well as a raising of his own morale. These rewards tend to fall within the orbit of communitas rather than social structure, and make the pilgrim a *primus inter pares*, not a person of higher rank.

The branch of Christianity which has traditionally been most committed to the pilgrimage process—that is, the Roman Catholic Church—has also conceived of the struggle for salvation as a life-long drama played out essentially in the individual soul but involving a huge cast of actors, some visible, some invisible, some natural, some supernatural: God; Mary, Mother of God; the angels; the saints; and the three divisions of the living Church, the Church Triumphant of the invisible souls in heaven; the Church Suffering of the invisible souls in purgatory; and the Church Militant of living mortals beleaguered in the world by flesh and the devil, and by human adversaries. The individual soul is seen as dramatically involved, until the moment of death, with all these persons, personages, and corporate groups. It has free will to turn to God or away from him. God in turn plies the soul with graces (either directly or through sacramental ritual), which are thought of as gifts aiding in salvation or in resistance to temptation. These may be freely accepted or rejected. The doctrine of the communion of saints presupposes that souls may help one another, by praying to God on each other's behalf. Members of the Church Triumphant, being themselves saints in heaven, are the most effective intercessors; but anyone may pray for anyone. One motive for going on pilgrimage is the feeling that a saint's shrine has a sort of "hot line" to the Almighty. One purifies oneself by penance and travel, then has one's prayer amplified by asking a saint at his own chief shrine to forward it directly to God. This theory is characteristic of the peculiar union of individualism and corporateness that made up the medieval Christian Church; ordinary mortals can augment the efficacy of their prayer by passing their request, preferably on behalf of someone else, upward through a mediator or chain of mediators of increasing sanctity, to the source of all creative power. The converse of this is that God became incarnate, moving down from the invisible spiritual realm to visible mortality as Jesus Christ. The paradigms of the imitation of Christ, and mystical union with Christ, are available for making saints out of "middling good" Christians; that is, they serve as extensions of the salvific, incarnative process, in the continuing life of the Church, the mystical body of Christ.

Pilgrimage is very much involved in this perennial, universal drama, cutting across cultures, societies, polities, language groups, and ethnicities. In the uncertainty regarding that drama's climax, pilgrimage itself is regarded as a "good work," in the theological sense of observance of the Church's precepts and counsels (especially the counsels to pray, to fast, and to give alms, all prominent features of pilgrimage). No one good work will ensure ultimate salvation; but in the popular view it ensures many occasions of grace as rewards for a good work done freely out of a desire for salvation and for the benefit of others.

In most tribal societies, save for those which are in the hinterlands of literate Great Traditions and have absorbed ideas from them (see Redfield 1956:69–72), initiatory and affliction rituals cannot be traced to any demonstrable historical foundation. Instead, there may be myths recounting the origin of a given ritual *in illo tempore*, the timeless, undatable time of cultural beginnings, when gods, demigods, and semidivine heroes walked the earth and initiated the central cultural institutions (Eliade 1971:4,21). In contrast, most pilgrimage systems have beginnings traceable in historical time. One must qualify this statement, of course, by underlining the fact that many of the pilgrimages of the historical world religions—like the hajj of Islam and the Guadalupe pilgrimage in Catholic Mexico—were established on the sites of pilgrimages belonging to earlier religions which, though more than tribal in theological scope and territorial range, did not yet possess the strain toward universality of their historical supplanters. At any rate, in the world religions with which we are now concerned, the beginnings of most pilgrimages can fairly confidently be ascribed to a particular historical period, and even, in many instances, to a precise date. Our contention is that the epoch of genesis is of crucial significance in determining the lines along which a specific pilgrimage has developed—that is, the nature of its processual structure.

CLASSIFICATION OF PILGRIMAGES

In a broad system of classification, we have identified four main types of pilgrimages, the first two of which occur in all the historical religions: (1) Those pilgrimages which, on the authority of documentary or widespread traditional evidence, were established by the founder of a historical religion, by his first disciples, or by important national evangelists of his faith, may be termed *prototypical* pilgrimages. Such pilgrimages, though sometimes founded on ancient pilgrimage sites, dramatically manifest—in their symbolism, charter narratives, ecclesiastical structure, and general form of international repute—the orthodoxy of the faith from which they have sprung, and remain consistent with its root paradigms. Prototypical pilgrimages (such as those to Jerusalem and Rome for Christianity, Mecca for Islam, Benares and Mount Kailas for Hinduism, and Kandy for Buddhism) must be distinguished from (2) pilgrimages which bear quite evident traces of syncretism with older religious beliefs and symbols. Among such pilgrimages we would place Glastonbury in England's Somerset, with its continuing Celtic pagan overtones; Croagh Patrick in the west of Ireland; Chalma in Mexico, with its evident Ocuiltecan and Aztec embellishments; and Pandharpur in the Deccan of India, whose equivocal deity Vithoba Bhave may well have Dravidian, pre-Indoeuropean associations. We call these ambiguous and syncretic pilgrimages *archaic* pilgrimages.

Within the Christian tradition, it is possible to distinguish two further types: (3) Many of the pilgrimages best known in the popular and literary traditions of the Christian world originated in the European Middle Ages and take their tone from the theological and philosophical emphases of that epoch; we need only instance here Canterbury and Walsingham in England, Compostela in Spain, Chartres in France, Loreto and Assisi in Italy, Einsiedeln in Switzerland, Cologne and Altötting in Germany, and Częstochowa in Poland. Pilgrimages originating, roughly, in the period A.D. 500–1400 we call *medieval* pilgrimages. (4) Finally, attention must be paid to a genus of pilgrimage which has grown steadily in the post-Tridentine period of European Catholicism, particularly in the nineteenth and early twentieth centuries. Such pilgrimages are characterized by a highly devotional tone and the fervent personal piety of their adherents, and they form an important part of the system of apologetics deployed against the advancing secularization of the post-Darwinian world. All surviving pilgrimage systems are heavily in debt to modern modes of communication and transportation, but

18

the late post-Tridentine pilgrimages have, almost from the beginning, been deeply involved with mass technological and scientific culture, both positively, in drawing upon it as a source of instrumental aids, and negatively, in seeing it as a challenge to the Christian, and indeed to the entire religious world view. This category we term *modern* pilgrimage. But we must emphasize that by "modern" we here denote postmedieval. In tone, these pilgrimages are actually antimodern, since they usually begin with an apparition, or vision, and they assert that miracles do happen.

A pilgrimage's historical origin, then, determines its design and modulates its later development. Nevertheless, whatever their origin, pilgrimages have never been immune from the influences exerted by subsequent periods, with their modes of thought and politics, patterns of trade, military developments, and the ecological changes brought about by these and other forces. Thus, we must consider, in identifying types, the relationships between a given historically derived pilgrimage paradigm and the influences to which history has subjected it. At this point the sociologist of religion must also have his say. There are certain crucial moments, key points, when the data themselves insist that we arrest our time machine, to examine the synchronic connections between economic, political, legal, religious, social, and ecological factors, and analyze them in terms of sociological theories. Inevitably, we do not have all the data required by modern standards of sociological research, but we can at least produce plausible approximations which may incite thought and encourage deeper research. We propose, therefore, to select examples from these four broad categories of pilgrimages, to regard them as roughly paradigmatic of their genre, and to treat them both historically and anthropologically.

We have chosen for intensive consideration pilgrimages in Mexico, England, Ireland, and France which either achieved historical preeminence or enjoy contemporary esteem—or, better still, satisfy both criteria. These pilgrimages exemplify the latter three of the four types discussed above. St. Patrick's Purgatory in Lough Derg, and Croagh Patrick, both in Ireland, are pilgrimages of the archaic sort; Walsingham in England is a medieval pilgrimage; and the pilgrimage to the shrine of Our Lady of Lourdes in the south of

France, visited by millions annually, is a fine instance of a modern, "apparitional" pilgrimage system. We will also refer on occasion to the immensely popular Irish pilgrimage to the shrine of Our Lady of Knock, in County Mayo, another modern, "apparitional" system. We have visited these places, observed the behavior of pilgrims there, and collected local and national archival documentation on them. Canterbury, which we also visited, has ceased since Henry VIII's time to be a pilgrimage center in the formal sense, but the streams of English visitors and foreign tourists (and many of them are "closet" pilgrims) who visit Canterbury Cathedral mainly to gaze on the reputed spot of St. Thomas à Becket's martyrdom, attest to the hardihood of the pilgrim spirit. As we hinted earlier, a tourist is half a pilgrim, if a pilgrim is half a tourist. Even when people bury themselves in anonymous crowds on beaches, they are seeking an almost sacred, often symbolic, mode of communitas, generally unavailable to them in the structured life of the office, the shop floor, or the mine. Even when intellectuals, Thoreau-like, seek the wilderness in personal solitude, they are seeking the material multiplicity of nature, a life source. Perhaps, like Walsingham and Glastonbury, the archiepiscopal see of Canterbury, center of the Anglican ecclesiastical structure, will experience a revival of its traditional pilgrimage, with processions, candles, and religious services devoted to the martyred cleric. No doubt there would have to be major changes in the relations between church and state, and between the Anglican and Roman confessions, before tourists could shed their current guise and present themselves as pilgrims; but the fact that both Roman Catholics and Anglo-Catholics have reinstated Walsingham and Glastonbury as pilgrim centers (and even timidly participate in joint processions on occasions at Walsingham) may be a straw in the ecumenical wind.

In addition to the British examples cited here, mention will be made of medieval pilgrimages on the continent of Europe, preceding or coeval with our British examples. Similarities and differences of history and structure can thus be the better revealed.

ANTHROPOLOGICAL APPROACHES TO THE STUDY OF PILGRIMAGE

Our field research on pilgrimages in Mexico has produced useful comparative material. In Latin America we have the spectacle of a Christianity introduced by missionaries from a Church already under attack, in its European base, by Luther and his Protestant successors. Such missionaries often seem to have regarded the New World as a *tabula rasa* on which to inscribe the pure forms of the faith. Yet their own local traditions, from the provinces of Spain and Portugal, combined with indigenous Amerindian customs and beliefs to generate a fascinating set of new syncretic variations on metropolitan Catholicism. Among the variations were the pilgrimage systems. These exhibited both continuity with the pre-Columbian past (notably in the communitas of the assembled pilgrims) and discontinuity (in their theological and cosmological paradigms). The potent indigenous tincture of many Latin-American pilgrimages relates them to European archaic pilgrimages, though examples of both medieval and modern pilgrimages may also be found in the Iberian New World. Here we should mention that when pilgrimages of all types coexist in the same religious field (in this case Catholic Christendom), each type influences all the others, so that a single pilgrimage system comes to absorb "prototypical," "archaic," "medieval," and "modern" features, with variable dominance at different points in time. Examples of this process will be given in subsequent chapters. Nevertheless, throughout its development, each pilgrimage continues to maintain a subsystem of beliefs and symbols derived from its historical origin; this subsystem within the wider system of all subsequent paradigmatic accretions can be described as the "nuclear paradigm" and exerts selective pressure on all subsequent borrowings. Glastonbury offers a case in point. From its early medieval beginnings, this pilgrimage has always had a broad penumbra of Celtic pagan and other pre-Christian associations, some of them figuring as important parts of the Arthurian and Grail legends. Even today, these associations continue to resonate—for example, in the countercultural pilgrimages which link the ruins of Glastonbury with adjacent prehistoric sites

21

and regard the whole complex as a cosmological schema laid out either by the lost Atlanteans or by extraterrestrial "Saucerians," to whom are also attributed the megalithic structures of Stonehenge and Avebury. Some will doubt the propriety of extending the notion of a pilgrimage system to embrace the entire complex of behavior focused on the sacred shrine. But we insist, as anthropologists, that we must regard the pilgrimage system, whenever the data permit us so to do, as comprising all the interactions and transactions, formal or informal, institutionalized or improvised, sacred or profane, orthodox or eccentric, which owe their existence to the pilgrimage itself. We are dealing with something analogous to an organism-environment field: here the "organism" comprises all the sacred aspects of the pilgrimage, its religious goals, personnel, relationships, rituals, values and value-orientations, rules and customs; while the "environment" is the network of mundane "servicing mechanisms"—markets, hospices, hospitals, military supports, legal devices (such as passports), sys ems of communication and transportation, and so on—as well as antagonistic agencies, such as official or unofficial representatives of hostile faiths, bandits, thieves, confidence men, and even backsliders within the pilgrim ranks.

A fully mature pilgrimage system, or "field," is comparable to a series of overlapping, interpenetrating ellipses whose common area of overlap has the shrine at its center. Each of these ellipses constitutes a pilgrimage route, or "way," with its own sociogeographical surrounds. Indeed, even when pilgrims return by the way they came, the total journey may still be represented, not unfittingly, by an ellipse, if psychological factors are taken into account. For the return road is, psychologically, different from the approach road. When the pilgrim advances toward his ultimate sacred goal, he tends to stop at every major way station, there to do penance, pay his devotion, and prepare for the holy climax at the central shrine. When he returns, so travelers' accounts repeatedly inform us, his aim is to reach home as swiftly as he can, and his attitude is now that of a tourist rather than a devotee. He has sloughed off his structural sins; now he can relax and enjoy himself, while looking forward to a warm and admiring welcome at home. The road is thus two roads; the apt metaphor is an ellipse, not a straight line.

Near the central shrine the ingoing routes become evermore beset with way stations (lesser shrines, chapels, holy wells, and the like), and the pilgrims' progress becomes correspondingly slower as they advance. These sacred valves and resistances are designed to build up a considerable load of reverent feeling, so that the final ingress to the holiest shrine of all will be for each pilgrim a momentous matter. In the older centers the inmost shrine is immediately surrounded by a complex of sacred places and objects, which must often be visited in a fixed order, in some cases after the climactic visit to the central shrine. It is the task of the anthropologist to discriminate the structure of this sacred complex, and to relate its labyrinthine ways to the progress of the pilgrim toward his devotional goal.

Pilgrimages, as we have noted, have several time dimensions, too. It is therefore necessary to delineate the diachronic profile of each pilgrimage, and to relate its consecutive phases to the larger histories by which it is encompassed. Every pilgrimage has a local and a regional history; responds more or less sensitively to a national history; and, especially in the case of the most important pilgrimages, is shaped and colored by international, even world history. We shall find echoes of world events in several of our British pilgrimages for example.

Like all sustained mass movements, pilgrimages tend to accrete rich superstructures of legend, myth, folklore, and literature. Legend may be defined as the corpus of written accounts of the marvels and miracles connected with the genesis and development of a pilgrimage system; myth, as the systematic oral tradition concerning these events; and folklore, as the assemblage of unsystematized (and often locally idiosyncratic) tales and yarns about happenings of an unusual sort along the pilgrimage way and about its saints. Finally, most of the greater pilgrimages have become seedbeds of the literature of "high culture." Everyone knows of the writings of Chaucer, Tennyson, T.S. Eliot, and Jean Anouilh, to cite but a few, having direct relevance to the origin and institu-

23

tionalization of the Canterbury pilgrimage. Similarly, the development of the Arthurian legend has seldom wandered far from its legendary homeland of Avalon, the cradle of the Glastonbury pilgrimage. Shane Leslie (1932) has listed a long line of literary references to St. Patrick's Purgatory—a line which includes Marie de France, Roger of Wendover, and Matthew Paris—and has further claimed (perhaps not altogether convincingly) that both Dante and Shakespeare, among the very great, were aware of St. Patrick's Purgatory. To these authors must be added the Spanish dramatist Calderón de la Barca, who wrote a play entitled *Purgatorio de San Patricio;* and the poet Ariosto in Italy. The French chronicler Froissart mentioned the grim island cave, while even the English printer Caxton noted it, however skeptically. Walsingham is less well endowed with literary tributes; yet its legend is enshrined in a fifteenth-century ballad printed by Richard Pynson; frequent mention is made of the pilgrimage in the Paston Letters (see below, chapter 5); and the brutal destruction of the shrine in the reign of Henry VIII is lamented in an elegy by Philip Howard, earl of Arundel. Few books have been written on Knock; however, a popular literature of tracts, plays, and verse—pioneered by four volumes on the shrine's history and personalities, by William J. Coyne (1935, 1948, 1953, 1957), founder of the influential Knock Shrine Society, and once a militant Irish rebel against England—has flowed in a steady stream for several decades. Since 1938, the *Knock Shrine Annual,* a record of important events at the shrine, sermons preached there, and articles by leading Catholic writers on the meaning of the pilgrimage, has appeared regularly. Our experience has shown that most major pilgrimage centers have become foci and sources of popular devotional literature, a copious source of data for the cultural anthropologist interested in myth and ritual. Often we have good historical records as well of events relating to the shrines. Light may be shed on the mythopoeic process by our comparing these records with the legends, myths, and literary compositions—products of both "folk" and "high" cultures, often transformations of one another—which have evolved in successive historical epochs. Legends and myths to account for a pilgrimage sometimes arise quite late in its history. Discrepancies among these accounts sometimes reveal the social tensions and cultural anomalies in changing pilgrimage fields. For most pilgrimages, tales of miracles abound, comparative analysis of which illuminates regional and national differences in culture, as well as changes in the temper of the times. Legends cluster round a pilgrimage's ending, too, as in the cases of Canterbury and Walsingham, which terminated in a burst of political and theological polemics. One advantage of studying a long-term sociocultural process such as pilgrimage is that one's attention is directed toward the dynamics of ideological change and persistence, rather than committed to analysis of static ideological patterns and cognitive structures.

While it may be useful to apply to pilgrimage systems the concept of organism-environment fields in space-time, it must not be forgotten that each pilgrimage has its own entelechy, its own immanent force controlling and directing development. A phased process can usually be traced, where the data is adequate. A pilgrimage's foundation is typically marked by visions, miracles, or martyrdoms. The first pilgrims tend to arrive haphazardly, individually, and intermittently, though in great numbers, "voting with their feet"; their devotion is fresh and spontaneous. Later, there is progressive routinization and institutionalization of the sacred journey. Pilgrims now tend to come in organized groups, in sodalities, confraternities, and parish associations, on specified feast days, or in accordance with a carefully planned calendar. Marketing facilities spring up close to the shrine and along the way. Secularized fiestas and fairs thrive near these. A whole elaborate system of licenses, permits, and ordinances, governing mercantile transactions, pilgrims' lodgings, and the conduct of fairs, develops as the number of pilgrims grows and their needs and wants proliferate. In the sacred domain, special prayers, novenas, litanies, rosaries, and other modes of devotion to the pilgrimage saint, Jesus, or Mary, multiply. The pilgrims' Mass itself is often the climax of an escalating series of devotions held at ancillary way stations and subordinate intrabasilican shrines. To cater for the fired-up pilgrim's spiritual needs, the merchants of holy wares set up booths in the market, where they sell devotional statuettes and pictures, rosaries, missals, sacred tracts, and a variety of other sacramental objects and edify-

25

ing literature. In major population centers today some travel agencies have as their sole function the organization of pilgrimage itineraries and the chartering of aircraft, boats, omnibuses, and trains to convey pilgrims to distant destinations. Even in the medieval period, as the narratives of Fra Felix Fabri and Canon Pietro Casola bear witness, it was customary for pilgrims to travel in organized parties on shipboard and in caravans. The Church absorbed pilgrimages into its system of salvation, and absolved grave sinners if only they would visit a distant holy shrine. Kings and great lords developed the taste for pilgrimage, and rode the pilgrims' way with great entourages. The arterial pilgrim routes became conduits of cultural transmission. Some scholars have held that the great roads extending from Germany and the Low Countries through France to Santiago de Compostela in Northern Spain did more to spread knowledge and appreciation of the Romanesque style of architecture than any other mode of communication.

It is our intent to trace these developments from vision to routinization, from antistructure through counterstructure to structure, in their several discernible dimensions (compare V. Turner 1974a:275–94). It is clear, for example, that the style of social interconnectedness changes as pilgrimage systems become more elaborate. Numbers bring diversification of functions, and the coordination of diverse functions brings bureaucracy and centralized control. Faith is often manipulated for political and economic ends. Nevertheless, it can also be shown that even amidst the materialism of declining pilgrimage systems—of the kind that Erasmus condemned at Canterbury and Walsingham (it is worth noting that he thereby helped prepare the way for Henry VIII's suppression of these and many other centers)—something of the original ardor and communitas persists, a thin trickle of popular devotion. Moreover, pilgrimages have been known to revive after a period of decline. It is rare indeed for a long-established pilgrimage to die out completely, unless it has fallen victim to sustained and merciless deracination. The histories of many pilgrimage systems provide evidence for this. The shrine of St. Anne de Beaupré in Canada (Leclerc 1907:539–40), for example, was the focus of a pilgrimage that made slow progress from its origins in the late seventeenth

26

century until 1875, when it developed astonishingly in keeping with the late post-Tridentine trend mentioned above. Another case is the pilgrimage to the shrine of Our Lady of Bonaria, in Cagliari, the capital and chief seaport of the island of Sardinia. This pilgrimage, which throve in the High Middle Ages, declined during the seventeenth and eighteenth centuries, but has recently revived quite significantly (Gillett 1952:205–11). Even extinguished pilgrimages may revive; there are evident signs that Walsingham and Canterbury, for instance, are about to flourish once more (Stephenson 1970:247; Henderson 1967).

Another dimension of change is in the nature and style of the symbolic forms prevailing in each period: ecclesiastical architecture, sculpture, paintings, abstract ornamentation, stained glass, and music, as well as the folk symbolism of dress, gesture, object, site, song, and dance, often associated with pre-Christian beliefs and practices. Pilgrimages are like cultural magnets, attracting symbols of many kinds, both verbal and nonverbal, multivocal and univocal. One of our aims here is to explore the changing symbolic systems associated with pilgrimage systems, and to examine their influence upon pilgrims individually and collectively. Here the study of personal documents such as the journals, diaries, and published narratives of pilgrims can be illuminating, if they are read in connection with the theological, pastoral, and liturgical literature of the period. Because the British data are very uneven, we have drawn on the rich resources of Irish, Continental European, and New World Catholic pilgrimage data to illustrate our argument. At some points we have utilized data from the pilgrimage systems of other historical religions, for there are striking similarities in pilgrimage processes and structures in all the world religions. As pilgrimages attract greater numbers and fall increasingly under ecclesiastical sway, ceremonial symbols multiply and are elaborated. The stream of social communitas, choked by the symbols arrayed in the ceremonial structures of the church, becomes, in some cases, a mere trickle of mobile "antistructure." Pilgrimages that develop to this point experience their major crisis, since critics are not slow to point out the disparity between their original and latter-day conditions. If such critics become iconoclastic, for whatever reason, and

27

develop. fear of. iconoclasm

manage to enlist adequate political support, the result will be destruction of the symbolic complex and of the pilgrimage in its present shape. If the critics aim at reform rather than destruction, however, there may ensue both a social reorganization of the wardenship of the shrine and a purification of its system of worship, veneration, and devotion. Muhammad's reform of the pre-Islamic pilgrimage to Mecca is a non-Christian case in point. We shall discuss Christian instances in some detail later. Any religious system which commits itself to the large-scale employment of nonverbal symbolic vehicles for conveying its message to the masses runs the risk that these vehicles will become endowed by believers with magical efficacy. And if these signifiers represent persons, they may become objects of idolatry, rather than of veneration. Indeed, much catechizing and homiletic is directed against the popular tendency to take symbols literally rather than metaphorically. Taken literally, symbols cease to mediate between the orders of being they are intended to conjoin. Symbol-vehicles which are viewed materialistically, in terms of self-serving interests, become increasingly opaque. Where they should be lenses bringing into focus the doctrines of the faith, they become blinders hindering the understanding. They themselves are felt to possess the powers to which they only point, and which are not man's to bestow. For their worshipers they become instruments by which to obtain material goals: they cease to be aids to salvation *from* the material order. Paradoxically, iconoclasts seem themselves to share a belief in the literal efficacy of symbol-vehicles, for why else would they rage so violently to destroy these visible objects? It is the reformers within a church who wish to retain iconicity while condemning iconolatry, though they are not averse to using the pruning hook whenever the growth of symbols has become overluxuriant. But, being intellectuals, their use of the pruning hook sometimes lays low symbol-vehicles which have become important objects of popular devotion, even of thoroughly orthodox devotion. In the eyes of the simple faithful, such intellectual reformers may seem no better than iconoclasts. Some thinkers have argued that the process of selection should be left to the popular judgment, to the collective taste, which bestows its favor now on one symbol-vehicle, now on another. This would be a cultural selection akin to natural selection. Many a pilgrimage center is littered with the images and icons of abandoned saints, while in a favored side-chapel or niche of the shrine candles blaze before the statue of some newly popular beatus. It is hard, however, to decide *a priori* in individual cases whether the multiplication of symbol-vehicles is by arbitrary ecclesiastical fiat or in response to popular demand. Patently both processes make their contribution: permission from a superior in the hierarchy must be granted before a popular new symbol-vehicle may be installed; while an enthusiastic bishop or priest may insist on establishing a devotion which exemplifies the latest theological ideas. This is why it is necessary to undertake, on a comparative basis, a series of intensive studies of various pilgrimage systems in order to determine, in each case, which process is paramount at a given phase of development. The answers may well prove to be important. One mark of a pilgrimage's decline may be an increase in externally imposed ceremonial symbols, while a major symptom of normal growth may be the proliferation of devotional symbols donated by ordinary pilgrims. Our observations of pilgrimage centers in Mexico and Britain suggest that this is indeed the case. Here those who are concerned with church renewal should proceed carefully, for their pruning may hack away the very roots of religious devotion, rather than the dead wood they are intending to destroy.

SOCIAL AND CULTURAL CONTEXTS

Finally, we shall consider the relationship between the entelechy of a specific pilgrimage and the major sociocultural changes in the environment. For the development of a pilgrimage may be accelerated or retarded by the intellectual and political climate. Just on the point of flourishing, for example, a pilgrimage may be denounced and destroyed by representatives of church or state, or even by revolutionary groups who see it as an organ of church or state. Pilgrimage systems are peculiarly vulnerable in that they do not have their own means to defend themselves by force. But they have one immense advantage: unless a pilgrimage center is systematically discredited and destroyed, the believing masses will continue to make

Pilgramage and cultural/political climate.

their way to the shrine. Mexico provides many examples of the per-severance of pilgrims in the teeth of antireligious governmental pressures. Some call this inertia, others faith, but the fact remains that on the great feast days pilgrimage centers have never been so crowded as today. Thus, a popular pilgrimage, supported by a range of homeostatic institutions, both formal and customary, may long resist the countervailing tendencies of an unpropitious environment. Something in the human condition, particularly as it is exemplified in the poor, responds to the root paradigms which nest within one another in any great pilgrimage. Regardless of the progress of the division of labor, the nature and degree of social stratification, the division between urban and rural milieus, and the distribution of wealth and property, human beings are subject to disease and death, and experience guilt as a result of their dealings with one another. From all these ills and sins, pilgrimage systems furnish relief—as well as the increased prospect of ultimate salvation, since the performance of pilgrimage is considered by Catholics to be a supereminently good work. Pilgrimage provides a carefully structured, highly valued route to a liminal world where the ideal is felt to be real, where the tainted social persona may be cleansed and renewed.

It is significant that Calvin, who declared that pilgrimages "aided no man's salvation," believed in predestination and shared the general Protestant emphasis on faith rather than good works as the key to salvation. The orthodox Catholic view, of course, has always been that no one can be sure of salvation until the very last gasp: on the one hand, the believer is plied with graces by God; on the other, he continually exerts his free will by accepting or rejecting them. Faith without good works is regarded as useless. Good works are performed in response to graces—the initiatives of God, who desires the salvation of all. Good works are defined as the "observance of the precepts and counsels." "Precepts" are rules of life and conduct necessary for all who wish to obtain salvation. The Ten Commandments are examples of such rules. "Counsels" are rules of life and conduct for those who, not satisfied with the bare minimum, aim at greater moral perfection by means of good works not commanded but commended—for example, abstinence from lawful

[Margin note: Predestination + Calvin]

pleasures. Observance of the counsels is held to be meritorious only if done out of a desire for salvation, rather than out of a wish to be highly regarded by one's fellow men. Protestantism, which professes justification by faith alone, naturally ignores the distinction between precepts and counsels. For Catholics, going on pilgrimage is a good work in response to a counsel. We mention this peculiarly Christian instance of theological infighting merely to emphasize that pilgrimage, though having initiatory features, is not, strictly speaking, an initiation rite (that is, "an irreversible, singular ritual instrument for effecting a permanent, visible cultural transformation of the subject"). Pilgrimages resemble private devotions—like those to the Sacred Heart of Jesus or the Immaculate Heart of Mary—in their voluntary character, but differ from them in their public effect. The decision to go on pilgrimage takes place within the individual but brings him into fellowship with like-minded souls, both on the way and at the shrine. The social dimension is generated by the individual's choice, multiplied many times. On pilgrimage, social interaction is not governed by the old rules of social structure. When a pilgrimage system becomes established, however, it operates like other social institutions. The social takes precedence over the individual at all levels. Organized parties make the journey; devotions at the shrine are collective and according to the schedule. But pilgrimage is an individual good work, not a social enterprise. Pilgrimage, ideally, is charismatic, in the sense that pilgrim's decision to make it is a response to a charism, a grace, while at the same time he receives grace as he makes his devotions.

For this reason, orthodoxy in many religions tends to be ambivalent toward pilgrimage. The apparent capriciousness with which people make up their minds to visit a shrine, the rich symbolism and communitas quality of pilgrimage systems, the peripheral character of pilgrimage vis-à-vis the ritual or liturgical system as a whole, all make it suspect. Pilgrimage is too democratic, not sufficiently hierarchical. In Catholic Christianity the sacramental system does have something of the irreversible character of tribal rites of passage, giving direction to social and personal life, and coordinating sacred and secular processes. Baptism, confirmation, ordination to the priesthood, all are irreversible, once-only rites of passage, which are declared dogmatically to "imprint an indelible character on the soul." It is significant that the sacraments most closely associated with pilgrimage are the Eucharist and penance. Neither of these is a rite of passage, and both are indefinitely repeatable. These sacraments in one aspect form an admirable system of instruments of social control. This is not true of pilgrimages, at least in their early stages. As we shall see when considering historical cases, there is something inveterately populist, anarchical, even anticlerical, about pilgrimages in their very essence. They have at times been linked with popular nationalism, with peasant and anticolonial revolt, and with popular millenarianism. They tend to arise spontaneously, on the report that some miracle or apparition has occurred at a particular place, not always a place previously consecrated. Pilgrimages are an expression of the communitas dimension of any society, the spontaneity of interrelatedness, the spirit which bloweth where it listeth. From the point of view of those who control and maintain the social structure, all manifestations of communitas, sacred or profane, are potentially subversive. We shall see, in this connection, how religious specialists have attempted to domesticate the primitive, spontaneous modes of peregrination, with their freedom of communitas, into orderly pilgrimage, more susceptible to ecclesiastical control. Their model is the structured ritual system. Individual Catholic pilgrimages have in the course of time been transformed into extended and protracted forms of such sacraments as penance and the Eucharist. Their voluntaristic, even miraculous, essence has been subjugated to doctrinal and organizational edict. Their charism has been routinized; their communitas, structured. Nevertheless, like Etna, old pilgrimages are apt to revive unexpectedly; and new ones erupt like so many Paricutíns—indeed, miracles attributed to the crucifix rescued from Paricutín village in Mexico have made of its present refuge, the church in San Juan near Uruápan in Michoacán state, a new pilgrimage center!

There is no simple answer to the question of how pilgrimages begin. Some pilgrimages indeed have no traceable ultimate origin, but are known to antedate the historical religions with which they are currently associated. Other pilgrimage centers exist today which have been superimposed on known older centers, like scions on a stock. This is true not only for the Mexican Catholic shrines of Guadalupe, Ocotlán, Chalma, and Ízamal, pilgrimage sites, but also for such world-renowned centers as Mecca, Islam's "navel of the world" (which was a pilgrim shrine long before Muhammad), and Jerusalem, frequented by Jewish pilgrims long before the birth of Christ. Wherever communitas has manifested itself often and on a large scale the possibility of its revival exists, even when linked to a different religious system. Recognition of this fact perhaps underlies Gregory the Great's injunction, via the monk Mellitus, to St. Augustine of Canterbury, missionary to the Anglo-Saxons—to tolerate those pagan practices which were not directly repugnant to Christian notions of morality, and to attach them to some feature of Christian belief or practice. To this letter may be owed the preservation of many wells held sacred to pre-Christian deities, wells which were later incorporated into the shrine-complex of local Christian saints. Such a practice of incorporation is referred to colloquially as "baptizing the customs" (this practice will be discussed more fully in chapter 2, in connection with Mexican pilgrimage).

However, the oldest pilgrim centers of the historical religions are generally places mentioned in sacred narratives as connected with the birth, mission, and death of the founder and his closest kin and disciples. In Hinduism, pilgrim shrines are associated with the cults of deities. The sacred narratives are paradigms of the salvific process. They concern the relationship between the timeless message of the founder, whose words and works show how to obtain release from time's suffering or how to use it to one's eternal advantage, and the concrete circumstances of time and place. Believers in the message seek to imitate or to unite with the founder by replicating his actions, either literally or in spirit. Pilgrimage is one way, perhaps the most literal, of imitating the religious founder. By visiting the sites believed to be the scenes of his life and teaching mission, the pilgrim in imagination relives those events. As we have noted above, pilgrimage may be thought of as extroverted mysticism, just as mysticism is introverted pilgrimage. The pilgrim physically traverses a mystical way; the mystic sets forth on an inte-

33

rior spiritual pilgrimage. For the former, concreteness and historicity dominate; for the latter, a phased interior process leads to a goal beyond conceptualization. Both pilgrimage and mysticism escape the nets of social structure, and both have at various times been under attack by religious authorities. Pilgrimage has its inwardness, as anyone who has observed pilgrims before a shrine can attest; while mysticism has its outwardness, as evidenced by the energetic, practical lives of famous mystics such as St. Theresa of Ávila, St. Bernard of Clairvaux, St. Catherine of Siena, William Law, al-Ghazali, and Mahatma Gandhi.

In the early stages of a religion's development, the prototypical shrines tend to predominate. Later, the places where saints and martyrs lived and died may become pilgrim shrines. Later still, places where visions, or apparitions, of the founder and those close to him—or of some manifestation of God or divine power—presented themselves to a believer, may become pilgrim shrines. All these types of shrines provide evidence for the faithful that their religion is still instinct with supernatural power and grace; that it has objective efficacy derived from the founder's god or gods and transmitted by means of miracles, wonders, and signs through saints, martyrs, and holy men, often through the medium of their relics.

SUMMARY

Pilgrimage, then, has some of the attributes of liminality in passage rites: release from mundane structure; homogenization of status; simplicity of dress and behavior; communitas; ordeal; reflection on the meaning of basic religious and cultural values; ritualized enactment of correspondences between religious paradigms and shared human experiences; emergence of the integral person from multiple personae; movement from a mundane center to a sacred periphery which suddenly, transiently, becomes central for the individual, an *axis mundi* of his faith; movement itself, a symbol of communitas, which changes with time, as against stasis, which represents structure; individuality posed against the institutionalized milieu; and so forth. But since it is voluntary, not an

34

comprise

compromise

obligatory social mechanism to mark the transition of an individual or group from one state or status to another within the mundane sphere, pilgrimage is perhaps best thought of as "liminoid" or "quasi-liminal," rather than "liminal" in Van Gennep's full sense.

Tribal rites know nothing of modern distinctions between "work" and "play" or "work" and "leisure"; episodes of joking, trickery, fantasy, and festivity mark the rituals of tribal societies. Yet within tribal societies ritual activities are themselves clearly considered to be a form of "work" and are thus described by any modern preliterate societies, as in the Tikopia's "work of the gods," quite as necessary to the group's welfare as subsistence activities and the judicial process. The ludic (as in Huizinga's term, 1950), or play, aspects, as well as the most solemn aspects of ritual, are most vividly represented in liminality—for example, in the masked dancing, with clowns of various kinds, in the riddles, joking speech, rites of reversal, and practical joking, found in puberty initiations, side by side with the telling of myths about the sometimes obscene and often tricky behavior of deities and founding ancestors. Now, in postindustrial societies, the spheres of work and leisure are sharply divided by the clock but, at least in the cities, have little to do directly with the seasonal cycle—being determined instead by the rational organization of industrial production, mainly mass production in factories (V. Turner 1974b:67–70). Religion generally has been moved into the leisure sphere, more and more subject to individual option ("a person's free time is his to do as he likes with"). Even weekly attendance at religious services is becoming increasingly voluntary; failure to attend is no longer a sin. Games, sports, pastimes, hobbies, tourism, entertainment, the mass media, compete to fill the leisure sphere. On the other hand, work, perhaps originally under the influence of the Protestant ethic, has itself become rationalized, highly serious, almost ascetic in its regulation of productive time, like canonical hours in a monastery, and has been totally segregated from religion. But leisure activities have been so influenced by the prestige of work that many of them are pursued with the same solemnity as work and demand at least an equal outlay of attention. Even leisure has become professionalized, and some pastimes require more technical skill and know-how than

work/modern obsession ∂ profesion ↓ loss of religion

many jobs. Thus, under the influence of the division between work-time and leisure-time, religion has become less serious but more solemn: less serious because it belongs to the leisure sphere in a culture dominated by the high value set on material productivity, and more solemn because within that sphere it has become specialized to establish ethical standards and behavior in a social milieu characterized by multiple options, continuous change, and large-scale secularization.

The history of pilgrimage illustrates this progress from the "ludergic" liminal to the "ergic" liminoid (V. Turner 1974b:83). The great medieval pilgrimages, in Islam as in Christianity, were usually associated with great fairs and fiestas as indeed they are in Shinto Japan. For example, in his article "Ḥadjdj" (hajj) in the *Encyclopaedia of Islam*, A. J. Wensinck (1966:32) writes: "Great fairs were from early times associated with the ḥadjdj, which was celebrated on the conclusion of the date-harvest. These fairs were probably the main thing to Muhammad's contemporaries, as they still are to many Muslims."

The Christian medieval fairs at such pilgrim centers as Chartres, Zaragoza, and Cologne on important feast days of Jesus, Mary, or major saints have their present-day successors in Latin America. We have seen almost at the portal of the church of Naucalpan (on the outskirts of Mexico City), where the venerable image of Our Lady of the Remedies is kept, troupes of brightly feathered Conchero dancers mime fights between Aztec warriors and French troops, while a skull-headed Death clowns wildly for the amusement of pilgrims. Fifty yards farther on, a full-blown fair was taking place, with ferris wheels, shooting galleries, and bumper cars, beside peddlers selling a wide range of goods. In describing the northern Brazilian pilgrimage to the shrine of Bom Jesus da Lapa in Bahia, Daniel E. Gross (1971:132–34) has given us a vivid picture of the juxtaposition of worship and commerce:

[Lapa is a] raw river town whose chief *raison d'être* is the annual flow of thousands of pilgrims to its religious shrine. . . . As the major festival of August 6 (which is, incidentally, the Feast of the Transfiguration of Our Lord Jesus Christ) draws near, more and more vendors from outside Lapa arrive and set up stands selling a great variety of wares. Some of these depend on the local trinket distributors, but others bring a large part of their merchandise, including a few items of artisanry such as saddles, leather hats and vests, hammocks, horse-blankets, spurs, and innumerable items fashioned from tin cans. . . . I used to count the numbers of stands on my way down a single street about one-half km. in length. On June 20, 1966, there were only five temporary stands set up on this particular street. By July 11, there were 43; a week later 78 had appeared, and by the end of July, 187. On August 5, the day before the procession, 346 vending stands could be counted along the same street, which became choked with pilgrims admiring the wares.

Gross also mentions that cabarets and bars thrive in the pilgrimage season.

Pilgrimage devotion, the market, and the fair are all connected with voluntary, contractual activities (the religious promise, the striking of a bargain, the penny ride on the merry-go-round), and with a measure of joyful, "ludic" communitas (see V. Turner 1974a:221–23). This extends even to the religious activities proper, for comradeship is a feature of pilgrimage travel. Chaucer noticed this aspect six centuries ago, and we have experienced it personally as members of pilgrim groups in Yucatán, Ireland, Rome, and Lourdes. Those who journey to pray together also play together in the secular interludes between religious activities; sightseeing to places of secular interest is one common form of "play" associated with pilgrimage. Anthropologists have learned that it is necessary to study the total field of a great ceremony, the nonritualized factors surrounding it, as well as the liturgical or symbolic action. If one applies this method to the study of pilgrimage, one finds that play and solemnity are equally present. Indeed, it is the ludic component which excited the wrath of many Christian critics of pilgrimage and perhaps prepared the way for the virtual abolition of pilgrimage in Protestant lands. One has only to name William Langland, John Wyeliffe, Erasmus, Hugh Latimer (bishop of Worcester in Henry VIII's time), and John Calvin, among the host of detractors (see below, chapter 4).

Today, pilgrimages, like so many other leisure-time activities, have been organized, bureaucratized, and subjected to the influence of the modern forms of mass transportation and communication, mediated by full-time travel agencies. On the whole, they have become more solemn in tone, especially in the Western European lands, where once they combined devotion with pastime and mirth. However, recent changes in the Christian outlook have aimed to transform pilgrimage by encouraging more informal dress, sermons with contemporary themes, and a relaxed atmosphere outside the precincts of the shrine.

One fact is certain and striking. The numbers of pilgrims at the world's major shrines are still increasing. That this phenomenon is not due merely to tourism can easily be seen in the voluminous literature published in connection with pilgrimage centers (Lourdes, Guadalupe, and Knock come immediately to mind as Christian examples).[3] The papers, journals, and annuals of these centers abound with devout articles, fervent religious poetry, and news about visits to the shrine by organized pilgrimages and celebrities of church and state. Sermons delivered on feast days at the shrine by famous preachers and bishops are printed verbatim. There are lively correspondence columns on questions of doctrine and on the social role of the Church. Despite obvious resemblances and historical connections between archaic, medieval, and modern pilgrimages, we would argue that there is a significant difference between pilgrimages taken after the industrial Revolution and all previous types. In the scientific and technological age, pilgrimage is becoming what Geertz (1972:26) has described as a "metasocial commentary" on the troubles of this epoch of wars and revolutions with its increasing signs of industrial damage to the natural environment. Like certain other liminoid genres of symbolic action elaborated in the leisure time of modern society, pilgrimage has become an implicit critique of the life-style characteristic of the encompassing social structure. Its emphasis on transcendental, rather than mundane, ends and means; its generation of communitas; its search for the roots of ancient, almost vanishing virtues as the underpinning of social life, even in its structured expressions—all have contributed to the dramatic resurgence of pilgrimage. It is true that bureaucracy has been

[3] According to René Laurentin (1973a:145), there are "about a thousand [Christian] sanctuaries which [each] receive a hundred thousand pilgrims a year."

pressed into the service of pilgrimage, and that comfortable travel has replaced penitential travel. Here, too, the stress has been on the communitas of the pilgrimage center, rather than on the individual's penance on the journey thither. In the earlier periods, pilgrimage still had liminal, even initiatory, aspects. Though it was one of the first forms of symbolic religious action to assign an important role to voluntary action, it was still, especially in its penitential aspect, deeply tinctured with obligatoriness. This was because the earlier pilgrimage systems, in all the major religions, were highly consonant with both the social and the religious systems, which in some measure they served to maintain. But in the present age of plural values, increasing specialization of function and role, and potent mass communication (the publication explosion, in particular, has brought the whole of man's past within the range of all literate people, in cheap paperbacks), pilgrimage—with its deep nonrational fellowship before symbols of transmundane beings and powers, with its posing of unity and homogeneity (even among the most diverse cultural groups) against the disunity and heterogeneity of ethnicities, cultures, classes, and professions in the mundane sphere—serves not so much to maintain society's status quo as to recollect, and even to presage, an alternative mode of social being, a world where communitas, rather than a bureaucratic social structure, is preeminent. Thus, out of the mixing and mingling of ideas from many traditions, a respect may grow for the pilgrimages of others. These may be seen as providing live metaphors for human and transhuman truths and salvific ways which all men share and always have shared, had they but known it. Pilgrimages may become ecumenical; and more devotees than the Swami from Madras, whom once we met in Chicago, will become palmers to the pilgrim shrines of all the great religions.

CHAPTER TWO
Mexican Pilgrimages:
Myth and History

⟨ornament⟩

IT WAS IN Mexico that our interest in the pilgrimage process was first aroused. Hence we make no apology for putting the cart before the horse and beginning with this study of modern Catholic pilgrimages in a formerly colonial territory. An anthropologist must begin with what he has seen, even if, in attempting to comprehend the phenomena he has observed, he later finds himself compelled to retrace their past in the visible record of what may nevermore be seen. (For Mexican materials we have included elsewhere in articles on pilgrimage, see V. Turner 1974a:166–230; 1974c:305–27; 1975b:107–27.)

Pilgrimage *lives* in Mexico. Millions of people every year journey to near or distant shrines, some of which date almost from Cortés's conquest, others from the latest rumored miracle. In Mexico, as elsewhere, various criteria determine whether a shrine becomes a pilgrimage center or not. Such centers, though numerous, represent only a small percentage of the total number of shrines, public and private, to be found in Mexico today. Some of the important shrines are the sites of reported apparitions (of the Virgin or other saints);

some possess statues, crucifixes, or pictures held to have miraculous properties; others (though this is rare for Mexico) have martyrs' or saints' relics believed to be endowed with curative powers; while still others have achieved fame through their antiquity and historic associations.

Pilgrimages in Mexico have both Old and New World antecedents. In certain cases it is possible to trace genetic links back through Spanish religious culture into the far past of Judeo-Christian tradition. For example, it is clear that the foundation narrative for the central, paradigmatic pilgrimage of Mexico—to the shrine of the Dark Virgin of Guadalupe, in a suburb of Mexico City—belongs to what Vincente de la Fuente (1879:41), the great historian of the Spanish cult of Mary, described as *el ciclo de los pastores* ("the shepherds' cycle"). Recently summarized by Steven Sharbrough (1975:7–11), whose synopsis we draw upon here, "the shepherds' cycle" refers to a body of legends, current between the ninth and thirteenth centuries, which describe the miraculous discovery of images of the Virgin Mary, mainly by shepherds, cowherds, and farmers. De la Fuente recorded numerous local traditions varying in detail, but all of them exhibited a strikingly uniform thematic structure. The holy images are "found in the ground by knocking a dirt clod aside, in caves while fetching lost sheep, in ponds, in streams, on islands, and in trees" (de la Fuente, as cited by Sharbrough, p. 7). Very often the shepherd is led to his discovery by a miraculous happening, such as the appearance of the Virgin in a vision; an unnatural light; an unexpected noise. This narrative genre had a very wide distribution in medieval Europe. Among the other distinctive features noted by de la Fuente (cited ibid.) were

mysterious lights, celestial harmonies, demonstrations of adoration and respect by some animals in a rustic and little frequented place, doubts and vacillation by the favored shepherd, attempts to carry the image and worship it privately, incredulity on the part of the people of the town when the miraculous vision is reported, attempts to carry the image to a more comfortable and accessible place, return by the image two or three times to the site of the vision, resolution to build a church in the designated place, and frequent veneration of the image there by the people of the town.
. . .

These motifs, variously combined, recur, as we shall see, in legends relating to the foundation of Mexican shrines.

Sharbrough also discusses the discovery of so many images in the ground: he confirms the explanation that during the Carolingian period, sacred images were buried to protect them from being profaned. This would explain the "black Virgins," for silver images would turn black through long exposure to the corrosive action of nitrates and other chemicals in the soil.

The shepherd component in this cycle of legends was referred by de la Fuente to the charter narrative of the birth of Christ in Luke 2:7–20. In that account, shepherds have a vision (of "an angel of the Lord"), and go on a kind of pilgrimage to witness the "sign" (the infant Jesus laid in a manger, traditionally in a cave), and to pay their respects to the holy family. An Old Testament prototype was the peregrination of Abraham, the pastoral nomad and exile seeking Canaan. Sharbrough further emphasizes the legendary and iconic associations, in the Middle Ages, of the Virgin Mary with domestic animals, and suggests that she may be linked with the earlier Mediterranean cults of the Great Goddess, the Magna Mater, who was, of course, concerned with the fertility of animals, both tame and wild. Some of the legends of the shepherds' cycle even relate that the Virgin's image was discovered by a bull (Sharbrough, p. 9).

OUR LADY OF GUADALUPE IN SPAIN

A graduate student colleague of ours in the Department of Anthropology at the University of Chicago, L. Plascencia, himself of Mexican descent, has probed the salient literature on the two major devotions of the Virgin of Guadalupe in Spain and Mexico. We abridge his unpublished paper (1974) here and note the sources he drew on in his survey.

The Spanish Guadalupe statue (properly speaking, a Madonna and Child) is now in a monastery shrine near Cáceres in the province of Estremadura (or Extremadura) in west-central Spain. The first account about this statue dates it to the sixth century, when the monk Gregory, who later became Pope Gregory the Great, is said to have venerated it in his private chapel (Herbert Leies 1964:378; J. I. Gallery 1960:3). Around A.D. 590, Gregory, now pope, sent the statue to his friend Leander (Leandro), archbishop of Seville. According to Gallery (pp. 3–4), the statue was venerated for more than a century in a chapel in Seville. When the Moors conquered Andalusia, around A.D. 711—the account relates—in order "to save the miraculous statue from profanation, one of the fleeing bands [of Christians] heading for the province of Estremadura carried it with them" (Leies, p. 379), and hid it in a cave in the side of a mountain. Leies notes that "the faces of Mother and Child are brown, since the original statue was carved from an oriental wood" (p. 377).

Now begins the narrative which places the history of the Spanish Guadalupe shrine firmly within the shepherds' cycle. Leies (p. 380) summarized the tale: One day a cowherd named Gil Cordero, from the town of Cáceres, found that one of his cows was missing, and he began to look for it. After three days of fruitless searching, he came upon the cow dead before a cave near the Guadalupe River. Nothing indicated the cause of death, and Gil Cordero resigned himself to stripping off the hide. All at once a lovely lady appeared in splendor before him, and told him that she was the Most Holy Virgin Mary. Unexpectedly the cow rose then to its feet. The lady told Gil to proceed to Cáceres and bid the priest and people to come to "the spot where the cow had lain" and to remove the stones hiding the nearby cave, which contained her sacred image. She instructed that a chapel be erected on that spot, and her statue be placed in it, so that she might be venerated there. On his way to Cáceres, Gil stopped at his home, only to find that his son had died and was to be buried that very day. Soon a priest arrived, already notified of the boy's death. But the son suddenly sat up, alive and well, and announced his desire to visit the spot where the Blessed Virgin had appeared to his father, so that he might thank her for restoring his life. The statue was found in a cave near the river Guadalupe, and was therefore named Our Lady of Guadalupe. A temporary hermitage was built—later replaced by a shrine and a monastery. In a short time it became yet another Marian pilgrimage center.

Other versions of the foundation narrative for the Spanish Guadalupe shrine exist. As summarized by Zsolt Aradi (1954:48), Gil

43

Cordero's vision occurred in 1326. In the vision, the Virgin told Gil to dig in the earth at a certain spot. When he did so, he found a buried iron casket. Opened in the village of Guadalupe, in the presence of bishops and priests, the casket was found to contain a statue of the Blessed Virgin that had been hidden six hundred years earlier by the Knights of Don Rodrigo, leader of the Visigoths, who had been defeated by the Saracens in 711. This was said to be the statue given to Bishop Leander of Seville by Pope Gregory the Great. Aradi adds that the image was placed in the custody of the Hieronymite Order, and that the devotion was at its height during the period of the discovery of the New World. According to Aradi, Columbus and the conquistadors carried replicas of the statue with them on their journeys, and the Franciscan missionaries who accompanied them spread the veneration of the Virgin of Guadalupe in the newly occupied countries, particularly in Mexico. Indeed, in 1493 Christopher Columbus renamed the Caribbean island of Karukera (now Guadeloupe) in honor of the miraculous Madonna of Guadalupe in Spain. Among the possible transmitters of her devotion must be considered Hernán Cortés himself. As Plascencia has pointed out (1974:19–20), Cortés was born in 1445, in the town of Medillín, then in the province of Estremadura, and his home is said to have been near the monastery shrine to Our Lady of Guadalupe. Moreover, in Gallery's view, Cortés had "more devotion to Our Lady of Guadalupe than ordinary Spaniards"; Gallery further maintains that most of Cortés's army, as well as most of the Spaniards living in Mexico in 1531, were from the neighborhood of the monastery of Guadalupe (Gallery, pp. 4–5; Plascencia, pp. 19–20).

The connection of the Spanish Guadalupe narrative with the shepherds' cycle is clear enough. Gil Cordero (lit., Gil Lamb) is himself a cowherd. He finds his dead cow after three days' quest. This recalls the three-day period of Christ's entombment. Gil's cow and son are also restored to life after three days. The symbolic importance of the cave—Christ was both born (in some legends) and entombed in one—is equally striking. The Virgin's involvement with domesticated animals such as the lamb and the cow is also a regular element in the cycle. Both the building of a chapel at the sacred place and the growth of a pilgrimage to the sacred image revealed by a miraculous apparition of Mary likewise fall within this tradition.

A further version of the Guadalupe foundation narrative is worthy of consideration. This is given under "Guadalupe" in volume 43 (1850:715–16) of the *Encyclopédie théologique*, by J. P. Migne—actually the first of two volumes devoted to pilgrimage. This version mentions the firm friendship between Bishop Leander of Seville and Pope Gregory the Great and describes how even at the height of fever Gregory used to send the bishop the newly written chapters of his commentaries on the Book of Job. On one occasion, it is reported, the pope sent with his envoy an "ancient and venerable" image of the Virgin, already "famous in Rome for the miracles produced by her intercession." On the way, shipwreck was prevented by the sacred image: the boat carrying the holy image and the precious manuscript would have perished had not a priest inspired the sailors with renewed "hope and confidence" by "gathering them round the miraculous image." The figure of the Madonna and Child was borne in triumph to the bishop at Seville. "But Leander, fearing that the Saracens would overrun the whole of Spain,[1] secreted the image in a rocky hollow near the episcopal town, along with some relics of his brother St. Fulgentius, and a bell. He also inserted some letters inventorying these treasures and testifying to their religious value for some future discoverer." Six centuries then went by before "the Holy Mother of God revealed her image to Spain, through the agency of a shepherd (*berger*) whom she chose to discover it." Appearing to him in the midst of a "new burning bush," the Virgin was

completely surrounded by sunbeams, and bade him tell his fellow citizens of Cazerra [Cáceres] of her appearance and show them the cave where her image had been. "As proof of the truth of my words," she told him, "you will find your son dead when you return home; but to induce those to whom you will announce this to believe, you will tell them that I will restore his life to him, and your son will immediately return from the dead." The shepherd was at first disinclined to believe; but, just as he was about to cut up an ox he had slaughtered, he felt his arms lose their strength,

[1] Since Leander died A.D. 599, and Spain was not invaded by the Muslims until the first decade of the eighth century, this was foresight indeed!

45

and he could not continue his work. However, rendered submissive by this punishment, he recovered the strength of his arms at the same time that faith returned to his heart. To avoid further chastisement, he hurried off to Cazerra and told the citizens what he had seen and heard. They made haste to go to the cavern and take out what it contained.

The people of Cazerra soon raised a chapel on that site. Alfonso XI afterward replaced it with a magnificent temple large enough to contain the large number of pilgrims who flocked there from all directions. This church was adorned with great quantities of riches of every kind: silver and gold vases, precious stones, splendid vestments for religious ceremonies, and the like.

The face of the holy statue is black . . . , "like an Ethiopian woman"; but she has such a divine expression that the most ferocious bandit could not contemplate it without feeling his heart melt with love.

Lévi-Strauss has familiarized us with the notion that variant forms of a myth possess the same structure. The same elements and motifs recur, but in different relationships. Thus, in the version of the Spanish Guadalupe foundation narrative summarized by Boris (1974), which we shall call version 1, the cow is resurrected—but apparently not in version 3 (Migne 1850). In version 1, a cow is dead when discovered by Gil Cordero; in version 3, the anonymous *berger* killed an ox (*boeuf*). In version 3, the herdsman's arms "wither" (*se dessèchent*), representing his unfaith; their use is restored when his faith revives. In version 1, it is the animal which revives. In version 1, Gil Cordero has to go home before he learns that his son is dead; the son revives when the priest comes to bury him, and he already knows of the Blessed Virgin's appearance to his father. In version 3, it is the Virgin herself who informs the herdsman that his son will be found dead and that she will restore him to life.

All these reversals, and more, are identifiable as aspects of the same myth. What they do is to underline the basic, nonrational Christian dogma of the resurrection, by associating it with the "death" and "burial" of the sacred image and its "restoration to life" by miraculous means. In both cases the intervention of the Theotokos, the Mother of God, was decisive: it was she who bore Jesus and helped to lay him in his sepulture in a cave; it was she

46

whose papally blessed image was for so long hidden in a cave, through the long "dormition" of the Saracen conquest.

But it is not the "structure" of the foundation narrative, revealed by its variants, that is of primary importance to those who undertake lengthy pilgrimages to the shrine in the hopes of a miracle—or, at the least, of a reinforcement of faith. It is rather the historical, theological, and phenomenological aspects of the tales which attest to the validity and efficacy of the pilgrimage. Indeed, each narrative is extraordinarily condensed and multivocal, operating simultaneously on several levels of significance. Theologically, as we have seen, the entire "shepherds' cycle" devolves from the root paradigm of the birth of Jesus and the adoration of the shepherds, as related in Luke 2:7–20, which itself has Old Testament precedents. The metaphorical extension of the Latin word *pastor* from "shepherd" to "priest" is not without significance here. In some tales it is fairly explicit. For example, Sharbrough cites de la Fuente's account of the foundation narrative of a pilgrimage to a holy well (la Fuente Santa, located outside Nieva, a small village near Segovia) in support of his view that the cultus of the Virgin Mary was frequently syncretized with pre-Christian cults of the Great Goddess as protectress of animals. In this narrative a poor man named Pedro was watching his sheep near Nieva in 1392, when the Virgin appeared to him and ordered him to pull a rush out of the ground. Immediately, a fountain of crystalline water sprang forth. (The reader will recognize an affinity with the foundation narrative of the Lourdes pilgrimage—in which Bernadette, at the Virgin's behest, scooped a hole in the ground near the grotto of Massabielle, and thus originated the renowned spring of miraculous water which still gushes out today with undiminished force.) Pedro, like Gil Cordero, also found an image of Mary (between two pieces of slate); and a chapel was built on the site. In a passage clearly meant to be read on two levels, Mary admonished Pedro not to neglect his humble profession and to take good care of his sheep. *Los pastores* were thought of as clerics as well as shepherds.

In the Spanish Guadalupe stories, two important clerical "shepherds" are mentioned: Pope Gregory the Great and Bishop Leander of Seville. Indeed, Gregory's *Regula pastoralis*, on the office and duties of a bishop, came to be used throughout Christendom and was translated into English by King Alfred. Both Gregory and Leander set considerable store on establishing good relations between the Catholic Church and the powerful Germanic peoples— the Lombards, Franks, and Visigoths, who had been devastating northern Italy, France, and Spain, respectively. Leander's main achievement was the conversion of King Recared, and many of his Visigoths, from Arianism. One of Gregory's important achievements was the negotiation of treaties with the Lombards; another, of course, was the sending of St. Augustine of Canterbury and forty other monks, probably from Gregory's own former monastery of St. Andrew on the Caelian Hill, to England to convert the Angles, Saxons, and Jutes.

It was not only with regard to their activities in the West that the two "pastors" had much in common. While on a mission to Constantinople in 583, Leander had met Gregory, who was then the papal *apocrisiarius* there, and had many discussions with him on doctrinal and, possibly, pastoral matters. Perhaps it was to commemorate this communion in the East that Gregory sent Leander "a statue carved from oriental wood."

Thus the seemingly simple foundation narrative of Guadalupe carries implications of the theological, social, political, and personal contacts between Western and Eastern Christendom, between the papacy and the episcopal peripheries, between Roman Catholic and Germanic pagan or heretical cultural systems. For example, the statue sent by Gregory to Leander bridges the interval between pre-Moorish, Visigothic Spain and the Spain of the Christian Reconquest; that is, between the earlier defense of the doctrine of the Trinity against Arian unitarianism and the triumphant reaffirmation of Trinitarian Christianity against monistic Islam. In a later chapter, we will refer to the importance of the Virgin Mary as Theotokos (Mother of God) in the key doctrine of the Incarnation, and will note the literally "crucial" bond between that doctrine and the dogma of the Trinity. Images of all kinds—panel paintings, stained-glass representations, murals, sculptured forms—served as "the Bibles" of the poor and illiterate, to make abstract doctrine concrete. Among the most important of such symbol-vehicles were the images of the Blessed Virgin, herself the very "vessel" of divine meaning because she was the instrument by which God had made the Word flesh. Out of the story of the Nativity grew the ambiguity of *pastor* as both shepherd of animals and guardian of the faithful. The humility of the Virgin, the humble circumstances of Christ's birth among the animals, the humility of the clerical "pastors" (Pope Gregory introduced the phrase *Servus Servorum Dei* to designate the papal incumbent), all are regularly stressed in the foundation narratives, iconography, and theology of Marian pilgrimages. In a sense every pilgrim is a shepherd going to Bethlehem, every priest both a pilgrim and a shepherd. As we shall see, too, in the European Middle Ages Mary was often regarded as the Church (Ecclesia) personified, made visible; and, like the Church, she acted as intercessor between man and God. Her shrines became centers for such intercession, holy places where persons humbled by affliction or humbling themselves through an act of enlightened will might seek graces and favors.

This system was well established in Europe, particularly in Spain (where great Marian pilgrimage shrines abounded, such as Covadonga, Montserrat, and Zarogoza), when the Spanish conquest of the Americas began. But, simultaneously, the Reformation was spreading in Europe, with its hostility toward pilgrimage, especially Marian pilgrimage. Furthermore, the Council of Trent (which, it must not be forgotten, was itself a Reformation within Catholicism, and not merely an attempt "to turn back the clock," as so many individuals, Catholics as well as Protestants, proclaim today), while it did not condemn pilgrimage outright, was little more than lukewarm about encouraging it, in view of the scandals concerning the sale of relics and pardons, scandals seized upon by Protestants and humanists to discredit the Church as a whole. Nevertheless, though pilgrimage was terminated in most of northern Europe and was markedly curtailed in southern Europe, it grew rapidly in the Iberian New World. The shepherds' cycle now enjoyed a new life. Its major source was clearly Catholic Europe; but features in the religious systems of the conquered Amerindian peoples blended with and reinforced the Old World "pastoral" beliefs so closely linked with pilgrimage.

One might argue, however, that pilgrimage in Mexico developed in spite of initial discouragement (perhaps under Tridentine influence) by the first missionaries. Robert Ricard, in his *Spiritual Conquest of Mexico* (1966:193), maintains that the Franciscan, Dominican, and Augustinian missionaries assigned to pilgrimage "only a rather secondary importance," and that their participation in its establishment and development was "much reduced." It seems that pilgrimage, or something akin to it, was already entrenched in the culture of Middle America before the arrival of Cortés. J. Eric Thompson (1970:135) summarizes the early eyewitness accounts, by Bishop Diego de Landa, Antonio de Herrera, and other Europeans, of Maya pilgrimage centers:

The conquerers . . . settled at Cozumel, Ízamal, Motul, and Mayapán, according to various sources. It is, I think, highly significant that Cozumel was the shrine of the moon goddess, Ixchel, which also drew pilgrims from all parts of the country. Landa compares the pilgrimages to Chichén Itzá and Cozumel with the Christian pilgrimages to Rome and Jerusalem. Furthermore, Ízamal, as the home of Kinichkakmo, a manifestation of the sun god, and of Itzamná, one of the greatest of Maya gods, was also a most important shrine. To these places came immense concourses of pilgrims, many of them from quite distant parts. As Itzamná and Ixchel were purely Maya deities, it is logical to suppose that these pilgrimages were in full swing long before the Mexicans came on the scene . . . . the focal point of these pilgrimages [to Chichén Itzá] was the sacred cenote, into which sacrifices, both of persons and valuables, were cast to propitiate the rain gods (p. 133).

When Cortés landed on the island of Cozumel (off Yucatán) in March of 1519—the first step in his conquest of Mexico—one of his first acts was to erect an image of the Virgin Mary in place of the cult image of the Maya moon goddess. The Virgin's appellation here was La Purísima, Mary Most Pure, or the Immaculate Conception. She was not depicted with the Christ Child; hence it could not have been a replica of the Estremaduran Lady of Guadalupe. The statue of Our Lady of Ízamal seen today is also a Purísima; as in most of the Mexican representations of the Immaculate Conception we have seen, Mary is portrayed standing on the crescent moon, an iconographic motif inspired by the Apocalypse 12:1: "And a great

50

sign appeared in heaven: A woman clothed with the sun, and the moon under her feet, and on her head a crown of twelve stars." It will be remembered that version 3 of the foundation narrative of the Estremaduran shrine of Guadalupe described the Virgin's apparition as "surrounded by sunbeams." Similarly, the miraculous painting of the Virgin of Guadalupe in Mexico is surrounded by alternately straight and wavy sunrays and has the "moon under her feet." While the influence of the Apocalypse inconography is evident here, pilgrimage links with the moon and sun deities of pre-Columbian Mexico have very likely played their part, too.

Pilgrimages seem to have existed on a regional scale in pre-Columbian Mexico. Not only the Maya of Yucatán but many other peoples went regularly to venerate certain deities at their shrines, and to propitiate them with gifts or sacrifices. Some of these shrines were later Christianized. It did not take the missionaries long to realize that pilgrimage was an effective instrument for maintaining regional cohesion, and their earlier misgivings gave way to enthusiastic support. After all, Gregory the Great himself had in effect sanctioned "baptism" of certain pre-Christian customs, when, more than nine hundred years earlier, he had written to the monk Mellitus (future archbishop of Canterbury), on his departure for Britain in A.D. 601:

When by God's help you reach our most reverend brother, Bishop Augustine, we wish you to inform him that we have been giving careful thought to the affairs of the English, and have come to the conclusion that the temples of the idols among that people should on no account be destroyed. The idols are to be destroyed, but the temples themselves are to be aspersed with holy water, altars set up in them, and relics deposited there. For if these temples are well-built, they must be purified from the worship of demons and dedicated to the service of the true God. In this way, we hope that the people, seeing that their temples are not destroyed, may abandon their error and, flocking more readily to their accustomed resorts, may come to know and adore the true God. And since they have a custom of sacrificing many oxen to demons, let some other solemnity be substituted in its place, such as a day of Dedication or the Festivals of the holy martyrs whose relics are enshrined there. On such occasions they might well construct shelters of boughs for themselves around the churches that were once temples, and cele-

brate the solemnity with devout feasting. They are no longer to sacrifice beasts to the Devil, but they may kill them for food to the
praise of God, and give thanks to the Giver of all gifts for the plenty
they enjoy. . . . If the people are allowed some worldly pleasures in
this way, they will more readily come to desire the joys of the
spirit. For it is certainly impossible to eradicate all errors from ob-
stinate minds at one stroke, and whoever wishes to climb to a
mountaintop climbs gradually step by step, and not in one leap
[quoted by the Venerable Bede, 1955 ed.:86–87].

Undoubtedly, Gregory's pastoral letter to Mellitus was considered
the charter for Catholic assimilation of certain material elements of
pagan tradition among peoples being converted to Catholicism.
This process of assimilation was particularly effective in polytheistic
cultures with relatively well-developed agriculture and craft traditions; in such cultures, Christian martyrs and saints could readily
be substituted for the patronal deities of caste, the communal base
of worship. Some Mexican examples are apposite here; we must
note, however, that in each of the three examples we shall discuss,
the pagan temple structure was not retained, but was destroyed and
replaced with a Christian building on the same site.

ZAPOPAN

The village of Zapopan (in Jalisco state), now caught up in the
suburban development of the great city of Guadalajara, was, in the
pre-Columbian period, part of a district tributary to the ruler of
Tonalá, a kingdom of ancient Mexico. Pilgrimages were made to
Zapopan from all parts of the district, to the shrine of the deity
Teopintzintl, "the Child God." In 1530, when Nuño de Guzmán
conquered the kingdom of Tonalá, its incumbent queen, Chihuapili
Tzapotzinco, ordered all her subordinate chiefs to render obeisance
to the Spanish Crown. The cacique of Atemajac, under whose jurisdiction Zapopan lay, soon complied with this order.

In 1541, the Indians rebelled against Spanish rule. During this
uprising, known as the Mixtón War, a Franciscan friar, Antonio de
Segovia, went among the Indians and urged them to make peace
with the Spaniards; on one occasion, Fray Antonio brought more
than six thousand Indians before the viceroy to seek his pardon.
Particularly relevant to our discussion is that Fray Antonio wore

around his neck an image of Our Lady of the Immaculate Conception—a small figure made, as were some images of the Indians' own deities, of *pasta de Michoacán*, bits of cornhusk smoothed and cemented together with glue (an indigenous form of papier-mâché, as it were).

In the course of the Mixtón War, the district around Zapopan was depopulated. Francisco de Bobadilla, the Spanish *encomendero* (commissioner) of Tlaltenango, obtained the viceroy's permission to repopulate Zapopan with Indians from Tlaltenango. When Zapopan was resettled—on the Feast of the Immaculate Conception, the eighth of December, 1541—Fray Antonio gave the newly settled colony his cherished Marian image, which he called La Pacificadora to commemorate his intercession with the viceroy on behalf of the six thousand Indians. Since that time this image, now known as Our Lady of Zapopan, has become increasingly important as a focus of unity for the Hispanic, criollo, mestizo, and Indian peoples of the whole state of Jalisco.

CHALMA

Chalma is a small village in Mexico state. Located at the mouth of a broad canyon about seventy miles southwest of Mexico City, the village consists solely of an Augustinian monastery and the houses and shops of the merchants whose livelihood derives from the thousands of pilgrims to the shrine of Our Lord of Chalma each year.

The literature on Chalma has been admirably summarized and evaluated by John Hobgood (1970a), who operates within Robert Redfield's conceptual frame, contrasting great and little traditions. The great traditions of Chalma were Aztec and Spanish Catholic; the little tradition was that of the Ocuiltec Indians, who occupied the canyon at the time of the Aztec conquest and were later integrated into the Aztec empire. In Hobgood's view (p. 2), "the contemporary culture of Chalma is a provincial manifestation of the Catholic European culture, overlaying and fusing with surviving elements of the Aztec great tradition and the local little tradition of Ocuiltec-Chalma."

Before the Aztecs entered the Chalma area, it had been inhabited

53

by Otomí Indians, who were largely displaced by Matlatzincas and Ocuiltecs, ethnolinguistic groups related to the Otomí, but not to the Aztecs, in language and custom. The area was settled by Ocuiltecs in 1439. The Aztecs did their best to impose their language on these Chalma peoples and, as was their practice, fabricated a history giving the conquered peoples the same origin as themselves.

The ancient Otomí, and presumably the related Ocuiltec, worshiped among their gods a pair called Old Father (Mixcoatl-Otonteuctli, "Cloud Serpent") and Old Mother (Xochiquetzal-Nohpyttecha, "Most Precious Flower"). These gods were considered the ancestors of all human beings. The Otomí believed that these two gods arose from caves. Old Father was a fire god and a god of the dead. Old Mother was the goddess of the earth and of the moon.

The Aztecs, like ancient Near Eastern peoples, tended to assimilate the gods of those they conquered to their own. It is known that Chalma was a major pilgrimage center in pre-Hispanic times, but it is not clear which of the syncretic Aztec-Ocuiltec deities were worshiped there. A tangled literature has sprung up since the time that Bernardino de Sahagún wrote his celebrated ethnography. Hobgood (p. 41) carefully weighs the evidence and suggests that the principal Aztec deity at Chalma was Huitzilopochtli (the war god and patron of the Aztec nation), and that his image, which was kept in a cave at Chalma, was replaced, after the conquest, by the Christ of Chalma—just as Tonantzin, mother of all the Aztec gods, including Huitzilopochtli, was replaced by the Virgin of Guadalupe at Tepeyac. It is possible that Huitzilopochtli had previously replaced Old Father.

The Aztec goddess of carnal love, Cihuacoatl-Tlazolteotl, had certainly been worshiped in the cave of Chalma. Her cult image in the cave was replaced with a statue of Mary of Egypt, the saint who had spent her early life in carnal sin and had lived her later years in penitence as a cave-dwelling hermit. The missionaries did not destroy the giant ahuehuete tree sacred to Cihuacoatl, however. The great tree, a few miles to the north of Chalma, still refreshes pilgrims today, and the cult of the goddess lingers on.

A number of pre-Columbian traditions are still discernible among

54

the present-day customs of Chalma and other Mexican shrines. For example, the umbilical cords of newborn babies often are sewn into little cloth bags that are hung from the sacred cypress by pilgrims on their way to Chalma—a practice probably alluding to the goddess Cihuacoatl's importance as the patroness of women in childbirth (Hobgood 1970a:35). We have seen a similar practice at Sacromonte (near Amecameca in Mexico state), a pilgrimage site centered on an image of the entombed Christ, enshrined in a cave. At Sacromonte, too, votive offerings (called *promesas*) in the form of umbilical cord contaıners are traditionally hung from two trees along the shrine's ritual routes (see plate 9). One of the trees is along the Way of the Cross; the other, beside the Way of Guadalupe (the stations on this path, which runs up the hill from the cave of the Cristo image to the "Guadalupe" chapel in the cemetery above, are marked by ceramic representations of incidents from the Mexican Guadalupe foundation narrative). Hobgood (personal communication) remarks that the Indians consider the Cristo of Sacromonte to be a "brother" of their "Father God of Chalma."

After the Spanish conquest, Chalma was for a while spared much contact with the Spaniards, because of its remote location and relative inaccessibility. Moreover, the early Franciscan and Dominican missionaries tended to learn Nahuatl rather than Ocuiltec. It was left to the Augustinians (who arrived later and thus had something of a marginal character themselves) to learn the local vernacular and proselytize the tribes which had worshiped at Chalma before Cortés came—the Chalmateca, Ocuilteca, Malinalteca, and Otomí tribes, and the Nahuatl-speaking peoples of the remoter valleys of Toluca and Mexico. According to both popular oral tradition and Augustinian records, a miracle facilitated the conversion of the Chalma area, a sanctuary for the old religion for several years after the Conquest. During the Feast of Pentecost, May 8, 1537, five and a half years after the apparition of the Virgin of Guadalupe, Fray Nicolas de Perea, bearing a wooden crucifix, led some Indians to the cave of Chalma, where he had previously been shown a stone idol described as Oztotéotl (lit. "the god of the cave"—not very helpful as a means of identification!). Perea planned to place the crucifix in the cave. Joaquin Sardo, an Augustinian father who in 1810 published a book on the devotion to Our Lord of Chalma, describes (pp. 19–20) the miracle that allegedly took place:

But O stupendous miracle! O admirable portent of divine omnipotence! As soon as the holy ministers and the Indians had set foot in the cave, they were astonished to see the same miracle that the Almighty had worked among the Philistines (1 Kings 5) [when the idol of Dagon was overthrown by the ark of the Lord]. They discovered the sacred image of our Sovereign Redeemer, Jesus Christ crucified, placed on the same altar where the detestable idol had stood before. The idol, dashed to the ground and reduced to fragments, was serving as a footstool to the divine feet of the sacred image. . . . The whole altar and the pavement of the cave was carpeted with a variety of exquisite flowers.

The day of the "miracle," May 8, is the anniversary of the apparition of St. Michael the Archangel, a feast of the universal Church. Hobgood (p. 11) suggests that there may also be a connection between San Miguel and Huitzilopochtli—who, like the archangel, is a warrior, and has sometimes been represented as flying and winged. St. Michael's image, like that of St. Mary of Egypt, is now kept in a cave chapel behind the hostelry.

In the precontact period it had been the custom for pilgrims to travel to Chalma with others from their village, on a given day of the year, and to conduct rituals there in a group. The Augustinians allowed this custom to continue after they had converted Chalma into a Christian shrine (see plates 1 and 2). Nowadays, January 6, the Epiphany, is the Chalma pilgrimage day for Aztec and Otomí villages from the state of Mexico; February 2, for the Zápotecs from the Isthmus of Tehuantepec; the first Friday in Lent, for pilgrims from the states of Morelos, Guerrero, Tlaxcala, and Puebla; and Pentecost (called *Pascua chica*, or "Little Easter"—a movable feast around the end of May or beginning of June), for the inhabitants of the Valley of Mexico. The organization of regional pilgrimages with respect to these dates in the Christian calendar was probably related, at least in part, to similar dates in the Aztec ritual calendar. Today several strictly Christian feast days also draw large numbers of pilgrims from many parts of Mexico. The feasts of St. Augustine, on August 28; St. Michael, on September 29; and Christmas, on December 25, are all occasions on which as many as thirty thousand pilgrims gather at Chalma. Like other great shrines, Chalma also receives, throughout the year, a steady stream of devotees who are motivated, by special vows or by illness, to make the pilgrimage on an individual basis.

OCOTLÁN

The sanctuary of Our Lady of Ocotlán stands, in the splendor of its churrigueresque facade and towers, on a hill outside the walls of the ancient city of Tlaxcala, capital of the state of that name. In pre-Hispanic times, Tlaxcala was a warrior state never subdued by the Aztecs. Later allied by treaty with Cortés, it was undeniably a major factor in his success. The rivalry between Aztecs and Tlaxcalans persisted after the Conquest, but, ironically, Mexico City prospered, while Tlaxcala fell upon hard times. Mexico City's Virgin of Guadalupe has become the major focus of pilgrimage devotion, and the dominant symbol of corporate identity, not only for all Mexico but for the entire Western Hemisphere, while Tlaxcala's Virgin of Ocotlán today mainly attracts the inhabitants of the former Tlaxcalan linguistic region. The shrine to Our Lady of Ocotlán is, nonetheless, one of the more important pilgrimage centers in Mexico.

We shall examine here two main versions of the narrative relating to the foundation of the Ocotlán devotion. Both tell of the miraculous appearance of the Virgin Mary to Juan Diego Bernardino, a humble Indian from the village of Xiloxochtla (just south of the city of Tlaxcala), who worked at the Franciscan friary at Tlaxcala. After taking steps to authenticate the apparition reported to them by Juan Diego, the Franciscan friars swiftly established a shrine to Our Lady of Ocotlán—a name derived from the burning ocote tree which figures, with some variation of detail, in both narratives.

The narrative now promulgated as the official version is the one related by Nicanor Quiroz y Gutierrez in his *Historia de la Aparición de Nuestra Señora de Ocotlán* (1940). This version associates the Virgin with the cure of disease, almost always an important factor in determining the popular esteem accorded to pilgrimage shrines. The Quiroz version relates that in the early months of 1541 the Tlaxcalan region was smitten with a plague of smallpox, which

57

killed nine out of every ten Indians. Indeed, as is well known, the Indian population was generally decimated by diseases introduced by the Spaniards, and many formerly populous areas became almost totally desolate. The local *curanderos* (medicine men) could do nothing to prevent the spread of the smallpox among the natives. Its burning fever drove the people into the rivers, some of which were believed by the Indians to have healing properties. Juan Diego obtained permission to go to the nearby Rio Zahuapan to draw water for his afflicted kin in the village of Xiloxochtla. He walked down the hill from the friary, filled his water jar in the stream, and continued on to Xiloxochtla. When he crossed the western slope of the Cerro de San Lorenzo (St. Lawrence—a martyr also connected with fire, for he was broiled to death on a gridiron), he entered a dense grove of ocote pines, and was immediately confronted by a beautiful queenly woman, who said to him, "May God preserve you, my son. Where are you bound for?" He replied that he was taking water from the Zahuapan to his dying kin. The lady then told him to follow her, and she would give him water to cure not only his own family but all who would drink of it. Her heart, she said, was always ready to help the sick, for she could not endure to see their misfortune. Just where the path approached a *barranca* (ravine), she showed him a clear spring. A mere drop of this, she assured Juan Diego, would restore those touched by it to perfect health. Before his departure, the lady told him to inform the religious of the friary that in the grove where she now stood they would find her image. If they placed it in the Chapel of San Lorenzo, it would manifest her perfections, and she would bestow favors and kindnesses by its means. According to the narrative, the water of the spring cured of the fiery plague not only Juan Diego's kin but everyone in Xiloxochtla. Next day, Juan Diego told the friars what he had seen and heard. They interrogated him most carefully, three times, and his story remained consistent. To test him further, they followed him secretly to the spring. In their turn they were followed surreptitiously by many local Tlaxcalans. When they reached the ocote grove, it seemed to be on fire, particularly one tree, the largest, which was burning along its whole length. Next morning, the Franciscans returned to the grove and found that the fire had apparently extinguished itself. One of the community had brought an axe and, at the guardian's behest, chopped down the large tree. In its trunk they found the promised image of the Virgin Mary. The guardian ordered the Indians to cut off ocote branches and walk in file singing hymns and chanting litanies, while the friars, bearing the image (made of ocote wood), brought up the rear. The image was then placed in San Lorenzo's chapel, in the niche of its titular patron, whose figure had been removed to make way for the image of the Virgin. Now begins an episode controlled by a motif found in many pilgrimage foundation narratives. The Indian sacristan of the chapel, resenting the removal of San Lorenzo's statue, replaced the saint's figure in the niche after taking down the image of the Virgin. Next morning, the figure of the Virgin was back in the niche, with the image of San Lorenzo to one side. The same thing happened on three successive nights (again, the traditional number three, perhaps based on the three days of Christ's entombment). This miracle confirmed the sacredness of the Virgin's image, which soon came to be called Nuestra Señora de Ocotlatla ("Our Lady of the Burning Ocote"), and is now known as Our Lady of Ocotlán; that is, of "the place of the ocote." Today, the ornate basilica of Ocotlán is freqented by tens of thousands of pilgrims on the major Marian feast days, and at night the pilgrims bear torches of ocote in their processions.

The other principal version of the Ocotlán foundation narrative is contained in a document dated 1547 and signed by Fray Martin Sarmiento de Hojacastro, then padre guardian of the Franciscan friary at Tlaxcala. Hugo Nutini (1970) has managed to obtain access to this document and has summarized Fray Martín's account (the original of which is now in the hands of Sr. Rafael Lozano Lavalle of Tlaxcala). Though Fray Martín does not deal with the theme of miraculous healing found in the Quiroz version, he is far more explicit about the syncretic aspects of the Ocotlán cult. Indeed, Nutini goes so far as to characterize as "guided syncretism" the means employed by the early Franciscans to convert the Tlaxcalan Indians. We shall take up the question of syncretism more fully in chapter 3. Here it is sufficient to note that among the Tlaxcalans, as among other Indian peoples, the Franciscan missionaries in the period following the

Conquest "consciously and explicitly" (to use Nutini's words) encouraged the equation of many elements of Catholicism with elements of the indigenous religion. (Of course, in that respect the friars were merely continuing the policy set down much earlier by Gregory the Great in his pastoral letter to Mellitus.)

To understand the syncretism in the Ocotlán cult, one must be aware of the pre-Hispanic antecedents (here summarized from Nutini 1970:3). On the hill now known as Ocotlán, overlooking Tlaxcala, there was, before the Christianization of the region, a temple dedicated to the goddess Xochiquetzalli. Primarily a goddess of the arts, and of flowers and games, she was essentially a benevolent deity and, after Camaxtli (the tribal god of the Tlaxcalans), she was probably the most venerated deity in the region. According to tradition, Xochiquetzalli would appear, in a burning ocote tree, to especially worthy individuals and would grant whatever they asked of her. She was always portrayed wearing a blue *huipil* (a blouselike upper garment) and a white *titixtle* (a wraparound skirt). Finally, and most important with respect to the Marian cult, Xochiquetzalli was sometimes considered "the mother of the gods,"[2] a designation that must have been known to the friars.

As we have not been able to see the document bearing Fray Martín's narrative, the account we give here is based on Nutini's summary. On the morning of May 12, 1541, the Virgin Mary appeared to Juan Diego Bernardino in a wooded area close to the site of the former temple of Xochiquetzalli (that temple, Fray Martín notes, had been destroyed in 1528, by order of Fray Martín de Valencia, then padre guardian at the Franciscan friary). Juan Diego was a *topil* (a messenger or attendant), whose job it was to keep the altars of the friary always decorated with flowers. He had been in the service of the friars for more than ten years when the Virgin appeared to him, and was, in Fray Martín's estimation, "as thoroughly Christianized as a person of his humble condition could be," given the proximity to paganism, many customs of which were still openly practiced by the local Indians. In the deposition Juan Diego gave to

[2] At least in the Tlaxcala-Puebla valley. Nutini notes that none of the sources pertaining to the goddess Chalchitlicue, Xochiquetzalli's counterpart in the Valley of Mexico, mention such an aspect.

the father superior of the friary, he stated that the Virgin, dressed in a blue *huipil* and a white *titixtle*, had appeared to him in a burning ocote tree, and had told him that a sanctuary to her should be built on the nearby ruins of the ancient temple. News of the apparition spread rapidly. Within a few days, thousands of pilgrims had come, from all over Tlaxcala. In response to the people's enthusiasm, the friars, headed by the padre guardian, soon took steps to authenticate the miraculous apparition. Within only three years the new cult of the Virgin of Ocotlán was established. By 1547 (the date of Fray Martín's account), there was a hermitage on the spot where the Virgin had appeared to Juan Diego, and plans were under way for a church on the site of the old temple. Nutini's summary ends, significantly, with the following comment:

At the end of the document, Fray Martín has the insight to say that although he is not entirely certain whether Juan Diego really saw and conversed with the Virgin Mary or with some other deity of his pagan past (he does not mention Xochiquetzalli specifically), it does not really matter, for even if the Indians have in mind something that is not entirely Christian when they come to pay homage to the apparition, eventually all will become clear to them, and they will truly come to understand what the Virgin Mary stands for [Nutini 1970:6–7; summarizing Fray Martín].

We can clearly see that the foundation narratives of the Ocotlán shrine recall certain details of *el ciclo de los pastores*, syncretized with indigenous, pre-Columbian motifs. Nutini (p. 7) points out the many parallels which assisted the syncretizing process: Xochiquetzalli and the Virgin Mary both were recognized as "mothers" (the former, "of the gods"; the latter, "of God"); both were associated with purity, goodness, and flowers, and could grant boons; the cults of both reached their yearly peak in May (the month of the Virgin's appearance to Don Diego); the apparition of Mary was near the site of the temple of Xochiquetzalli; the Virgin appeared in a burning ocote tree, just as Xochiquetzalli was believed to do; when the Virgin Mary appeared to Juan Diego, she wore the garb traditionally associated with the Tlaxcalan goddess; and, in Nutini's words, "the personality, condition, and social status of Juan Diego correspond identically to those worthy individuals to whom Xochiquetzalli appeared."

Nutini also stressed Juan Diego's role as *topil* in the convent of a religious order especially devoted to the Marian cultus, where he must have heard the friars frequently speak of the Virgin Mother of God. Nutini considers, too, that Juan Diego's Christian name of Bernardino is significant, since San Bernardino, syncretized with Camaxtli, was intimately associated with the syncretized Xochiquetzalli–Virgin Mary.

These examples illustrate the syncretic process, both spontaneous and "guided," through which the Spanish shepherds' cycle was indisseverably linked with indigenous pre-Columbian beliefs about encounters between humans and superhumans. In one important respect, Gregory's pastoral instructions to Mellitus were not followed in Mexico: the temples of the pre-Hispanic deities were nearly always destroyed, and churches were erected in their place. But the *tabula rasa* ideal propounded by the early missionaries soon had to come to terms with the cultural and ritual complexity of the indigenous culture. Compromises were made: theology changed, and syncretism saved the communitas of pilgrimage.

A TALE OF TWO VIRGINS AND ONE CITY: OUR LADY OF GUADALUPE, OUR LADY OF THE REMEDIES, AND MEXICO CITY

We have found that pilgrimage systems, at several levels of complexity and organization, can often be fruitfully studied as binary sets of oppositions. Such sets are usually associated with political cleavage and segmentation. For example, Muslim pilgrimage as a whole is opposed to Christian pilgrimage in the West, and to Hindu pilgrimage in the East, while within Christendom the Roman Catholic Church and the Eastern Orthodox compete for control and influence over the Holy Places of Palestine. Similarly, in Mexico, the shrine of the Virgin of Guadalupe (situated just within the northern limits of Mexico City), though unquestionably the main focus of all Mexican pilgrimage, can be studied as one member of a contrasting pair with each of several other major shrines in turn—for example, Our Lord of Chalma; Our Lady of Ocotlán (we have already noted how this shrine reflects the political status of Tlaxcala with respect to Mexico City); and, as we shall now see, Our Lady of the Remedies, a "rival" shrine in Mexico City itself.

We first became aware of the very interesting symbolic opposition between Our Lady of Guadalupe and Our Lady of the Remedies in the course of a political-anthropological study of symbolic processes in the Insurgencia, the Mexican struggle for Independence from Spanish overlordship in 1810 (see V. Turner 1974a: chapter 3). The Mexican insurgents, led by the priest Miguel Hidalgo y Costilla, fought under the banner of Our Lady of Guadalupe, snatched by Hidalgo from a country church; while the Spanish viceroy invested the tiny image of Our Lady of the Remedies with a marshal's baton, and made her the spiritual commander of the Spanish forces. But the opposition between the two Virgins is far older than this. The Indians' devotion to Our Lady of Guadalupe is inseparably connected with the visions of an Aztec Indian named Juan Diego Cuauhtlatohuac, a catechumen of the Franciscan missionaries, ten years after Cortés's conquest; while the image of Our Lady of the Remedies was once, according to tradition, the "saddle Virgin" carried by one of Cortés's conquistadors, Juan Rodriguez de Villafuerte (saddle Virgins, or *virgenes arzoneras,* were small images of the Virgin which were traditionally attached to the high pommel of the *caballeros'* saddles). As the story goes, Juan Rodriguez hid his saddle Virgin among the leaves of a cactus during the Noche Triste, July 8, 1520, when the Aztec army, in their one major victory, drove the invaders in rout from Tenochtitlán. Later, it is said, the image was found by a venturesome Indian ("a converted Indian chief," according to Behrens 1966:19–20) and was treated with reverence by the Indians. But its Spanish genesis, contrasted with the reputedly indigenous origin of the Mexican Guadalupe cult, has played an important role in its history and in that of Mexico. The politicization of these cults has long prompted criticism from Catholic spokesmen (see Jesus Garcia Gutierrez 1875, 2d ed. 1940; and Miguel Flores Solis 1972), who have regarded such polarization as a deviation from the Church's universal teaching on the devotion to the Virgin. When Marian shrines have achieved national eminence, they have, indeed, sometimes became a source of ecclesiastical embarrassment, for the notion of motherhood has been almost everywhere associated with the notion of national community. Thus, instead of serving as symbols of universal *ecclesia*, they may act to divide and dismember that mystical body by stressing nationalism and regionalism. The granting of papal privileges and coronation honors to images of the Virgin in important pilgrimage shrines became widespread in the early nineteenth century.[3] Since then we have had a spate of nationalistic Virgins. At Knock, Our Lady, Queen of Ireland; at Częstochowa, Our Lady, Queen of Poland; and at Guadalupe, Our Lady, Queen of Mexico; all have become foci of mystical nationalism. (It is interesting to note that all these countries lacked a secular royalty at the time the images were crowned.) By crowning these famous images in elaborate ceremonies, and by the granting or withholding of indulgences, an important stimulus of pilgrimage, the ecclesiastical hierarchy of course hoped to demonstrate, in a symbolic fashion, that the shrines were all integrated with the universal Church.

In Mexico, during the Insurgencia, Catholics fought against Catholics, following rival Virgins. As often happens in religious systems (whether polytheistic or monotheistic) with a multiplicity of symbol-vehicles or "signifiers," the sensorily perceptible vehicles took on lives of their own, and the original "meaning," or "signified," became attenuated. The images of the Virgin soon became personifications of opposed political interests, even of conflicting ethnicities. It was not a clear case of Spanish Los Remedios versus Indian and mestizo Guadalupe, however. Its characterization as such seems to have been a product of the anticlericalism of the era of President Calles (1924–28), and was uncritically accepted by Ricard (1933). Rather did the viceroy Venegas and the creoles who supported the Spanish cause succeed in persuading a population descended mainly from the Aztecs that Hidalgo's following were Chichimecas, descendants of northern barbarians, who would destroy them all. The viceroy attempted thus to "divide and conquer." Today, as in past centuries, Our Lady of the Remedies has a huge Indian and mestizo following, especially in Mexico City. On the

---

[3] Our Lady of Guadalupe at Tepeyac had received papal privileges since the time of Pope Gregory XIII (1572–85), however, long before her coronation in 1895 (see Leies 1964:407–16).

great pilgrimage feast of the Nativity of the Blessed Virgin Mary, we have heard a Dominican preacher, in the pulpit beneath the image of Our Lady of the Remedies (in the Church of San Bartolo Naucalpan, just outside the city boundaries), proclaim to his largely brown-skinned congregation that she "is not the Lady of the Whites, nor the Lady of the Indians, nor the Lady of the Mestizos; she is the Mother of God and the Lady of all Christians. . . . the same Mary as Our Lady of Guadalupe, Our Lady of Zapopan [near Guadalajara], and Our Lady of the Candelaria [at San Juan de los Lagos]." We must look behind her image, he said, to the Queen of Heaven, our own mother ever since Our Lord commended her into the care of St. John the Apostle at Calvary, for John stood at that time and place for all of us mortal men. Thus that preacher, like other Catholic spokesmen before him, attacked the view that Our Lady of the Remedies was for Spaniards and Our Lady of Guadalupe, for Indians.

Both Guadalupe and Los Remedios go back, as Christian pilgrimages (Tepeyac, the site of Guadalupe, was a pilgrimage center in pre-Columbian times as well),[4] to the period immediately following the Conquest. Simone Watson, in *The Cult of Our Lady of Guadalupe* (1964:19), points out that there are more than twenty indisputable references to Our Lady of Guadalupe in the literature of the sixteenth century, including one by the English seaman Miles Philips, who was abandoned, with some companions, by Sir John Hawkins in October, 1568, on the coast of the Gulf of Mexico. Philips's account, recorded by the Renaissance historian and geographer Richard Hakluyt (1598–1600; repr.1926:vol.6,pp.314–15), is the earliest account in English of this great Mexican devotion. Referring to "Our Lady's Church" in Mexico City, whither he and his fifteen companions had been brought as prisoners, Philips, a non-Catholic and an enemy of Spain, declared in his diary:

Whensoever any Spaniards pass by this church, although they be on horseback, they will alight and come into the church and kneel before the image and pray to Our Lady to defend them from all evil;

---

[4] In the literature it is not difficult to find scholars who attest to the early existence of these pilgrimage centers; see, for example, Leies 1964:137–38, Maza 1953:14, Vaillant 1953:262, and Madsen 1969:378.

so whether he be a horseman or a footman he will not pass by, but first go into the church and pray as aforesaid, which if they do not they think they shall never prosper: which Image they call in the Spanish tongue Nuestra Señora de Guadalupe.

This account clearly indicates that Spaniards, too, were devoted to the cult of the Virgin of Guadalupe less than four decades after the traditional date of its founding (1531).

Mariano Cuevas, in his *Historia de la iglesia en México*, cites a number of references to the cultus of Our Lady of the Remedies in the sixteenth-century literature (see Flores Solís 1972:58), as do José Bravo Ugarte (1947), Joseph H. L. Schlarman (1951), Mario Colín (1967:213), and other modern historians. Actually, the devotion to Mary as Nuestra Señora de los Remedios (in English, "help," "cure," "refuges," as well as "remedies") is known almost from the beginning of Spanish colonization in the New World. Cuevas (1946:334) asserts that the first diocese in Mexico was that of Santa María de los Remedios in Yucatán. With the approval of Pope Leo X,[5] a church was built in Cozumel and dedicated to Our Lady of the Remedies in 1518, three years before the fall of Tenochtitlán (which became Mexico City). Even earlier, in 1514, Captain Diego Velasquez, who accompanied Columbus on his second voyage, had founded the town of Remedios in central Cuba. As the name suggests, Los Remedios was sometimes associated with hospitals. In 1544, a hospital dedicated to Our Lady of Remedies was founded in Campeche, a town on the Gulf Coast, by the first Franciscan missionaries to this Maya-speaking area. At a later date, the Carmelites founded a hospital with that name in the city of Puebla. Soon many churches were named after Our Lady of the Remedies, each containing an appropriate devotional image of the Virgin Mary. Quite often these images are identified with Nuestra Señora del Patrocinio (Protection); for instance, at the mining city of Zacatecas. Today there are churches dedicated to Our Lady of the Remedies in the cities of San Luis Potosí; Comonfort in Guanajuato; Durango; Tlalpujahua and Zitácuaro in Michoacán; and Cholula in Puebla state.

[5] According to Cuevas, Pope Leo X approved the erection of the church in Cozumel in his bull *Sacri Apostolatus Ministerio* of February 25, 1518 (see Cuevas 1946 ed.: vol. 1, p. 293).

There may well be others, unrecorded in our sources. The conjunction between hospitals and the devotion to Our Lady of the Remedies is probably not unrelated to the plagues and diseases introduced by the Spaniards, which wiped out literally millions of Indians in a few decades following the Conquest. The Spaniards brought both the diseases and the remedies. Our Lady of the Remedies is, then, essentially an imported devotion which took root with the conquistadors in Mexico and, like them, rejuvenated the local population, previously decimated.

Unlike Our Lady of Guadalupe, whose image, we shall see, is unique and had an indigenous origin, Our Lady of the Remedies is multiple in expression, with considerable variation in the form of her images. Although miracles are attested in the history and legend of the image of Our Lady of the Remedies in Mexico City, the cultus was not founded on a single grand supernatural event as was that of Guadalupe, but rather on a series of happy "accidents," behind which Mexican believers readily saw the workings of God's grace and plan. Churches dedicated to the Virgin of Guadalupe possess paintings (and, occasionally, statues) faithfully replicating the features of the miraculous painting at Tepeyac. The churches honoring Our Lady of the Remedies have statues of varied forms and styles, though all the images are, like the statue at the shrine in Mexico City, diminutive in character; Hector Arroyo (1971:28) has described the Lady of Mexico City as *una deliciosa y menudita Virgen Española* ("a delightful and tiny Spanish Virgin —see plate 3). The small scale of these images is related to their origin as saddle Virgins. (Cortés himself carried on his person a medallion of the Virgin[6] through all his adventures.) Several of the Mexican images of Our Lady of the Remedies to be seen today are, in fact, of early sixteenth-century, popular Spanish workmanship. But, as if by way of compensation for their humble craftsmanship, the images are in-

[6] Ricard (1966:15) has stated that Cortés "always carried on his person an image of the Virgin Mary, to whom he was strongly devoted." Cuevas (1928:vol.1,p.111), on the basis of written accounts left by Bernal Diaz del Castillo, the sixteenth-century historian and companion of Cortés, has published a picture of the gold medallion reputedly carried by Cortés; the medallion bears an image of the Virgin Mary holding the infant Jesus and carrying a scepter.

variably dressed in the richest garments imaginable, and are often hung and encrusted with jewels and ornaments—a practice of Spanish origin,[7] though in execrable taste, in the view of some Mexican scholars. The Virgin of Guadalupe, in contrast, is dressed in a simple blue mantle and a rose-tinted tunic draped in great folds about her feet. Reproductions of that miraculous painting in the Basilica of Guadalupe are to be found everywhere in Mexico at all levels of devotion and cultures—from faded copies above domestic shrines in the huts of peasants, to small prints on the windshields of taxicabs, to transfers on the toolboxes of auto repairmen.

The popular tradition associated with Our Lady of the Remedies was set down in writing in 1788 by Antonio de Alcedo, a member of the Real Academia de Historia, and we draw upon that account for the summary presented here. The image of Our Lady of the Remedies was found under a cactus, as we have noted, by an Indian, a cacique whose Indian name was Cuautli ("eagle"). He was a recent convert to the Catholic faith and had received the baptismal name of Juan de Tovar. He was a native of the town of San Juan Teocalhuican, a short distance to the west of Otoncapulco. Some earlier accounts, among them the Jesuit father Francisco de Florencia's *La Milagrosa Invención de un Tesoro Escondido en un Campo* [the miraculous discovery of a treasure hidden in a field], published in 1685, assert: "Our Lady of the Remedies appeared several times to this noble Indian . . . asking him to make a hermitage (*ermita*) for her little image, where she would be able to receive the cultus which she merited as queen of heaven and special protectress of the conquistadors of Mexico" (quoted by Genaro Garcia 1909:664; Garcia synthesizes Fr. Florencia's account with another by Fr. Cisneros).

All accounts agree that Cuautli built a tiny hut (*caxoncito*) for the little image and made it offerings ("in ignorant simplicity," as Alcedo comments) of maize cakes and gruel (*atole*), as he might have done for an Aztec deity. One day, though, he came home from work and found the statue gone. The account tells that the statue

[7] Carlos Callejo (1958:92,95) tells us that the custom of dressing the image of Our Lady of Guadalupe in Estremadura was established toward the end of the fourteenth century.

had gone to seek the place where he had first found it. On seeing it back in its original place, he was astonished and he spread the tale around the area. Eventually the people of Mexico City decided to build a sumptuous church on the site. Our Lady of the Remedies was made the city's patroness, and the king of Spain ordained that a solemn feast be celebrated in her honor every September 1st. Whenever the city was endangered by plagues, droughts, wars, and the like, the image was brought to the cathedral from its shrine three leagues to the west of Mexico City (Alcedo 1788:409–10).[8]

The figure of Our Lady of the Remedies is a wooden sculpture about eleven inches in height, made of fire-hardened wood gilded and then polychromed—a now almost obsolete technique called *estofado*, involving the painting of *relievos*, raised work or reliefs, on a gilt ground. Traces of green, blue, red, and gold paint are still discernible on the wood. Since the seventeenth century, when it be-

[8] Our Lady of Guadalupe had a similar role. In the devastating flood of 1629, Leies tell us (1964:182–87), Our Lady of Guadalupe was "taken prisoner"; she was first brought to the archbishop's oratory, along with the statue of St. Catherine which was to keep her company, and was afterward placed in the cathedral. One could easily relate this account to the basic polarity between Our Lady of the Remedies and Our Lady of Guadalupe. As Braden has noted (1930:297), Los Remedios is sought for protection against drought, and Guadalupe for protection against floods (see also Maza 1953:31). To leave the matter here, however, would be to ignore the role of Our Lady of Guadalupe in other states of emergency as well. For example, we find that in the epidemic of 1544 (an epidemic which may have killed over 800,000 people), local officials organized a solemn procession of children, not to the shrine of Our Lady of the Remedies but to Our Lady of Guadalupe at Tepeyac (Ricard 1966:189).

A particularly interesting account of another state of emergency is given by Leies (1964:190–93). A great plague struck Mexico City in August, 1736, causing so many deaths that on December 17 the local officials and clergy decided that supernatural aid alone could save the city. The call for aid was first made not to Our Lady of the Remedies but to Our Lady of Loreto. A solemn novena was offered, but the plague raged on. Early in January, 1737, Our Lady of the Remedies—presumably possessing greater supernatural efficacy than Our Lady of Loreto—was brought to the cathedral; "but no relief followed." Out of desperation a suggestion was then made to bring the Virgin of Guadalupe captive to the city. Instead it was resolved "to have the Guadalupan Virgin publicly and solemnly declared 'Patroness of the City of Mexico.'" The Virgin of Guadalupe was transported from Tepeyac to the cathedral of Mexico City (on the 25th of May) and, as the account goes, this resulted in "the truly miraculous cessation of the great plague."

In this narrative we can see a hierarchical structuring of the devotional images, at least in terms of their efficacy or power. The proceedings bear a resemblance to African processes of divination to determine the appropriate ritual in cases of affliction.

came popular in Spain and the colonies to vest sacred images in richly embroidered robes, Our Lady of the Remedies has been said to excel all others in the sacred fashion parade. Once she had sixteen complete changes of vestments, each garment carefully itemized and described. The image became an index of the waxing fortunes of Mexico City during the colonial era, and was regarded as a potent influence against the city's misfortunes, whether they were due to culture or to nature.

Not only have pilgrims from the city always come to Los Remedios in great numbers during the octave of the Nativity of the Blessed Virgin Mary, from September 1 to September 8, but, as we have already noted, the image has often been borne from her sanctuary in the Church of San Bartolo Naucalpan to the capital, when calamity threatens. Between 1576 and 1922, it has been estimated, the image traveled to the cathedral in the great square of the Zócalo a total of seventy-five times, always amid deep solemnity.

In the unsanitary conditions of preindustrial Mexico, pestilence was common. For example, in 1576–1577 a plague carried off more than two thousand persons, and the physicians of the Hospital Real could not identify the plague or its cause. In the spring of 1577, the archbishop of Mexico, Don Pedro Moya de Contreras, and the viceroy, Don Martín Enriques, decreed that the image of Our Lady of the Remedies should be taken to the cathedral. There a novena was conducted, invoking the intercession of Our Lady of the Remedies, under the special title "Health of the Sick." When the image was returned to its sanctuary, in early April, the rains burst forth and continued through November, purifying the air and ending the pestilence. The role of rainmaker (in which Los Remedios perhaps succeeded the Aztec and pre-Aztec deity Tlaloc) was taken up by her again in 1597 and 1616. Drought and plague were always intimately related in Mexico, as were their opposites: rain, health, and abundance.

It is not for us to determine the validity of such miraculous claims. What is important for our purposes here is that the beliefs associated with Los Remedios reveal several themes widely recurrent in the charter legends of other pilgrimage devotions, both in Mexico and elsewhere. One theme, the concealment of a cherished sacred object when it is endangered by foes of the faith, is particularly active in Mexico today, as we have had ample opportunity to ascertain.

If we may digress briefly from Los Remedios, we have observed, in a cultus centered in Tlaxcala, another interesting and illuminating example of the theme of concealment in Mexican Catholic folk belief. When we visited the cathedral of Tlaxcala, we noticed that much attention was being paid, in a side chapel, to a small figurine of the Child Jesus, known as the Niño Santo (see plate 14). Many candles burned before this image clad in a white dress and cap; many letters petitioning him for help were affixed to the walls; worshipers rubbed the glass protecting the image, and prayed before it *milagritos* (small metal votive offerings representing parts of the body—arms, legs, and so on—cured by the Child's intercession) were displayed.[9] Children were lifted up to kiss the glass near the face of the image. An aged cripple on crutches, sombrero in hand, stood praying and licking his hand, which must have recently touched the glass (all over the Catholic pilgrimage world we have seen such evidence of belief in the tactile transmission of grace; it is not to be thought of merely as contagious magic, for it is mediated through a carefully learned theology of incarnation which recognizes that selected components of the material order were sanctified through the bodily sacrifice of Jesus—at any rate, demythologizing processes have not yet ventured into these holy quarters!).

We were intrigued by the cultus of the Niño, and through our research assistant, Jorge Serrano, we asked the lady vending sacred objects near the entrance of the cathedral if she could tell us anything about the devotion. We shall try to preserve the flavor of her reply in this translation:

The Niño came out of private life when the Callistas [followers of the anticlerical dictator Plutarco Calles] came here and intended to burn the sacred images in Tlaxcala.

Before those days, the Niño was not in a church or a public place, but in the private home of a little girl, as a private devotion. She

[9] This last practice goes back to the ancient Greek cultus of Asklepios, god of medicine, in the pre-Christian Mediterranean region.

71

used to talk with him: the talking was in a very nice, friendly way. She used to ask him personal, private questions, such as: "Why don't you want me to change your clothes more often?"—because the little girl liked to change his clothes and clean them often. Sometimes it was difficult; the Niño became angry because of the jokes and sayings of the girl. The baby Niño jumped from her and went away. This was the first time that the Niño started his career.

The second time was the time of the Callistas. The Child ran out of the house—walking around in this area, hiding himself from his persecutors. People were then saying he was bewitched or that somebody had practiced witchcraft on him. After some days, though, the same girl found him walking somewhere. She brought him back home and told what she had found. Her parents were afraid and called the parish priest. She told him everything that had happened when she changed the baby. The parish priest was also afraid and exorcised the doll (muñeco)—no, not the doll, the Niño. Then he kept the image secluded in the church. To his surprise, next day the Niño was not there. He found him on top of the tabernacle of the church, moved from the altar on which he had been at first. He was holding in his raised hand the selfsame cross with which he had been exorcised! Previously his hands had been just stiff, attached to his body.

The child also grows. He used to be only twenty centimeters long, and the little girl used to keep him in a shoe box. Now he is about thirty-five centimeters long.

Wood-carvers used to come to the girl's house before this, selling holy images. The people in the house bought this image. The girl used to tease the Niño, saying, "Why are you so ugly?" The image was then not so good as you see it now. While the little girl was teasing him, he gradually became better in shape and size. Now he is very famous, people even come from Enseñada, Baja California, to see him. People like him very much because of his playful behavior and also because of his wanderings. There was once a booklet about him, but now it is out of print. I asked the parish priest to reprint it. He said he would ask authority from the bishop. The bishop of Tlaxcala said, "Don't bother me, another time!" He said the same about the printed prayers of the Niño. [Perhaps we may see here a post-Conciliar stance!]

The Niño has a broken finger on his left hand. Why? Several times they have repaired the image, but he doesn't like it and drops the new piece of finger immediately.

The little girl (whose name was Concepción, she used to live where the post office is now, and died in maturity) used to treat the Niño as a toy sometimes. She played with him, chatted with him, dressed him up. They called him Andaloncito, "the great little walker," because of his habit of walking away. People often ask me, "Have you ever seen him walking?" I say, "Never." I have never asked him to walk. But people who are very devout and saintly see him walking. But not me, how could I see him? [Laughter.]

The woman's tone, quick, gay, sometimes excited, in no way solemn or pious, reminded us keenly of the way African villagers speak of and address their ancestral spirits. It was the tone of a culture in which the religious domain is accepted as naturally as any other. Puritanism, in alienating religion from the realm of the magical and miraculous, has also, paradoxically, alienated the everyday realm from the religious. We mention the Niño of Tlaxcala not only to illustrate how the peregrinal theme of concealment has persisted for centuries but to give the reader something of the smack of Mexican folk religion. People must have talked of the Virgencita (Little Virgin) of Los Remedios, much as the woman in Tlaxcala Cathedral spoke of the Niño, whose devotion began as late as the 1920s.

The Virgencita and the Niño Santo are also representative of yet another important religious theme—the potency of the small and the weak, especially children. This theme is rooted deeply in the Judeo-Christian tradition: "A little child shall lead them" (Isaiah 11:6); "Suffer these little ones to come unto me" (Mark 10:11); and "He who offends one of these little ones, it were better that a millstone should be hung around his neck" (Matt. 18:6)—not to mention the story of the birth and infancy of Jesus himself. But the concept has pre-Columbian associations as well: children were sacrificed to the rain god Tlaloc and to his wife Chalchihuitlicue because it was believed that the parents' love for the children produced sacrificial tears which made rain in the land and benefited everyone else's children. When Christianity introduced its concept of the sacred power of the worldly powerless (the teaching of Jesus is charged with metaphors of childhood innocence as a premonition of heaven), images representing human littleness inevitably became associated with the general good, the total community's welfare, as opposed to selfish or sectional interests—and thus with the fertility of men, animals, and crops, as well as with their preconditions: peace in the cultural order, and rain (not excess rain, only "little" rain) in the natural realm.

Littleness has still another symbolic function: it represents the

73

beginning of the life-cycle, often equated with the seasonal cycle. In her study *The Transformations of the Hummingbird* (1976), Eva Hunt has shown that a song (recorded in the region of Zinacantan) equating a hummingbird with a large white hawk is not a paradox but represents part of the debris of an ancient myth cycle in which the hummingbird = the sun in the early spring, and the white hawk = the sun in its midsummer brilliance. Hunt relates this to the Aztec cult of Huitzilopochtli, the sun god and war god, whose name means "hummingbird on the left hand." The tiny bird grows into the great predator. In anthropomorphic representations, Huitzilopochtli is often depicted as a child. Farther north, among the Navajos, the deity called Changing Woman is represented as moving through all the phases of the female cycle.

Another prevalent theme common to the foundation narratives of the Remedios and Niño Santo (Tlaxcala) devotions is that the sacred figure chooses the location of its shrine. In the annals of Christian hagiography, great emphasis is placed on the geographic site of pilgrimage centers, and the "charter legends" often relate that the choice of the site by the saint in question—or by Christ or Mary if the devotion is to either of them—was revealed by miraculous means. Juan de Tovar, the converted Aztec chief who discovered the abandoned image of Los Remedios, had his own views about where to store it, and he worshiped it as a pagan Aztec might have worshiped the goddess Chalchihuitlicue, with regular offerings of maize cakes and gruel. But the image, like the Niño of Tlaxcala, had a life and will of its own. It chose for the place of its veneration the spot where the Spaniard had first concealed it. This tricksterlike behavior—a metaphor for the apparently whimsical action of grace itself—is also reminiscent of the Niño of the Tepozteco, about whom there is a whole myth cycle mentioned by Redfield (1956).

As anthropologists, we have often been disconcerted to find that pilgrimage motifs and themes which we felt sure were of indigenous origin are shared at the popular level by Catholics everywhere. This is true for the peregrinal motif of "little images" as well as for that of "roving images choosing the site of their shrine." An interesting example of the former is the Santissimo Bambino d'Aracoeli (see plate 19)—which we have seen, in its little chapel in the

Church of Sta. Maria d'Aracoeli in Rome, an ancient church exemplifying for Romans the triumph of Christianity over the pagan world. Tradition holds that the figure of the Bambino was carved in the late 1400s by a Franciscan friar in Jerusalem, from olive wood from the garden of Gethsemane. Following an ancient custom in Rome, the image is carried on request to the bedside of the sick. From Christmas to Epiphany (January 6), the Bambino is placed in its historic crib. Thousands of Roman children file past it, reciting the traditional "Poem of the Crib." As in Tlaxcala, hundreds of letters can be seen in the little chapel of the Bambino. They are requests for favors from afflicted individuals in all parts of the Catholic world. The Bambino of Aracoeli is the Niño of Tlaxcala writ large. But the Bambino, unlike the Niño, is not said to move under its own power. Each image of a sacred scriptural personality represents an idiosyncratic combination of mythemes, both universal and regional. Personhood characterizes the signifiers; theological and ethical universals characterize the signified.

Little Virgins, of course, abound in European iconography. (In Latin America, too, they are common; "saddle Virgins" are by no means the only diminutive images there.) Perhaps among the most pertinent for Mexico are the small images in Spain, especially the beautiful little wood figure of Our Lady of the Pillar, in Zarogoza— said to have been given by Mary herself, while still on earth, to St. James the Apostle, on the bank of the Ebro, on January 2, a. d. 40, to encourage his flagging mission in Spain. The image of Our Lady of Montserrat, of great antiquity (written records of her go back as far as A.D. 932) and still widely popular as a miracle-worker, is thirty-seven inches high, exquisitely carved and gilded, and elaborately adorned. The faces of Mother and Child have been blackened by age and by exposure through the years to the smoke of innumerable candles. Similar to the Virgin of the Remedies in size and decoration, she resembles, in her aspect of La Moreneta (the Little Dark One), the Mexican Virgin of Guadalupe, which is known as La Virgen Morena, from her brown coloring. Sometimes the color of these Virgins is associated with the line "O thou art black, my love" from the Song of Songs; but this association is probably a fallacy of the *post hoc, ergo propter hoc* variety. This theme is often linked with another important motif—that of the protective concealment of a sacred object by retreating defenders of the faith; this motif characterizes both the Spanish Guadalupe and Los Remedios narratives. To this must be added yet another widespread motif—the object's rediscovery by a humble person (the shepherd Gil Cordero in the Spanish example, and the Indian Juan de Tovar in the Mexican). Many are the tales of ancient images and paintings found again after long burial or abandonment. Usually some supernatural sign indicates the whereabouts of the sacred object—bright lights flashing from a storeroom or vestry where it has been abandoned or discarded; an apparition of the Virgin, as in the cases already mentioned; and the like. As we noted earlier, these motifs characterized the medieval *ciclo de los pastores*.

OUR LADY OF GUADALUPE: SPAIN AND MEXICO

The Mexican Guadalupe devotion resembles the Spanish—as well as many other Catholic Marian devotions—in that both tell of the apparition of the Madonna to a poor peasant. But there are many crucial differences between the two cults, as Mexican scholars have not hesitated to stress. (The Spanish affinities of Los Remedios are much stronger than those of the Mexican Guadalupe, though the Indian cacique and the maguey cactus in the Remedios story do have pre-Columbian implications.) Apart from the identity of name [10] and the reference to a Marian apparition, the Tepeyac devotion established itself as uniquely Mexican even in its earliest traditions. Since this pilgrimage has assumed the dimensions of a national, even pan-Ibero-American, cult, around which controversy has raged for centuries, it has become the focus of an immense literature, apologetic, polemical, poetical, and scholarly. This chanting and brawling of clerks has had little effect on the pilgrimage's pop-

[10] Callejo (1958:16) and Gallery (1960:4) say that Guadalupe means "hidden river"; López Beltrán (1966:86) tells us it means "river of light"; and, lastly, according to a dictionary on the etymology of Spanish proper names (Tibón 1956), it derives from the Arabic *Uadi al-lub*, meaning "rio de cascajo negro"—in English, "black gravel river."

OUR LORD OF CHALMA, MEXICO. PILGRIMS WORSHIPING OUR LORD OF
CHALMA, THE BLACK CHRIST WHICH CAN BE SEEN ON THE HIGH ALTAR (UPPER
LEFT) OF THE AUGUSTINIAN CHURCH OF SAN MICHEL. (THE CRUCIFIX HAS BEEN
CONSTRUCTED TO INCLUDE PORTIONS OF THE MIRACULOUS IMAGE FOUND IN
THE PAGAN CAVE OF CHALMA IN 1537.) FROM A DISTANCE OF ONE MILE, THE
PILGRIMS HAVE APPROACHED THE SHRINE ON THEIR KNEES.

PLATE 1

WAY STATION ON THE ROAD TO
CHALMA, MEXICO. THE CROSSES
ARE PAINTED GREEN, TRADITIONALLY
SYMBOLIZING RAIN AND FERTILITY.

OUR LADY OF THE REMEDIES,
MEXICO. THIS DIMINUTIVE VIRGIN—
ELEVEN INCHES HIGH—STANDS IN A
GLASS-ENCLOSED NICHE ON THE HIGH
ALTAR OF THE CHURCH OF SAN BAR-
TOLO NAUCALPAN, ON THE OUTSKIRTS
OF MEXICO CITY. SHE HOLDS THE
CHRIST CHILD, AND A FIELD MARSHAL'S
BATON. HER GARMENTS ARE EN-
CRUSTED WITH JEWELS AND HUNG
WITH A ROSARY.

PLATE 2

Ex-votos to Our Lady of the Remedies, Mexico. MANY OF THESE VOTIVE OFFERINGS, IN THE CHURCH OF SAN BARTOLO NAUCALPAN, VIVIDLY DEPICT THE FAMOUS IMAGE OF THE VIRGIN, WITH CHRIST CHILD, MARSHAL'S BATON, CRESCENT MOON, AND THE CACTUS WHERE, ACCORDING TO TRADITION, THE IMAGE WAS FOUND BY AN INDIAN.

Ex-votos to Our Lady of the Remedies, Mexico. VICTORIOUS CYCLISTS AND FOOTBALL PLAYERS ACKNOWLEDGE OUR LADY'S HELP BY PRESENTING THEIR CHAMPIONSHIP SHIRTS.

Pilgrims to Our Lady of the Remedies, Mexico. INDIAN PILGRIMS PREPARE THEIR EVENING MEAL UNDER AN AWNING OUTSIDE THE CHURCH OF SAN BARTOLO NAUCALPAN.

Plate 3

STATUE OF ST. MICHAEL THE ARCHANGEL, MEXICO. ST. MICHAEL GUARDS THE MAIN APPROACH TO THE CHURCH OF SAN BARTOLO NAUCALPAN (THE SHRINE OF OUR LADY OF THE REMEDIES) ON THE OUTSKIRTS OF MEXICO CITY. A VENDOR DISPLAYS HIS SELECTION OF BRIGHTLY COLORED WOMEN'S HAIRBANDS ON THE BASE OF THE STATUE. ON THE HILLSIDE BEHIND CAN BE SEEN THE BATTLE SLOGAN OF THE CRISTEROS, "VIVA CRISTO REY."

CONCHERO DANCER, MEXICO. OVERNIGHT PILGRIMS IN THE CHURCHYARD OUTSIDE SAN BARTOLO NAUCALPAN WATCH A DANCER IN TRADITIONAL INDIAN COSTUME.

PLATE 4

EX-VOTOS ON THE WAY OF THE CROSS, SAC-
ROMONTE, MEXICO. STRIPS OF CLOTH, SOME
CONTAINING UMBILICAL CORDS AND CHILDREN'S
SHOES, ARE HUNG ON EXPOSED TREE ROOTS. THE
CROWNS OF FLOWERS THAT PILGRIMS WEAR ON THE
LAST MILE OF THE JOURNEY ARE ALSO HUNG HERE.

DEATH-DANCER AT A MEXICAN SAINT'S FES-
TIVAL. THIS DANCER LEAPS ABOUT GROTESQUELY
AND THREATENS CHILDREN. ON THE SIDE OF THE
SKULL-LIKE MASK ARE DESIGNS REPRESENTING ELEC-
TRONS IN THEIR ORBIT, WHICH SIGNIFY THE NUCLEAR
BOMB.

PLATE 5

BASILICA OF GUADALUPE, MEXICO. ABOVE
LEFT: THIS PHOTO, TAKEN IN 1970, SHOWS THE POSI-
TION OF THE MIRACULOUS PAINTING OF THE VIRGIN OF
GUADALUPE ON THE HIGH ALTAR OF THE BASILICA
(WHICH HAS SINCE BEEN REBUILT). ABOVE RIGHT:
ENLARGED VIEW OF THE "BROWN" VIRGIN OF GUADA-
LUPE. BELOW: PENITENT PILGRIMS MAKING THEIR WAY
ON THEIR KNEES AT THE BASILICA OF GUADALUPE.

PLATE 6

DORMITION OF THE VIRGIN, CHURCH OF OUR LADY OF ÍZAMAL, YUCATÁN. OUR LADY SLEEPS ON THE EVE OF THE FEAST OF ASSUMPTION. AT HER FEET ARE OFFERINGS OF MELON, PUMPKINS, AND BREAD. THE IMAGE WILL, ON THE FOLLOWING DAY, BE PLACED IN AN UPRIGHT POSITION TO RECEIVE THE VENERATION OF THE PEOPLE.

OFFERINGS OF CORN TO OUR LADY OF ÍZAMAL, YUCATÁN.

PLATE 7

El Niño Santo of Tlaxcala. This image of the child Jesus, in a side chapel of the cathedral of Tlaxcala, is revered as a great miracle-worker.

Plate 8

ular appeal. According to one estimate, an average of 15,000 persons visit the shrine of Guadalupe each day of the year; in our opinion this is no exaggeration, though some of these visitors must be reckoned as tourists, not full-fledged pilgrims.

Both the history and the present social organization of the pilgrimage are centered on the holy picture of the Virgin. To quote the article on Guadalupe in the 1910 edition of the *Catholic Encyclopaedia*, the image of the Virgin "really constitutes Guadalupe . . . . It makes the shrine: it occasions the devotion. It is taken as representing the Immaculate Conception, being the lone figure of the woman with the sun, moon, and star accompaniments of the great apocalyptic sign, and in addition a supporting angel under the crescent." As these references to dogmatic matters suggest, the Church has been attentive to the growth of this devotion for a considerable time. Indeed, the immense popularity of the cultus among Mexicans of all backgrounds has required the Church, especially its Congregation of Rites, to keep a watchful eye, for Catholicism's long history has been spotted with visionaries, prophets, and enthusiasts whose teachings have conflicted with orthodoxy and whose eager followers have disrupted orderly civil and ecclesiastical life.

The most coherent narratives of the genesis of the Guadalupe devotion emerged from the Apostolic Process the Church conducted in Mexico City in 1666. The Process was in response to a request, sent by 13 prominent Mexican Catholics to Pope Alexander VII in 1663, that December 12, the traditional date of the miraculous appearance of the painting on an Indian's cloak, should be kept as a day of precept with a proper Mass and Office. In canon law, a precept is a command given to a single person by his ecclesiastical superior. Unlike a law, it binds the person everywhere, even outside the territory of the superior. But it cannot be enforced judicially, and it ceases with the authority of the superior, unless it is imposed by a legal document. Nevertheless, the granting of such a request represented, in the eyes of Rome, a major step toward the official recognition of Guadalupe as a devotion sanctioned by the Universal Church. It therefore called for serious scrutiny by the influential Congregation of Rites, especially since the request was accompanied by an episcopal decree from the bishop of Puebla (the see of Mexico City was vacant at the time), authoritatively affirming "the truth of the apparitions and the faithful devotion of the Mexican people" (cited in Simone Watson 1964:30). The result was a rescript by the Congregation of Rites to begin a plenary and formal investigation of the apparition. On January 7, 1666, one hundred and thirty-five years after the alleged miraculous events, the Canonical Chapter ordered the judiciary process to be opened.

To "demythologized" twentieth-century skeptics, positivists, and jurists, the proceedings must seem passing strange: a highly rational investigation, with due regard to the rules of evidence, into a set of testimonies which assumed the objective existence of a supernatural order. But for the anthropologist the evidence is invaluable; we do not foreclose issues on account of contemporary philosophical, religious, or political biases, but leave all open. Life is short, science long. In the case of Guadalupe, the evidence is systematically laid out, and fascinating from the standpoint of comparative symbology—the study of the verbal and nonverbal ways through which men seek a common understanding of their vital situation and social predicament. Part of the reason for the Catholic Church's endurance has been its flexible capacity for tapping the emotional power of local, regional, and national symbols to energize its major dogmas, doctrines, and tenets, as we shall see further in chapters 3 and 5. Local patriotism, focused on an icon or image related to a local miracle, is pressed into the service of loyalty to the universal Church. This is "sublimation" at the cultural level, translating ingroup solidarity into pan-Catholic normative communitas.

The Guadalupe Process had the task of testing the validity of the tradition of the Mexican Church with respect to the miracle. Since the examiners could not summon eyewitneses, they first sought the testimony of those they called "ear-witnesses," very old people who had heard of the events from senior kin who were contemporaries of Juan Diego. We would need at least a chapter to study just the testimony of the twenty aged Indians from the town of Cuauhtitlán, home of Juan Diego, the prime visionary; some of these Indians were alleged to be over a hundred years old—for example, Andrés

Juan, reputedly 115, would have been born only twenty years after the miraculous events. These elderly Indians testified that Juan Diego had lived, and that the story of the apparitions was common knowledge. Pablo Juárez, governor of Cuauhtitlán, said that the story was "so public and well known . . . that even the little children sang it" in the lifetime of his own grandmother (cited in Watson 1964:30). After the Indians, a number of clerics and religious were examined, including Luis Becerra Tanco and Miguel Sánchez, both of whom had written books on the cultus on the basis of "ancient sources," mainly oral. Then the royal physicians of Mexico, Don Lucas de Cardenas, Don Gerónimo Ortiz, and Juan de Melgarejo, testified that the damp and salty air around the site of the hermitage was not "a natural help in preserving it . . . it should have caused its total ruin . . . and the fineness of [the painting's] colors should have been dulled by the action of the nitrate" (*Informaciones de 1666*, p. 140). The implication of this testimony, of course, was that the painting was preserved by miraculous means.

On April 14, 1666, the findings of the judiciary process, together with Becerra Tanco's written version of the traditional account of the apparition, were sent to Pope Alexander VII. Rome exercised its usual prudence, however, and nearly a century passed before Pope Benedict XIV, in his brief *Non est equidem*, dated May 25, 1754, finally acceded to the request of the Mexican hierarchy that the "Most Blessed Virgin, approved and confirmed with Apostolic Authority, should be elected [by the Congregation of Rites], under the title of Guadalupe, as Patroness and Protectress of New Spain" with a special Office and Mass of her own. The testimonies of 1666 were thus retrospectively validated by Rome.

The Apostolic Process had the effect of establishing one narrative as the basic Guadalupan canon. This narrative began with the *Nican Mophua*, so called from the first two words of the account, written in Nahuatl by the scholarly Aztec Don Antonio Valeriano (a student of the famous Sahagún), probably within a decade of the apparitions. The original manuscript disappeared in 1847, during the war between the United States and Mexico, when it was removed, with twenty-five other documents from the collection of Don Carlos de

79

Siguenza y Gongora, from the Royal University of Mexico; it is thought to be in the archives of the U.S. State Department in Washington, but no one is sure. Fortunately, copies had been made (two are in the New York City Public Library in the manuscript collection, *Monumentos Guadalupanos*), and several early Spanish translations exist. The first publicly printed account of the Guadalupe tradition in Spanish was that by the mystic-minded Fray Miguel Sánchez in 1648. Sánchez claimed that he had used ancient sources, but he did not specify them. In 1649, Luis Lazo de la Vega published an account in Nahuatl, *Huei Tlamahuicoltica*, which is now thought to be a transcription of the Valeriano original; this publication greatly stimulated the development of the cult. Finally, Fray Luis Becerra Tanco, who had also read the Valeriano original, translated Lazo de la Vega's Nahuatl account into lucid Castilian, as one of the key documents of the Apostolic Process. This was later to be known as *La Felicidad de Mexico*, and was published as a book in 1865. These authors, Valeriano, Sánchez, Lazo de la Vega, and Becerra Tanco are often spoken of as "the four evangelists of the good tidings of Tepeyac." The Nahuatl and Spanish texts, allegedly based on the original Valeriano account, have almost scriptural authority in Mexican folk Catholicism, and quotations from the Becerra Tanco version are to be found in churches and homes all over Mexico.

The Guadalupe narrative has a lilting, humorous, tender quality, difficult to convey in translation. It describes the encounters on and near the hill of Tepeyacac (now Tepeyac) between an Aztec commoner, Juan Diego, about fifty-five years old, and a maiden of about fifteen, whom he soon came to recognize as Mary, the Mother of God, from her words, deeds, and attributes. In his translation of Lazo de la Vega's Nahuatl version, Becerra Tanco succeeded in communicating what Bernardo Bergoénd (1967:46) has called *todo el sabor ingenuoso del texto primitivo* ("all the naive flavor of the primitive text"). Indeed, the tone strongly reminds us of the Ndembu folk tales and explanations of divination and ritual which we collected in Zambia, some of which we have published (see esp. V. Turner 1975a).

The narrative opens with Juan Diego, an Aztec Indian—whose Nahuatl name is given in other sources as some variant of Cuauhtlatohuac ("Singing Eagle")[11]—on his way from his home town of Cuauhtitlán, eighteen miles to the northeast of Tenochtitlán.[12] The reader will recall that the Aztec cacique who rediscovered the image of Our Lady of the Remedies was also called Juan (de Tovar) and Cuauhtli, or "Eagle." When we recall further that the "humble Tlax-calan commoner" who discovered in a burning ocote tree the mirac-ulous statue now venerated as Our Lady of Ocotlán, was tradi-tionally called Juan Diego, we understandably begin to wonder about the duplication of names. We may be in the presence of a body of tales which Lévi-Strauss would see as transformations of one another, various combinations and permutations of a set of themes. The mysterious "author" of this body of legend would be some Meso-American avatar of "l'esprit humaine," that invisible collective being who, Lévi-Strauss suggests, "plays" with a bundle of themes and relations, presenting, inverting, and variously com-bining them to generate a body of apparently concrete, quasi-his-torical stories, which clearly underline the "structural" themes cru-cial to the articulation of Mexican culture and, indeed, characteristic of all mankind's "pensée sauvage." We have at the root of the Gua-dalupe and Los Remedios devotions an indigenous "Eagle," whose Christian name is Juan Diego (John James) for Guadalupe, the para-digmatic Mexican devotion, and Juan for Los Remedios; while at Ocotlán we find another Juan Diego.[13] It will be recalled, moreover, that in Christian iconography the eagle is the traditional symbol of

[11] Behrens (1966:148) gives this meaning and spelling for the Nahuatl name; Walt-son (1964:18) tells us it was Cuauhtlatohuac, and that it means "he who talks like an eagle", Maza (1953:26) believes that Cuauhtlatontzin is the correct form—this is probably the diminutive form of the name, for -tzin is a diminutive suffix (see Lazo de la Vega 1926:36).

[12] Juan Diego, described as the "Immortal Ambassador of Holy Mary of Guada-lupe" on the plaque of his statue in Cuauhtitlán (see Leies 1964:131), was born in Cuauhtitlán, but apparently did not reside there. According to Maza (1953:57) the route from Cuauhtitlán to Tlatelolco does not pass by Tepeyac; Maza further suggests that Juan Diego actually lived in Tulpetlac.

[13] It is also interesting to note the duplication of the name Juan elsewhere in the foundation narratives. In the Guadalupe narrative we find not only Juan Diego, but Juan Bernardino (Juan Diego's uncle) and Juan de Zumárraga, the bishop of Mexico; for Los Remedios, there is not only Juan de Tovar but Juan Rodríguez de Villafuerte (the conquistador who is said to have brought the statue from Spain)—thus the statue went from the hands of one Juan to those of another Juan.

St. John the Evangelist; thus Spanish "Juan" = Nahuatl "Eagle." On the other hand, it has been shown by historians that Indians were received into the church in large groups in the early days, all the men in one group being given a single name or pair of names, such as Juan or Diego or Juan Diego; it is therefore likely that many early Indian converts were indeed called Juan. Nevertheless, corrupted as we are by structuralism, we find the identity of names in the foundation narratives of these three devotions suggestive, at the least. The name Cuauhtli, or "Eagle," further recalls the famous foundation myth of the Aztec empire: when the wandering tribe of barbarians (chichimecas) were looking for a sign to tell them where to build their city, they saw, on a small island in Lake Texcoco (now all but dried up), a huge eagle crouched on a prickly pear, in its beak a twisting snake. This sign is now embroidered on the national flag. If we were focusing on the comparative symbology of Mexican pilgrimage systems, instead of on their social and historical processes, there would be a great deal more to say about the syncretism here, for both Christian and Aztec traditions are replete with eagle symbolism. But for now it is enough for us to emphasize that an Aztec catechumen called at once Eagle and John, after the Evangelist (who was also, it must be remembered, thought to be the author of the Apocalypse, with its well-known Marian reference, Rev. 12:1, which some say has influenced the iconography of the miraculous painting of Our Lady of Guadalupe: "A woman clothed with the sun, and the moon under her feet"), stood at the human heart of Guadalupe and Los Remedios, while another Juan Diego was the recipient of the fiery vision of Ocotlán.

John James Eagle, then, representing Catholic evangelist, Spanish patron saint, and the Aztec nation, went walking from his home town to receive instruction in Christian doctrine from the friars at the Franciscan center of Tlatelolco (now deep in Mexico City), and to hear Mass. On his way he had to climb the hill of Tepeyacac just at the crack of dawn. What follows is quoted from Becerra Tanco's narrative, interlined with our literal translation of the Spanish:

Al llegar junto al cerrillo llamado Tepeyacac, amanecia;
When he approached the little hill called Tepeyac, dawn began;

y oyó cantar arriba del cerrillo; semejaba canto de
and he heard singing above the hill; it seemed the song

varios pájaros preciosos; callaban a ratos las voces de
of different choice birds; at times the voices of

los cantores; y parecía que el monte les respondía.
the singers were silent; and it seemed that the mountain echoed
them.

Su canto, muy suave y deleitoso, sobrepujaba al del
Their song was sweet and pleasing, surpassing that of the

coyoltótotl y del tzinizcan y de otros pájaros lindos que
coyoltótotl [bellbird?] and tzinizcan and other lovely singing

cantan. Se paró Juan Diego a ver y dijo para si:« por ventura
birds. Juan Diego halted to look and said to himself: "Am I,

¿soy digno de lo que oigo? ¿Quizas sueño? ¿me levanto de dormir?
perchance, worthy of what I hear? Maybe I'm dreaming? Did I

¿Dónde estoy? ¿Acaso en el paraíso terrenal que dejaron
rise from asleep? Where am I? Maybe I'm in the earthly

dicho los viejos, nuestros mayores? ¿Acaso ya en el cielo? »
paradise which the elders of our people spoke of? Maybe in

Estaba viendo hacia el oriente, arriba del cerrillo, de dónde
heaven?" He was looking toward the east, above the hill, whence

procedía el precioso canto celestial; y asi que cesó,
came the marvelous, heavenly song; and as soon as it ceased,

repentinamente se hizo el silencio, oyó que le llamaban de
suddenly there was silence, he heard someone calling him from the

arriba de cerrillo, y le decian:« Juanito, Juan Dieguito »
crest of the hill and saying: "Little John, little John James."

Luego se atrevió a ir a dónde le llamaban: no se sobresaltó
Then he dared to go whence he was being called: he did not in

un punto; al contrario, muy contento fue subiendo al
any way exceed himself; on the contrary he was quite happy to

cerrillo a ver de dónde le llamaban.
climb the hill to see the source of the voice calling him.

Cuando llegó a la cumbre, vio a una señora, que estaba allí
When he reached the top, he saw a lady who was standing there

de pie y que le dijo que se acercara.
and who told him to draw near.

Llegado a su presencia, se maravilló mucho de su sobrehumana
When he approached her, he wondered much at her superhuman

83

grandeza: su vestidura era radiante como el sol; el
greatness: her garments were as brilliant as the sun; the

risco en que posaba su planta, flechado por los resplandores,
steep rock on which she put her foot—fledged with sunbeams—

semejaba una ajorca de piedras preciosas; y
seemed like a Moorish anklet of precious stones; and it

relumbraba la tierra como el arco iris. Los mezquites,
sparkled on the ground like the rainbow. The thorny mesquite
trees,

nopales y otros diferentes hierbecillas
prickly pears, and other kinds of

que allí se suelen dar, parecían de
plants which are wont to grow there, seemed to be [made] of

esmeralda; su follaje, finas turquesas; y sus ramas
emerald; their foliage of fine turquoises; and their branches

y espinas brillaban como el oro.
and thorns shone like gold.

Se inclinó delante de ella y oyó su palabra muy blanda y
He bowed before her and heard her extremely mild and courteous

cortés, cual de quien atrae y estima mucho. Ella
speech, which charmed him and utterly delighted him. She

le dijo: «Juanito, el más pequeño de mis hijos,
asked him: "Little John, the smallest of my children [xocoyo-
te = "younger son"],

¿a dónde vas?» El respondió: «Señora y niña mía,
where are you going?" He replied: "Lady and my

tengo que llegar a tu casa de México Tlatelolco, a
daughter, I have to reach your house of Mexico Tlatelolco, to

seguir las cosas divinas, que nos dan y enseñan nuestros
follow the divine things that our priests give and

sacerdotes, delegados de Nuestro Señor.»
teach us, ministers of Our Lord."

Ella luego le habló y descubrió su santa voluntad; le dijo:
Then she spoke to him and made her will plain; she told him:

«Sabe y ten entendido, tú el más pequeño de mis hijos, que yo
"Know and take heed, littlest of my children, that I am the

soy la siempre Virgen Santa María, Madre del verdadero Dios
ever-Virgin St. Mary, Mother of the true God,

por quien se vive, del Creador cabe quien
through whom there is life; of the Creator through whom

está todo; Señor del cielo y de la tierra.
everything exists; Lord of heaven and earth.
Deseo vivamente que se me erija aquí un templo, para en
I deeply desire that a temple be built for me here, so that in
él mostrar y dar todo mi amor y compasión, auxilio y
it I may show and bestow all my love, compassion, aid, and
defensa, pues yo soy vuestra piadosa madre, a ti, a todos
protection, for I am indeed your merciful mother, yours, your
vostros juntos los moradores de esta tierra y a los demás
fellow-dwellers' in this land and my other
amadores míos que me invoquen y en mí confíen: óir allí sus
lovers' who plead with me and confide in me: that I may hear
lamentos, y remediar todas sus miserias, penas y
in it their griefs, and mend all their miseries, pains, and
dolores. Y para realizar lo que mi clemencia pretende, ve
afflictions. And to fulfill what my mercy seeks, go
al palacio del obispo de México y le dirás cómo yo te envío
to the palace of the bishop of Mexico and tell him how I sent
a manifestarle lo que mucho deseo, que aquí en el
you to declare to him what I so much desire, that here in the
llano me edifique un templo: le contarás
plain [of Mexico] he build me a temple: and you will tell him
puntualmente cuanto has visto y admirado, y lo que has
exactly what you have seen and wondered at, and what you have
oído. Ten por seguro que lo agradeceré bien y lo
heard. Regard it as certain that I will reward you well and
pagaré, porque le haré feliz y merecerás mucho
pay you, so that you may be happy and deserve
que yo recompense lo que te ecomiendo.
much to recompense you for what I have entrusted to you.
Mira que ya has oído mi mandato, hijo mío, el más
See to it that you have heard my command, my son, the littlest
pequeño; anda y pon todo tu esfuerzo.»
one; go and put all your heart into it."

  Al punto se inclinó delante de ella y le dijo:
  He promptly bowed before her and told her:
«Señora mía, voy a cumplir su mandato; por ahora me
"My Lady, I will obey your command; for the present I
despido de ti, yo tu humilde siervo.»
bid you goodbye, I, your humble servant."

This excerpt is enough to convey something of the simple peasant tone of the original, which is too often translated into frilly, ultra-pious English. Throughout, Juan Diego alternates between calling the Virgin "my lady" and "my daughter" (a translation of the Nahuatl *xocoyota*—the feminine form of *xocoyotl*, meaning "smallest of my sons," the term used by the Lady in addressing Juan Diego). There is a fascinating interplay between Juan Diego's awe for the Lady's office as "Mother of the true God," the Theotokos of the Ephesian Church Fathers, and his emotional reaction toward her appearance as a young woman of about fifteen years old, brown-skinned like himself, and speaking Nahuatl. The signifier seems to him to be disparate with what is signified. The same sort of paradox, of course, occurs throughout Christian theology— How could God the eternal Creator have deigned to be born a helpless babe among humble barnyard animals? Juan Diego does not seem to doubt for a moment that the Mother of God has appeared to him. But he is not above trying to play a harmless deception on her, as we shall see!

We shall briefly summarize the rest of the well-known story. Juan Diego went straight off to Fray Juan de Zumárraga, a Franciscan religious who had been appointed as first bishop-elect in the state of Mexico, to tell him the words of the Lady of Heaven. After he had been kept waiting for a good while by the bishop's servants at the episcopal palace, he was finally admitted to Zumárraga. The bishop heard him out but remained skeptical, though he said, kindly enough: "My son, come again when I'm less busy; but I'll think about your motives for coming to see me." Juan Diego went away, sad at the utter failure of his mission. When he reached the hill where he had first seen the Lady, she was awaiting him. He fell on his knees and said:

"Lady, littlest of my children, my daughter, I tried to fulfill your command, but found it hard to get to the bishop's chair. I saw him and gave him your message, just as you taught me. He received me kindly and listened attentively, but it was obvious he wasn't sure about it all. He said to me: 'Come again another time when we'll have more leisure and I'll look thoroughly into what it is you want.' It was quite plain to me from the way he replied that he thinks that

86

it's perhaps just my own invention, and not your order, that you want a temple made for you here. So I pray you, Lady and daughter, most earnestly (*encarecidamente*), that you ask some big shot (*alguno de los principales*), famous, respected, and honored, to take your message—then they might believe him. For I'm only a little fellow (*hombrecillo*), a piece of cord, a wooden stepladder, I'm the tail-end (*cola*), a leaf, I'm common folks (*soy gente menuda*), and you, my daughter, the littlest of my children, Lady, sent me to a place where I couldn't go and did not stop. Pardon me for causing you all this trouble and falling under your displeasure, Lady and my mistress."

But the Lady persisted in sending Juan Diego to the bishop, saying that though she could send anybody, he was her particular choice. Eventually, he succeeded in getting through to Zumárraga that something extraordinary had happened to him on the road. The bishop, who was beginning to believe the account, told him to ask the Lady for some sign of proof. On his return home, Juan Diego found that his uncle, Juan Bernardino, was ill with a burning fever. He went at once for a *curandero* (a native herabalist), but the *curandero's* medicine did not work, and Juan Bernardino pleaded with him to go to Tlatelolco and fetch a priest to confess him, for he felt near death. When Juan Diego approached the hill where the Lady usually met him, he said to himself: "If I go straight on, as I ordinarily do, I'm certain to see the Lady, and she'll persuade me to take the sign (*señal*) to the bishop. But first let's get rid of our affliction; I'll go first to call the priest for my poor uncle, who's certainly expecting him along."

With this, Juan Diego turned onto another path at the foot of the hill, to take a short cut to Mexico City toward the east, and not be detained by the Lady. It is a perennial source of amusement to Mexicans that Juan Diego was so simple as to think he could dodge an omnipresent being. The lady of course intercepted him, saying: "*Xocoyote mío*, where are you off to?" Juan Diego was rather shamefaced at being caught, but replied fairly spiritedly that he had to get a priest for his uncle. He begged her to be patient with him until he had done his duty, and he would attend to her tomorrow. The Virgin, who was not in the least offended, assured him that his uncle was already well. Greatly relieved, he told the Lady that the bishop wanted him to carry back some sign from her. She then told him to climb to the top of the hill. There he would find many kinds of flowers, which he was to pick and bring back to her. He did as he was told, not without wonder—for, though December is the cold season, he saw on the hilltop "different roses of Castile . . . fresh, open, fragrant, and precious." He picked them, wrapped them in his *tilma* (the Nahuatl word for a mantle of *ayate* (a cloth woven of maguey fibers), and carried them down to the Lady. She took them in her hands, gathered them together, and laid them once more on his *tilma*. Then she told him that the flowers were the sign requested, that he was to take them straight to the bishop and not open his mantle in anyone else's presence, and that he should tell the bishop how he had been told to climb the hill to pluck the flowers. This, she said, would persuade the bishop to build the church she asked for.

Once more the bishop's servants gave Juan Diego a hard time. He had to wait for hours, and they even tried to open his *tilma* to see what sort of proof he had of the miracle, which they all had heard about by this time. They glimpsed the roses of Castile, and coveted them because they were out of season. Three times they sought to seize the blooms; but whenever they attempted to touch them, they seemed not to be flowers but painted or worked or sewn onto the mantle. Eventually Juan Diego came before the bishop and told him the whole tale. "Here are the roses," he ended by saying, opening his white *tilma*. As the roses dropped onto the floor, so the narrative relates, "there suddenly appeared [on the *tilma*] the precious image of the ever-Virgin St. Mary, Mother of God, just exactly as it is even now in her temple of Tepeyacac, in her church which is named Guadalupe" (see plate 11).

The bishop, according to Lazo de la Vega's account in 1649, wept and asked forgiveness for not having done the Lady's bidding at once, then untied from Juan Diego's neck the *tilma*, on which was printed the figure of "the Señora of heaven," and carried it into his chapel. Next day Juan Diego showed them the place where the Lady wanted her church built. Then he hurried off, followed by a crowd of people from the bishop's palace, to see how his uncle was.

Juan Bernardino, now perfectly well, told them that he too had seen the Virgin, and that his cure had occurred at the very moment when the Lady had spoken of it to Juan Diego. Juan Bernardino added that the Lady told him that the blessed image (on the *tilma*) should be called Santa María de Guadalupe. Ecclesiastical scholars have surmised that a Nahuatl designation was used here by Juan Bernardino—who, like his nephew, claimed that the Lady spoke in this tongue. The designation might have been *Xanta Malia Tecuauhtlanopeuh*, "Saint Mary who appeared on the rocky summit." The Nahuatl phrase sounds rather like "Guadalupe," [14] a name familiar to the Spaniards from the famous shrine in Estremadura. [15]

According to widely held tradition, many miracles of healing attended the establishment of the miraculous painting in the crude adobe hermitage built by Indians on the site where the Lady had stood—the first miracle being the curing of a wounded Indian on

[14] López Beltrán (1966:86) gives the suggestions of several scholars concerning the possible Nahuatl origin of the Mexican "Guadalupe": Tequatlanópeuh = *la que tuvo origen de la cumbre de las peñas* ("the woman who originated on the rocky summit"); Tequantlaxópeuh = *la que auhyentó o aparto a los que nos comian* ("the woman who removed or frightened away those who ate us"); Coatlallupeuh = *la que auhyentó a la serpiente* ("the woman who frightened the serpent away"); and Coatlaxópeuh = *la que quebrantó, a la que halló, a pisoteó a la serpiente* ("the woman who discovered, crushed, or trampled the serpent").

[15] While there does not appear to be a primary, direct connection between the Guadalupe devotions of Spain and Mexico, their foundation narratives do share a number of themes, some of which are given here:

(a) In both narratives we find the theme of death or near-death: in the Tepeyac narrative, Juan Diego's uncle was near death; while in the narrative of Estremadura, Gil Cordero's son died." One version of the Spanish narrative tells us that Gil Cordero's son arose from death and said "he wished to go to the spot where the Blessed Virgin had appeared to his father" (Leies 1964:380), which seems to suggest that he received a message or a vision of the Virgin herself. In the Tepeyac narrative, it is explicitly stated that Juan Bernardino received a visit from the Virgin—a relatively important visit, for it was then that the Virgin revealed her name as "Guadalupe."

(b) The number three figures importantly in both traditions. Gil Cordero had been searching for his lost cow for three days before the apparition; Juan Diego saw three apparitions before the sign (the image on the *tilma*) was revealed to him, on his third visit to Zumárraga's house; the servants of the bishop-elect tried three times to remove the roses from Juan Diego's *tilma*.

(c) In both cases, the Virgin asked that a shrine be built in her honor. This appears to be a general, if not universal, theme in Marian devotion.

(d) Gil Cordero and Juan Diego both expressed doubt about their credibility in the eyes of those to whom they were supposed to relay the message of the Virgin (with regard to Gil Cordero, see Pérez y Gomez, 1965:3).

December 26, 1531, the very day on which the painting was transferred from Zumárraga's church. For several years Juan Diego was the caretaker of the hermitage. Like the Virgin of the Remedies, the Lady of Guadalupe speedily revealed herself as a protectress of Mexico City: its citizens attributed to her their deliverance from a disastrous inundation in September, 1621; and from a decimating plague, in 1737, in which forty thousand persons were estimated to have died (Velasquez 1931:279). Both of these miracles have been officially recognized by the Church.

It is tempting to draw up a list of oppositions between Our Lady of the Remedies and Our Lady of Guadalupe. The image of Los Remedios was hidden by a Spaniard and found by a converted Aztec chief; Guadalupe was, according to the evidence of her representation, Amerindian in physical type, and appeared speaking in Nahuatl to an Aztec commoner, but her devotion was legitimated in the presence of a Spanish bishop. Los Remedios has a simple foundation narrative, Guadalupe a complex one. The Dark Virgin of Guadalupe is often regarded as *mestiza*, a prototype of the millions of Mexican mestizos to come, while Our Lady of the Remedies is called La Gachupina, "spur" (a slang term for a native of Spain; when Hidalgo decided that it was time to begin the Insurgencia, he is said to have shouted, "Well, gentlemen, there is no help for it—we must go get ourselves some *gachupines*"). Guadalupe has a life-size painting, Los Remedios a tiny wooden image; the former is in a good state of preservation, the latter battered and obviously ancient. The image of Guadalupe is undecorated; the figure of Los Remedios has many changes of vestments. The painting of Guadalupe is believed to be of miraculous origin; the statue of Los Remedios is known to have been carved by human hands in Spain. Guadalupe is believed to have saved Mexico City from floods (the blue color of Guadalupe's robe is traditionally linked with rain and moisture); Los Remedios, from droughts. The Guadalupe picture has seldom been moved from Tepeyac; the image of Our Lady of the Remedies traveled from her shrine in the Church of San Bartolo Naucalpan seventy-five times between 1576 and 1922, when such processions were forbidden. Perhaps because her image has so often been taken to the cathedral of Mexico City, Los Remedios has been linked with the upper bureaucracy of New Spain. She has certainly been connected with antirevolutionary movements for some time. When French troops invaded Spain in 1809, for example, the image of Our Lady of the Remedies was taken from her sanctuary to Mexico City and was circulated through convents belonging to the various religious orders—possibly to protect the image from molestation at the hands of home-bred revolutionaries inspired by events in France. The religious at the Convent of St. Jerome dressed the figure (Mother and Child) with the insignia of a captain general of the army of New Spain. The regalia became very popular, and so remained for some time. Indeed, the military and imperialist associations of Los Remedios were augmented on October 31, 1810, when the insurgent leader Hidalgo and his troops were advancing on Mexico City. The viceroy, Venegas, had detailed a body guard of thirty lancers to the shrine of Our Lady of the Remedies, but then decided to have this peripatetic Virgin removed to the cathedral—ostensibly to save her from "atrocities," but perhaps to prevent her from becoming, like the Virgin of Guadalupe, a patroness of the mainly Indian and mestizo insurgents.[16] Venegas approached the image on his knees and placed in her tiny hands his own military staff, begging her to preserve the city from ruin. Journalists of the *ancien régime*, some of whom had previously compared Hidalgo with Attila the Hun, had a field day; comparisons of Venegas with Pope Leo I (who, according to tradition, turned the barbarian Attila and his hordes from the gates of Rome by supernatural means) were not wanting, for Hidalgo, without significant military opposition to his drive, turned back voluntarily almost at Mexico City's gates.

Our Lady of Guadalupe, on the other hand, has always been associated with the insurgency of the common people. When Hidalgo, at the very outset of his brief career of glory, had taken the town of Dolores, and was passing with his still negligible troops

---

[16] According to Hamil (1966:161), Venegas tried to bring *both* images of Mary into the city, but the canons of the basilica of Guadalupe saw no reason to remove their Virgin from her shrine. Their refusal was based partly on the fact that the insurgents were approaching Mexico City on the opposite side from the basilica, which was therefore not threatened.

through the hamlet of Atotonilco, he snatched up from the local church a banner bearing a picture of the Virgin of Guadalupe. Behind it then rallied many thousands of peasants, mostly of Indian descent but no longer tribally organized. A century later during Zapata's uprising in Morelos, the sombreros of the Zapatistas were decorated with embroidered facsimiles of the Guadalupe painting. On a less radical level, a process for the beatification (the first step toward sanctification) of Juan Diego, who is undoubtedly thought of as representing indigenous Mexicans, has long been promoted. We believe that its slow progress must reflect a prevalent view in the Vatican that Juan Diego's role in the foundation narrative of Guadalupe is more suggestive of structural and mythical relations than of historical facts. At all events, there is certainly, in the devotion to the Dark Virgin, a convergence of Mexican nationalism, indigenism, and peasant insurgency, in striking contrast to the Hispanic, conservative character of Los Remedios. It is interesting to note that devotees of Our Lady of the Remedies were influential in the right-wing Cristeros movement of the 1920s, a movement which violently opposed, to the point of armed rebellion and guerilla warfare, the anticlerical measures of Calles and other postrevolutionary presidents. Even when we visited the shrine of Our Lady of the Remedies in September, 1970, more than forty years after the time of the Cristeros, we saw their battle slogan written on a nearby hillside with large white stones—*Viva Cristo Rey*, "Long Live Christ the King" (see plate 7).

Both Guadalupe and Los Remedios are believed to protect the people of Mexico. It may be said, however, that Los Remedios has protected them insofar as they have participated in a hierarchical, paternalistic structure, dominated by *gachupín* whites in the colonial period, and by creoles with white affinities and associations in the postcolonial period. The Virgin of Guadalupe, on the other hand, being brown and Nahuatl-speaking in her origin, hardly superior to an Aztec commoner, protects and advances the interests of the lower classes. She was first recognized by Zumárraga, a member of the Franciscan Order, itself initially concerned with the poor; and she represents the first-known appearance of the Virgin Mary to inhabitants of the New World. In broad terms, then, Los Remedios is "structure," Guadalupe "communitas."

But history, as it often does, has partially reversed this ideal dichotomy, in that the Guadalupe pilgrimage today is far more coherently systematized and structured than the Los Remedios pilgrimage. Two major causes exist. On the one hand, there has been almost an excess of ecclesiastical approbation for the cultus, from the time of Bishop Zumárraga onward. On the other, because Guadalupe has served as a rallying point for Mexican nationalism, systematization of the pilgrimage has paralleled the ever-stricter organization and articulation of the republic under the Partido Revolucionario Institucional. One may call this a union of opposites, of structure and antistructure; indeed the very tension between such conflicting ideas and styles often generates and sustains great religious symbols. Transcendence of this type always defies logic, since it recognizes emotional and conational unisons, as well as cognitive integration.

Fray Alonso de Montúfar, the Dominican successor to Zumárraga as bishop of Mexico (missionary friars were seconded to the secular hierarchy in those pioneering days), strongly supported the Guadalupe devotion, defended its miraculous nature, and spread the cultus (Tornel y Mendivil 1849:142). A memorandum of 1575, written by Fray Everardo Mercuriano, provost general of the Society of Jesus, to Fray Pedro Sanchez, provincial of the Society in Mexico, is the earliest-known testimonial of papal interest in Guadalupe; this document indicates that Pope Gregory XIII extended the indulgences previously granted by the Holy See to the hermitage of Guadalupe (Demarest and Taylor 1956:243). Later popes—Urban VIII, Innocent X, and on February 6, 1664, Alexander VII— expressed their awareness of Guadalupe through the granting of indulgences and by other means. In 1667, Clement IX granted Mexico a plenary jubilee indulgence for December 12, the date of the miracle of the *tilma*. Altogether, twenty-two popes most significantly have given official blessings in one way or another to Guadalupe. The Indian maiden of the apparition has now become not only Queen and Patroness of Mexico but Empress of the Americas, by papal decree. Pope John XXIII placed all the works of the Episcopal Commission of Latin America under the protection of the Virgin of Guadalupe, and the Commission has given much ammunition to radical members of the lower clergy. Undoubtedly the support from

93

the Mexican hierarchy and the papacy has contributed both to the popularity of the devotion among the vast majority of ordinary Mexicans and to its use as a legitimating device for the various types of Mexican nationalism. Nationalism is never "pure and simple," but is always alloyed with ethnic, class, and local considerations. There are creole, mestizo or Ladino, Indian, and mulatto Mexicos, rich and poor Mexicos, and northern, southern, and Yucatecan Mexicos. But all find their point of convergence, their common perspective, in Our Lady of Guadalupe.

Nationalist developments in Mexico, have been aptly summarized by Frederick C. Turner (*The Dynamic of Mexican Nationalism* 1968:142):

The Virgin of Guadalupe has gained prominence as miscegenation has turned Mexico into a mestizo nation. Hidalgo made her the symbol of his revolt in 1810, and in the Revolution of 1910, Maderista and Zapatista troops carried her picture into battle on banners and on medallions attached to their hats. Now, with the new compatibility between church and state which has gradually emerged from the Revolution, deep devotion to the Virgin of Guadalupe throughout Mexico evidences the conjunction of loyalties.

In an anthropological analysis of the Guadalupe data, Eric Wolf has argued that in the course of history the Guadalupe devotion has come to "link together family, politics, and religion: colonial past and independent present; Indian and Mexican. It reflects the salient social relationships of Mexican life, and embodies the emotions which they generate. It provides a cultural idiom through which the tenor and emotions of these relationships can be expressed. It is, ultimately, a way of talking about Mexico: a collective representation of Mexican society" (Wolf 1958:39).

As a national symbol, the Guadalupe pilgrimage has become highly organized. One has only to thumb through the basilica's Mass schedule for December, 1971, to see how many modern Mexican institutions are represented before the altar. Take December 16 of that year as a typical day: at 7:30 A.M., the auxiliary police attended in large numbers; at 11:00 A.M., electrical equipment firms; at noon, employees of the San Juanico Omnibus Company "of first and second class"; at 1:00 P.M., religious of the order of La Merced;

at 2:00 P.M., the Mexico City branch of the old firm of Levi-Strauss, (no relation to the structuralist from Paris); at 3:00 P.M., the Union of National Lottery Ticket Sellers; at 4:00 P.M., workers of the Pavements and Highways Department; at 6:00 P.M., the publishing house of Jus in Mexico City; at 6:45 P.M., the Piedad de Cabadas Bus Company; at 8:00 P.M., the New Porcelain Company, San Isidro; at 8:45 P.M., the Cummins Service. Nearly four hundred masses for special groups were conducted in December, 1971. We have acquired runs of three journals published in connection with the Guadalupe pilgrimage. These publications (*La Voz Guadalupana, Juan Diego,* and *Tepeyac*) contain, in addition to much interesting information on the history of the devotion, day-to-day records of the organized parties of pilgrims coming to the basilica from all over the world. They show, for example, that every diocese in Mexico has its allocated pilgrimage day in the annual schedule, as do hundreds of individual parishes from all over Mexico. They also indicate the scope of the activity of the Comite Oficial de Peregrinaciones Guadalupanas in organizing pilgrimages to the basilica from other Latin American nations, as well as the United States and Europe.

THE QUERÉTARO PILGRIMAGE TO GUADALUPE

The pilgrimage to Guadalupe is also highly organized at its points of departure. To illustrate this aspect, we quote from the article "Fifty Years of Guadalupan Pilgrimage," which appeared in *La Voz Guadalupana,* the basilica's official publication, in July, 1940, and describes (p. 16) the pilgrimage to Guadalupe from the city of Querétaro, capital of the state of that name:

Year after year, from 1890 onwards, the Guadalupan devotees of Querétaro have made the pilgrimage on foot from their city to the sanctuary of Tepeyac. In eight days they traverse the rough road, 260 kilometers in length—the old royal road, broad and austere—which joins Querétaro to the metropolis. Eight days during which the weariness of the body is submitted to hard, voluntary discipline, loosening the bonds of matter to liberate the spirit. The rhythm of the march is set by collective prayers chanted in the plains under the mid-day sun, in the cool dawns when leaving

95

towns, in the evenings at the end of a day's journey. It is a march of religious folly in which the Indian—who comes on it propelled by his strong will and better nature—is freed from his bonds, while the rich man punishes his own softness by the austerity of prayer and walking.

This year, the fiftieth of the pilgrimage, the number of pilgrims was greater than ever. Two thousand five hundred pilgrims set out from Querétaro on June 23rd and reached Tepeyac on July 1st. They were divided into 25 groups of a hundred, each with its leader, and all under the general authority of Fr. Joaquin Ugalde, administrator of the sanctuary of Guadalupe at Querétaro. The pilgrimage was a model of order. Advance parties went ahead to arrange minimum hospitality—often no more than a piece of ground—in the villages on their way. A patient burro served as their field ambulance. A loud bell gave the necessary commands. Everything is penetrated by a fervor, an impulsion, an eagerness shared by all. The Dark Virgin.

A visceral faith grows from the pilgrimage (*brota de la peregrinación*). This is quite palpable during the journey's last stage, approaching the Villa de Guadalupe. When they cross the last hill, "the hill of the Pardon," from which they can see for the first time the sanctuary, the pilgrims shout out at this point. The whole immense column trembles. Their sweat-dimmed eyes shine, and their bleeding feet seem lighter. And as if they were merely at the beginning of their long journey, they break into a lively trot. And a unanimous chorus breaks out, intoning an ancient, traditional quatrain, the beautiful greeting to the Virgin at their longed-for arrival:

> *Dios te salve bella aurora.*
> God bless you, lovely dawn,
> *Dios te salve luz de día;*
> God bless you, light of day;
> *Dios te salve gran señora*
> God bless you, great lady,
> *y Dios te Salve María.*
> and God bless you, Mary.

The song is profoundly loving, intimate, charged with faith. It wanders through the maize-fields like a fresh breeze. It spreads along the broad sundrenched road like gentle water. The rough voices of strong men, the pure voices of children, the slow voices of old people chant it with the same fervor. And what one has gone to see from idle curiosity leaves the soul shaken. And a deep, magnetic, supernatural emotion becomes visible, as though materialized as water.

At the door of the sanctuary the pilgrimage receives a resplendent banner. The bells of the basilica scatter their glory on the massed heads. And when they enter the temple of the Virgin, the pilgrims throw themselves on their knees and in this way pass through the church to the very feet of the Virgin. The organ renders even more spiritual the moving scene. And the song surges up anew; it puts in their mouths an old stanza which Brother Antonio Margil taught the people of Querétaro in the eighteenth century: *Pues concebida fuiste sin mancha—Ave María llena de gracia.* "Surely thou wert conceived without stain—Hail Mary, full of grace."

I met an elderly man, Burgos, who was one of the founders of the pilgrimage and has never missed one since. He has a venerable white beard, his eyes are sunken. "They'll have to bury me on that road," he says. Now a group of children has come, about fifty of them, as an advance guard. And, in summary, I have seen in this pilgrimage the only possible classless society. The industrialist, the merchant, the professional man, beside the Indian, next to the worker. On the road, they walk, suffer, and pray together. In the inns, they throw themselves down side by side on the same piece of ground. And even their dress is the same. A wide sombrero to protect them from the sun, and a "Chirgo," a peasant raincoat of palm-leaves, on their shoulders. A humble pilgrim's staff [*bordon* = Jacob's staff] to help on the march. A triumph of the only real equality which is from the spirit and grace.

The solemn ceremony of the pilgrimage takes place in the basilica on the second day. The famous Querétaro choir sings the Mass in four parts in honor of [the Mexican saint] Philip of Jesus by the Querétaro composer Fr. Valázquez; at the organ is another Querétaro maestro: Julián Zuniga. And the sermon is preached by the Very Revnd. Salvador Salazar.

Thus does Querétaro, with its people, render up its art, its faith, its fervent annual homage to Our Lady of Guadalupe.

We can vouch for the accuracy of this description with respect to the emotional tone of the pilgrimage. One has only to arrive with a group of pilgrims at a Mexican shrine (or indeed at centers elsewhere in the world, as we shall describe in later chapters) to feel the strength of "collective representations" such as those mentioned in the Querétaro narrative. This account vividly displays the communitas within the structure, the "flow" within the "frame."

The Virgin of the Remedies, as we have said, often symbolized the Spanish side of Mexican history. After Mexican independence, there was a great falling off in popular devotion to her image. But in the twentieth century, particularly in the past few decades, there has been a marked revival in her cult. We have attended and photographed the ceremonies and festivities around the shrine of Our Lady of the Remedies, in the Church of San Bartolo Naucalpan, during the period from September 1 through September 8, the Nativity of the Blessed Virgin Mary, a universal Holy Day of Obligation for the Roman Catholic Church. This period is set aside for special devotions to Our Lady of the Remedies. It is also the occasion for a great market and fiesta, or *quermes* (like the Dutch *kermis*—a term derived ultimately from the *kerk*, church, and *mis*, Mass—an outdoor festival held on the feast day of a local saint), complete with giant ferris wheels, shooting galleries, merry-go-rounds, and the rest. Thousands of pilgrims (including many Indians) travel, often hundreds of miles, by every imaginable means of conveyance, ancient and modern, to spend the entire eight days at the shrine. Hundreds of Indian families, most of them with small infants, jam the courtyards round the church; at night, sleeping shoulder to shoulder or head to toe on mats of woven grass; by day, observing and taking part in the traditional dances in the plaza, and attending the numerous Masses celebrated in honor of Our Lady of the Remedies. Nobody returns home without having waited in line, at least once, to climb the flight of steps behind the main altar and do homage to the tiny figure, which is approached from behind. The line starts by a wall hung with homemade ex-votos (just like those in the basilica of Guadalupe)—paintings representing pilgrims' infirmities, or injuries, often with a stylized representation of Our Lady of the Remedies in the upper left-hand corner. In these images, the Virgin stands on a crescent moon resting on a maguey plant; she is crowned, and her crowned Child rests in the crook of her left arm. These ex-votos are signs of gratitude for favors received from Our Lady of the Remedies, as are the numerous championship shirts hung here by teams that regard their victory in soccer, bicycle-racing, or other sports as due to Our Lady's intervention (see plate 5). The public display of such ex-votos and of *milagritos* form part of the fulfillment of a *promesa* (vow) to go on pilgrimage to Los Remedios if the Lady renders the supplicant the favor requested. (Another way of showing gratitude is by putting an advertisement in a newspaper or in a column reserved for this purpose in a publication connected with the shrine; such notices mention the favor received and some of the circumstances surrounding it.) Every step of the way to the devotional image is surrounded with symbols. As the pilgrims move on from the *milagritos*, they pass an image of Jesus as the Infant of Prague, much venerated. They pass the sacristy, full of oil paintings and busy priests, and farther on enter the *camarín*, a small richly decorated room where the sacred images are dressed and the ornaments destined for that purpose are kept. There are many ancient religious murals on the walls. The pilgrims then file past a representation of the Sacred Heart and one of the Archangel Michael, spearing a hydralike dragon, whose seven heads represent the Deadly Sins. Passing a Franciscan saint's image, the pilgrims climb a flight of stairs to a glass-enclosed niche containing the authentic image of Our Lady of the Remedies, which seems beautiful and glowing after the dim ascent. Each pilgrim touches the glass protecting the image, then crosses himself. A priest, on the image's right, receives gifts from the pilgrims and hands each of them a paper with a prayer written on it. The pilgrims descend the stairs on the opposite side, pausing to venerate a Cristo immediately below the Virgin's niche. This image, of the type known as Ecce Homo ("Behold the Man") represents Christ scourged, in his purple robe with a reed in his hand. The Cristo is protected by a glass partition, for his feet have been rubbed through to the plaster by generations of pilgrims, and cannot survive much more of this treatment. Finally, the pilgrims file past the baptistry, where baptisms go on continually during the great feasts, for pilgrims, mainly Indians, may wait for almost a year after birth to have their babies christened at an important or favorite shrine. This symbolic journey is a minipilgrimage within the main pilgrimage, and it is undertaken with great reverence and fullness of participation.

Brilliantly costumed dancers, organized into societies (we counted ten separate troupes on one occasion in the atrium of San Bartolo Naucalpan), perform reputedly traditional, even "pre-Columbian," dances—as a perpetual *promesa*, or *manda* (vow), to the Virgin. The most prominent troupes are known as the Concheros (see plate 4); others are the Apaches and the Chichimecas. They travel to various pilgrimage centers on the great feast days. For example, they journey in box cars all the way from Mexico City to perform at the famous Candelaria festival (the Feast of the Purification of the Virgin) at San Juan de Lagos in Jalisco state. They consider themselves pilgrims and venerate both Virgin "bulwarks" (*baluartes*) of Mexico City—Guadalupe and Los Remedios. They do not dance for pay, they say, but to fulfill their vow and "visit Our Lady." An anthropologist from the Autonomous University of Mexico has recently been studying Conchero groups and is publishing an account of their initiation rites, secret language, and code of conduct. A constant feature of the dance performances is a masked skeletal figure of Death, who chases and terrorizes onlookers, especially children, though merriment is always mixed with the dread. Sometimes a Clown, Fool, or Harlequin is introduced who fights with Death. In these comic figures, the traditional Death's Fool of the medieval Dance of Death, which was popularly performed on feast days, is syncretized with the Aztec deity Mictlanteotl, the skull-faced Lord of the Dead.

Many other details of the scene around the shrine of Los Remedios suggest to us that despite its manifold connections with Hispanic culture—including a gigantic statue of Christ the King and a column surmounted by a huge crown symbolizing the same concept, both central to the Cristeros rebellion against the anticlerical government of Calles—Los Remedios has become increasingly Mexican in character and rich in communitas, as if to compensate for the ever-growing internationalization of Guadalupe. We have a strange dialectic here: the Spanish Virgin becomes more Indian, as the Dark Virgin who revealed herself to an Indian becomes increasingly a symbol of mestizo Mexico and of Latin America as a whole (as well as of the Philippines and other parts of the Latin world). Perhaps we have here a cultural analogy to Freud's notion of "the return of the repressed." The devotion to Guadalupe, which originated in a miracle in the presence of the Spanish bishop Zumárraga, and served to reconcile conquistadors and conquered Mexicans and to convert the Indians to Christianity, has revealed its mestizo aspect progressively since Independence; while the cultus of Los Remedios, centered on an image hidden in a maguey bush and found by an Indian, has become more indigenous, more creolized and Indianized, as covert opposition has increased toward the reigning mestizo regime of the Partido Revolucionario Institucional. In Los Remedios, one may perhaps see an alliance of ethnic strains, rather than a miscegenation of them. We have already mentioned the ex-votos representing Our Lady of the Remedies; these popular art forms perhaps illustrate what we have said before—that iconography sometimes reveals unrecognized and unlegitimated social values, even a kind of social, if not "collective," unconscious, which persists in culturally transmitted, though unexplained, symbols. The Virgin and the Child in the ex-votos are both crowned, representing papal recognition of the Mother and the kingship of her Son—symbols of the Cristeros movement against the anticlericalism of Mexican liberals and socialists alike. We did not mention that in both the image and the ex-votos, Los Remedios carried in her hand the marshal's baton, nor that her tunic and the Child's dress were white—again standing for the historical Spanish colonial connection. The pilgrim has also represented himself as wearing a white shirt, thus emphasizing his identification with these Spanish aspects. The Virgin stands on a white crescent moon; here circum-Mediterranean, though undoubtedly unconscious, affinities with pagan mother goddesses such as Ishtar, Artemis (in her early forms), and Isis, as well as with the Moorish dominant symbol, become palpable. Beneath the moon is a huge maguey plant. Here Los Remedios and Guadalupe are at one, for the maguey is also associated with the Dark Virgin. Now we are back in pre-Columbian times. The maguey, or century plant, was an Aztecan symbol of Tonantzin (her name means "mother" in Nahuatl), the goddess who gave birth to Huitzilopochtli and all the other gods and was also a deity of the earth and corn. One of her shrines, a pre-Columbian pilgrimage center where human sacrifices were made to her, was—the reader will recall—on the hill of Tepeyacac, where the Virgin appeared to Juan Diego. The white, milky sap of the maguey, called "Virgin's milk" by Mexican villagers, is the source of the mildly intoxicating *pulque* liquor. According to William Madsen (1960:231), in the village of Tecospa in the Valley of Mexico, not far from Mexico City, "the Virgin of Guadalupe [is believed to] care for dead children, who are dressed in saints' costumes (as once they were dressed in the regalia of the gods), and put in coffins with toys and a bottle of mother's milk to relieve their trip to the other world. Once in heaven the Virgin nurses them with her own milk in the Garden of Flowers until they can be weaned and raises them as if they were her own."

Mexicans believe that the mantle of Juan Diego, the *tilma* on which was stamped the image of the Virgin of Guadalupe just as she appeared to the Aztec catechumen, was made of maguey fibers. In popular art the Virgin of Guadalupe is often shown beside or above a maguey plant, and in the gardens on the hill of Tepeyac today many fine specimens of several varieties of maguey have been planted to commemorate this connection. Once more the symbolic union of Spanish and Aztec cultures is emphasized, since the maguey (in Nahuatl, *metl*) on the hill of Tepeyac is contrasted with the miraculous "roses of Castile" which the Dark Virgin bade Juan Diego gather in his mantle.

Despite all their differences of origin and history, both Guadalupe and Los Remedios remain as symbols of communitas for Mexicans. On the pilgrimage routes and at the shrines, the view expressed by the author of the article on the Querétaro pilgrimage to Guadalupe—that here is "the only possible classless society"—is widely shared by the participants. Indeed, we have heard many similar comments by pilgrims of other religions. But, of course, as in other pilgrimages across the globe, communitas here is channeled by the beliefs, values, and norms of a specific historical religion. At the shrines of Guadalupe and Los Remedios it is only Catholic Christians who renew their sentiments of solidarity at various organizational and structural levels and at various places and times of pilgrimage. Members of other religions would not be welcomed as pilgrims here, only as tourists, "outsiders" (just as non-Muslims are unwelcome, even as tourists, at the holy places of Mecca). Perhaps the rather precise delineation of rules and norms— of the goals of the pilgrimage and the means of attaining them—is essential if the pilgrims are to attain that sense of "flow," that union of action and awareness, which is one of the most fulfilling of human experiences.[17]

[17] In his *Beyond Boredom and Anxiety: The Experience of Play in Work and Games* (1975b:36), M. Csikszentmihalyi discusses the conditions under which, in a variety of cultural contexts, there arises the holistic sensation of "flow" that people feel when they act with total involvement. Among these conditions is the centering of attention on a limited stimulus field—a condition which certainly exists in pilgrim travel and devotions.

The concept of flow originated with John MacAloon.

CHAPTER THREE

St. Patrick's Purgatory:
Religion and Nationalism in
an Archaic Pilgrimage

In its discussion of Archaic pilgrims.

THIS CHAPTER is in keeping with the Malinowskian anthropological tradition (in which we have developed) of eliciting the general from the particular. The particular in this case is an Irish pilgrimage of great antiquity, St. Patrick's Purgatory in Lough Derg in
County Donegal, a pilgrimage which has persisted through numerous changes in its religious context (see the chronology in Appendix B). St. Patrick's Purgatory belongs to the category of pilgrimages which we have labeled "archaic," and is distinguished
from the "prototypical" pilgrimages, those directly connected with
the life and teachings of the founder of the faith and of his principal
disciples, companions, and immediate successors. Archaic pilgrimages, as we have noted, bear evident traces of earlier religions, in
their foundation narratives, attendant folk beliefs, liturgies, and
symbolism; in the nature of the way stations along the pilgrim
roads; in the location and attributes of the principal shrine; and in
the positioning of their major feast days in the calendar.

Since the "archaic" and "prototypical" categories are only ideal models, many pilgrimages actually partake of the attributes of both. The Christian pilgrimage to Jerusalem, for example, is an obvious heir to the ancient Jewish pilgrimages to the Temple on the feasts of Passover, Pentecost (Shabuoth), Tabernacles (Sukkoth), while its *via crucis* component is just as obviously an imitation of Christ, the founder. Likewise, long before the time of Muhammad, Arab pilgrims had traveled to Mecca to worship various deities, including Kuzah, the ancient Semitic thunder god (Wensinck 1966:32). Yet the prototypical aspect (and the totally innovative role of the religious founder) in these and other pilgrimages soon became preeminent and was firmly linked to the theological structure of the later, dominant religion. Visible traces of the graft between archaic stock and historical scion all but vanish, and zealots are iconoclasts to the old pilgrim symbols, but iconophiles for the new. (An example in the Catholic tradition is Bishop Diego de Landa in Yucatán, who destroyed the images of the Maya deities and substituted for them those of Catholic saints.)

There often remains a profound sense of continuity with the earlier tradition, however. Stratification of pilgrimage may involve the simple addition of new to old features, but often involves syncretism as well. Hugo Nutini (1972:7–9) has defined syncretism as a process with three distinct developmental stages: the first involving confusion or identification of the ideological and structural orders of the interacting religious traditions; the second, "a structural interplay of elements intrinsic and extrinsic to the syncretic matrix in question" (here, the pilgrimage system being studied); and the third, assertion of a new theological order, with the structural elements of the second stage syncretized and interpreted within this new context. Nutini's own basic data are from Mexico. Across the Atlantic in Ireland there are other examples of archaic pilgrimage and syncretism. What we have called the "archaic pilgrimage" of Lough Derg may well be a pilgrimage system in Nutini's "second stage," where there is still competition between the archaic and evangelizing religions and ambiguity (or, at least, "structural interplay") of the ritual structures of the pilgrimage. Nutini's developmental paradigm frequently remains incomplete, however, for

105

his "second stage" often becomes, in actuality, a permanent state when nationalist or regionalist forces remain active in the "field," or dynamic environment, of the pilgrimage in question. Perhaps the new theological order has been asserted, but a pilgrimage is very much more than its theology. It is a field of social relations and cultural contents of the most diverse types, formal and informal, orthodox and heterodox, dogmatic and mythical, often juxtaposed rather than fused, interrelated, or systematized. Attempts to revive a national or regional culture and language may select elements of the otherwise "receding" (Nutini, p. 13) structural and ideological orders for renewed emphasis in pilgrimage beliefs, behavior, and symbolism. There may be a deliberate "arrest" of the syncretic process, in which unassimilated elements of form and meaning may retain political significance. "Archaism" may, indeed, be an attribute of the contemporary political situation, a symbol of certain aspects of the present, rather than merely a "folk survival." We hope to show that nationalistically revived, reinforced, or even invented "archaism" may also be associated with what we have called "normative communitas" and "ideological communitas," especially when they are in active opposition to alien political attempts to dominate and restructure the group from which the pilgrims are drawn. Pilgrimage, under such circumstances, is like a vertical shaft driven into the past, disclosing deep strata of ancient symbols, potent signifiers (sacred symbol-vehicles such as images, paintings, proper names, and places) which reinforce nationalistic sentiments. A pilgrimage devotion may be rendered even more potent by the juncture of these sentiments with the ethical and moral system of the universal, historical religion. For instance, what the Irish call "the faith of our fathers," the Catholic religion, has an international legitimation, though this phrase is often taken as referring specifically to the much persecuted faith of the Irish in particular. Here we have the paradox: If harm is from outside, help may also be from outside.

Ireland has many archaic and ancient pilgrimages, most of which are mentioned by Maire MacNeill in her fascinating study of Irish Christian syncretism, *The Festival of Lughnasa* (1962). Easily the best-known are the two principal "Patrician" (dedicated to St. Pat-

106

rick) pilgrimages—Croagh Patrick in County Mayo and St. Patrick's Purgatory in County Donegal. These still flourish in zeal and numbers, though the pilgrimage to Knock in County Mayo (scene of the reputed apparition, in 1879, of Mary, Joseph, John the Evangelist, and the Lamb on the Altar, to about a dozen villagers) has become, since Irish independence, the numerically dominant pilgrimage of Ireland (see plate 16). The Patrician pilgrimages survived the years of British persecution with éclat. To give the reader a hint of the patriotic feeling involved, let us quote a passage from F. P. Carey's pamphlet *Lough Derg and Its Pilgrimage* (p. 3), published in 1939 by the Dublin office of the *Irish Messenger*, a nationalist newspaper. The passage begins with this quatrain by the poet Thomas D'Arcy McGee:

> *Oh, would you know the power of Faith,*
> *Go, see it at Loch Derg.*
> *Oh, would you learn to smile at death,*
> *Go, learn it at Loch Derg.*

"The writers and poets of many centuries," Carey comments, "have hastened to reveal and extol to the world of their times the real charm of Loch Derg, but few have disclosed the secret with the eloquent truth to be esteemed in those lines written by Thomas D'Arcy McGee, *Nation* poet, upon conclusion of a pilgrimage made while his country suffered the ruthless measures taken by the British Government to suppress the Insurrection of 1848." Carey was referring to the desperate attempt of the Young Irelanders to win self-government by armed insurrection. Their attempt began and ended in a futile fray at Ballingary in County Tipperary, at the height of the famine in which the Irish population was reduced by two million. McGee was given sanctuary in America, where he wrote the poem. He had previously been given sanctuary on Station Island in Lough Derg, the site of St. Patrick's Purgatory, the theme of his poem. This pilgrimage shrine combines religion and nationalism in a unique way which we shall try to unravel in this chapter.

Judging from the nineteenth-century literature on St. Patrick's Purgatory, the pilgrimage was then the focus of an acrimonious polemic between Irishman and Englishman, Protestant and Catholic. For example, Philip Dixon Hardy, an Anglican clergyman, wrote of the site, in his *Holy Wells of Ireland, containing an Authentic Account of Those Various Places of Pilgrimage and Penance Which Are Still Annually Visited by Thousands of the Roman Catholic Peasantry* (1836), the following: "If penance and not repentance could save the soul, no wretch who performed a pilgrimage here could, with a good grace, be damned. Out of hell the place is matchless; if there be a purgatory in the other world, it may very well be said, there is a fair rehearsal of it in the county of Donegal in Ireland" (p. 24). This polemic followed a long series of violent incidents during the post-Reformation centuries, incidents interspersed with legislation forbidding the pilgrimage. Attacks on the pilgrimage cannot be blamed solely on the English, however. After an adverse report from a Dutch monk in 1494, the notorious Borgia pope Alexander VI issued, in 1497, a papal order that the cave where pilgrims kept vigil be closed up. What is of interest to us is that neither bans nor adverse propaganda had much effect on the Irish pilgrims, who continued to visit the Purgatory over the centuries. The "real charm" of Lough Derg extolled by the patriot-poet McGee may well escape those not schooled in Irish tradition.

TOPOGRAPHY OF THE SHRINE

As we have noted, Lough Derg (literally, "Red Lake," though the antiquary John O'Donovan believes that its true sense is "Lake of the Cave") is located in County Donegal, in northwestern Ireland. The lake is about five square miles in area, surrounded by low, heather-clad mountains, which isolate it from the outside world. Only one main road leads to the lake, from the small town (four miles distant) of Pettigo, on the little river Termon. The name Termon is the Irish form of the Latin *Terminus,* and refers to a place where three things come together: a king, a bishop, and a people; or church land. "Termon crosses" marked the boundaries of these units. The river Termon derives its name from the old territory of Termon-Dabheoc, named after one of the saints important to the Lough Derg pilgrimage. The pilgrim route from Dublin, a hundred miles distant, is via Enniskillen, to the southeast of Pettigo. Nineteenth-century sources (Hardy 1836:14) describe how pilgrims were

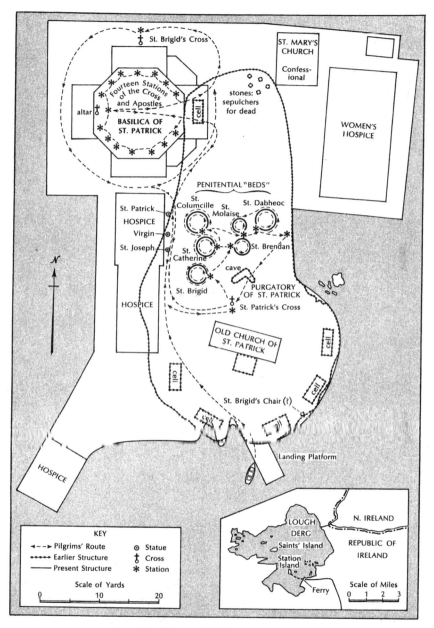

St. Brigid's Cross

ST. MARY'S CHURCH
Confess-
ional

WOMEN'S HOSPICE

Fourteen Stations of the Cross and Apostles

altar

BASILICA OF ST. PATRICK

cell

stones: sepulchers for dead

PENITENTIAL "BEDS"

St. Columcille
St. Molaise
St. Dabheoc

St. Patrick

HOSPICE

Virgin

St. Joseph

St. Catherine

St. Brendan

cave

St. Brigid

PURGATORY OF ST. PATRICK

St. Patrick's Cross

HOSPICE

OLD CHURCH OF ST. PATRICK

cell

cell

St. Brigid's Chair (?)

Landing Platform

HOSPICE

N

KEY
- - → Pilgrims' Route   ⊙ Statue
++++ Earlier Structure   ♱ Cross
——— Present Structure   ✳ Station

Scale of Yards
0   10   20

LOUGH DERG
Saints' Island
Station Island
Ferry

N. IRELAND

REPUBLIC OF IRELAND

Scale of Miles
0   1   2   3

ST. PATRICK'S PURGATORY

109

wont to walk barefoot to Lough Derg, carrying staff and scrip (a white wallet slung over the shoulder)—just as medieval pilgrims in Europe once did and modern pilgrims to Chalma in Mexico still do.

The lake is dotted with forty-six small islands, most of which are bare rocks projecting from the water. Two are important for the pilgrimage: Station Island and Saints' Island. Several modern scholars have taken the view that Station Island's sacred topography is only a copy of an older pattern on Saints' Island. Ludwig Bieler, in an article in *The Irish Ecclesiastical Record* (March, 1960), after surveying the relevant medieval literature (Peter of Aldgate, George Chrissaphani, Laurence Rathold de Pasztho, Antonio Mannini, and so on), concludes that the Purgatory was originally on Saints' Island, and was transferred to the smaller island sometime between the end of the twelfth century and 1230. Though Saints' Island may have been the original locale of the pilgrimage's penitential exercise, today the rites are performed on the much smaller Station Island, and no longer in a cave. Saints' Island is associated in legend and tradition with St. Patrick, though firm evidence is lacking. As anthropologists we are of course unperturbed by lacunae of this kind, for we study beliefs and myths as legitimate data in themselves. The fictitious folk-etymologizing which relates the name of Lough Derg (*dearg* means "red") to the blood of a serpent slain in its waters by St. Patrick, is as much grist to our mill as well-documented historical fact and scientific linguistic analysis. What scant historical evidence we have, fails to show conclusively that St. Patrick traveled to Lough Derg. The earliest saint associated with the locality was not Patrick at all, but the local saint Dabheoc, or Davog. It was not until the twelfth century, when Dabheoc's monastery on Saints' Island was taken over by Augustinian canons regular, that the legend linking St. Patrick with the cave on Saints' Island began to circulate. Basically, according to this legend, Patrick had been given, in the cave on Saints' Island, a personal and miraculous glimpse of Purgatory, where the suffering soul lay in unspeakable torment. His experience was later repeated by the Norman Knight Owen, who visited the cave in 1153, and spread its myth as a superstitious if glamorous curiosity all over Europe, considerably influencing (in the view of some scholars) the literature of the high culture, the European "Great Tradition." There may be echoes of the myth in Dante's *Divine Comedy*, for pilgrims were believed to have had visions and dreams of hell and purgatory while in the cave. Philippe de Felice, however, in *L'Autre Monde* (1906), makes a plausible case for finding the origin of the legend in pre-Christian mythology and pagan ideas of life after death. As has been stated elsewhere (V. Turner 1974a:289), what passes for the Great Tradition is often no more than a transformation of some Little Tradition. The reverse also holds true. What we need to hold to is the concept of a single, multileveled, religiomythical field, in which all the parts are interdependent, to some degree.

Station Island measures only about 126 yards long by about 22–45 yards wide (O'Connor 1903:207).[1] But on it are crammed a plethora of sacred structures and ancillary buildings (see map 2), and beneath these are evident traces of former holy sites and objects. When the pilgrim leaves the large rowboat which has ferried him from lakeshore to jetty, he first sees the hospices and the old Church of St. Patrick, directly opposite the landing place (see plate 15). Transportation is deliberately left unmodernized, and the large rowboats, each christened after an Irish saint, can carry up to a hundred and fifty passengers. Facing the old church is St. Mary's Church, where the pilgrims go to confession. Patrick and Mary are closely connected here, as at many levels of Irish symbolism. Between the two churches are the famous stone "beds," otherwise known as the penitential rounds. Six in number, the beds are of circular formation, and are dedicated to SS. Dabheoc, Brigid (Bridget), Columcille (Columba), Catherine, Brendan, and Molaise, the largest bed being that of St. Columcille. Each bed is a grassy area, 6 to 9 feet wide, surrounded by the low remains of a wall, broken for entry by a narrow doorway. Marble statues of the Virgin Mary, Joseph, and St. Patrick stand sentinel in front of the main hospice. Quite near the old Church of St. Patrick is St. Patrick's Cross, evidently of great antiquity; the cross lacks head and arms, which were broken off during the government seizure of 1632,

[1] Descriptions of Station Island may be found in O'Connor (1903), Gibbons (1937), Leslie (1932), and Curtayne (1944).

111

when the Augustinian canons (who had presided over the pilgrimage since 1135) were forcibly ejected by English soldiers.

The new basilica of St. Patrick, completed in 1931, is of an ornate octagonal design in the Hiberno-Romanesque style—its copper roof, surmounted by a gold cross, rising above the buildings in which the pilgrims make their retreat. Pius XI, in 1931, declared this church to be a Minor Basilica "in cherished memory of the traditional piety of the people of St. Patrick." The basilica stands on a projecting platform built out over the lake on piers sunk into the rocky bottom. Rowboats pass beneath it, guided at night by electric beacons. It can, and often does, accommodate two thousand pilgrims. It has a stately high altar, and lesser altars to SS. Mary, Patrick, Dabheoc, and Thérèse of Lisieux, all in marble (a substance held almost sacred in Christian churches, doubtless following the ancient Roman example), as are also the communion rails, puplit, and wall facings. Fourteen windows under the spacious galleries represent the Stations of the Cross, their stained glass the work of a well-known Dublin artist, Harry Clarke.[2]

The ritual topography, or cultural landscape, of St. Patrick's Purgatory exemplifies certain general features of pilgrimage symbolism, with some uniquely Irish touches. As Robertson-Smith observed almost a century ago (*The Religion of the Semites* 1889), pilgrimage shrines are often connected with striking natural features, such as mountains, caves, wells, river sources, and mesas. St. Patrick's Purgatory, as we have already noted, was founded in association with a cave—a topographic feature linked with the afterlife in pre-Christian mythology. It is located, moreover, on a barren island in a lake in the northwesterly part of Europe's westernmost major island. The not inconsiderable number of pilgrims from mainland Europe in the Middle Ages tended to regard Ireland as a stage on the soul's journey after death to its ultimate destination in the farthest west—in Christian terms, as an entry to purgatory—and the island cave on Lough Derg as the very gate to that western

[2] Curtayne wrote (1944:156–57): "Harry Clarke, before he died, was considered the greatest stained-glass artist in the world. As the lake and its surroundings are an almost unvarying monochrome of brown or grey, the wealth of colour in these windows is a particular joy."

netherworld. Many literary works and allusions, diligently researched and inventoried by the Catholic convert Shane Leslie,[3] clearly reveal the symbolic importance of the topography of St. Patrick's Purgatory: a cave (both womb and tomb for the penitent, as we shall see) on an island, within a lake, within a ring of hills, in the northwest of an island, to the west of Europe, whose mythology regards the sunset as the path to the Land of the Dead, and the soul as journeying westward after death. (Many European folk tales also tell of penitent ghosts journeying to St. James's shrine at Compostela in the far northwest of Spain—in Galicia, whose name bespeaks its ancient Celtic connections; see King 1920: vol. 3, pp. 246–52.) This is liminal indeed!

In the "economy of salvation" in pre-Reformation theology, living souls require penitence as the dead require purgatory. For the pilgrims who seek out Station Island, it is not merely a symbolic purgatory, but a real one for living penitents. When Cardinal Logue, primate of all Ireland, visited Station Island (on June 30, 1913), he said: "I believe any person who goes through the routine here on Lough Derg, the penitential exercises, the fasting, and the prayers for which so many Indulgences are granted—I believe if he died after leaving it, he would have very little to suffer in the next world" (Gibbons 1937:70). What the Cardinal suggested, the people implicitly believe.

Like most other major pilgrimage centers, St. Patrick's Purgatory is composite in character, containing not one focus of worship but several. It is also characterized by stratification, for later structures are often either physically superimposed on earlier ones or, if located on new sites, functionally displace them, the older structure then being assigned a different function (a building once used for worship may become a museum or a storehouse) or else being allowed to molder gracefully away into a hallowed ruin. History is thus conserved in a spot symbolizing timelessness. Even the blem-

---

[3] For many years, Lough Derg lay within the lands of Shane Leslie's Protestant family. His father, Sir John Leslie, claimed proprietary rights over Station Island in 1881. The claim was subsequently withdrawn (the action was settled out of court), but was revived again by Sir John in 1917, when Judge Cooke K. C. dismissed his claim. Sir John appealed, and again settled the case with the bishop of Clogher, this time in the Lifford Courthouse (Gibbons 1937:52).

ishes resulting from the violence of foes of the pilgrimage are preserved, the better to illustrate faith triumphant. Station Island preserves its mutilated St. Patrick's Cross, for example, just as the basilica of Guadalupe preserves the bent and twisted bronze crucifix which, the faithful believed, defended the holy painting of the Virgin of Guadalupe from destruction by an anarchist's bomb in 1921—Christ sacrificially saving His mother, as the pilgrims think of it. Thus, history, both of good and evil, God's will and man's disobedience, is conserved in the symbolism of the pilgrimage center. In a sense, all times are believed to coexist there, for the drama of salvation is the same in all ages: man's free will rejects or cooperates with God's grace, resulting in damnation or salvation. Yet the duration of an individual's life or a nation's history provides many opportunities to repent of the evil choices, time being "the mercy of Eternity," as William Blake once wrote. This paradigm is reflected in the sacred topography of St. Patrick's Purgatory, in its juxtapositions and stratification. The symbolic density of the total area of a major pilgrimage shrine is very high; a few "signifiers" have many "signifieds," as some linguists might put it, or, more simply, a few objects stand for many things. If we were to apply the techniques of symbol exegesis that we used in the study of African ritual (V. Turner 1967a: ch. 1) to the constellation of symbolic objects we have just described for Station Island, we would require several volumes to decipher the multivocality of these objects. For in literate cultures a specialized hermeneutic develops whose interpretations are deeply influenced by nonreligious, as well as religious, factors; by church and state politics; by economic processes and changes; and by secular philosophy and science. The pilgrims require no such analysis, however; for them the powerful "signifiers" are arrayed as a battery of sacred forces and holy persons who may aid them or their kin or friends—that is, of course, if the pilgrim's penance is sincerely undertaken and his disposition good. In some kinds of liminality, as Barbara Babcock has recently pointed out (1978, in press), we find a surplus of signifiers: in carnival, for example, a surplus of masks and disguises. In pilgrimage, we would add, there is a surplus of solemn representations of what for the pilgrim is the fundamental "signified"—personal sanctification through self-sacrifice.

114

The stone "beds" on Station Island are just such a surplus of signifiers. All the saints with whom the beds are associated were, like their divine exemplar Jesus, heroes of self-sacrifice; some of them were even martyred for the faith. The saints' beds also touch on the Irish question raised earlier; on the whole question of archaism in pilgrimage in general; and on how that relates to communitas and continuity. But before we can deal with these questions, we must first envision the elaborate devotional ritual performed by all pilgrims to the island.

THE PILGRIMAGE RITUAL

Alice Curtayne's vivid account of the Lough Derg pilgrimage (1944:167–78) holds good for the present and, in the main, for the early nineteenth century as well. The principal modification of earlier practices is that the pilgrimage is now a three-day affair, whereas six- or even nine-day periods of sojourn were typical for the pilgrims in the early nineteenth century. A pilgrim now stays on the island from three o'clock on the afternoon of the first day to about eleven on the morning of the third day. This three-day schedule has been related explicitly to St. Patrick's special devotion to the Trinity (also symbolized by his use of the three-lobed shamrock leaf to symbolize the Trinity, in a sermon said to have been delivered on Croagh Patrick, site of the other major Patrician pilgrimage in Ireland). As we have noted before, a three-day span also represents the period of Christ's sojourn in the tomb after the crucifixion—a period in which, according to tradition, he "harrowed hell"; that is, descended into limbo and brought out of it the souls of the good pagans born before his incarnation. The Lough Derg pilgrim imitates Christ in being "crucified" and becoming "dead" to worldly things, and in descending into a limbo, or liminoid state, where he undergoes penance in order that he may rise up again, renewed in spirit, on the third day. Initiations of this sort reverse nature; the tomb of one's past self becomes the womb of spiritual rebirth.

On arriving at Station Island, the pilgrim's first duty is to remove his shoes (this is a diminished form of the ancient ritual whereby the whole journey was made barefoot); and he must remain barefoot until he is about to leave. Having fasted since the previous nightfall, he may not take food again until he has made at least one "station" (a term for a special place of prayer in pilgrimage, to be distinguished from the Stations of the Cross of the universal Church) on the island. The first rite of the first station is, in the idiom of Catholic religious speech, "to visit the Blessed Sacrament" at the high altar of the basilica; that is, to pray before the consecrated Host. This rite is common to the whole of Catholic Christendom and usually begins the final cycle of devotions at Catholic shrines. But on Station Island the Irish note sounds soon thereafter. For the pilgrim must next walk to St. Patrick's Cross, the maimed relic mentioned earlier, poor but cherished, with a top made of rude iron, and a stone shaft perhaps dating from the ninth century (on the evidence of spiral tracery incised on the column and three parallel bands forming the capital). The pilgrim kneels before what remains of the cross and recites one Our Father, one Hail Mary, and the Creed—today these are recited not in Latin but in Gaelic (the official national language of Ireland) or in English.

The pilgrim's next stop is St. Brigid's Cross, set in a niche in the north outer wall of the basilica. This cross, of Roman type, was cut, probably in the twelfth century, from a stone slab taken from the wall of the old Church of St. Patrick. Similar ways of symbolizing continuity are of course common to most ritual systems: a fragment of something sacred and old is joined to the totality of something sacred and new, perhaps to speed up its sacralization, like yeast in the dough, leaven in the lump! (In the Sudanese Republic, Nuer tribesmen carry earth from an old village site to a new one. In circumcision rites, the Ndembu add a pinch of medicine from an ancient container to newly manufactured medicine in a new container.) The sacred power of past liminality "boosts" or "accelerates" or "amplifies" the power of a new liminality. The Lough Derg pilgrim kneels before the ancient cross of the Celtic saint Brigid and says three Our Fathers, three Hail Marys, and the Creed. He then rises, turns, faces the lake with his arms outstretched in the stance of crucifixion, and three times repeats aloud the ancient Catholic formula renouncing the world, the flesh, and the devil. (Students of the Muslim hajj may be reminded of the station of the Mecca pilgrimage known as the Stoning at Mina; according to tradition, Ishmael three times stoned Satan at Mina, and is

116

imitated by pilgrims, who cast stones at three pillars representing the devil.) Of course, the formula repeated by the Lough Derg pilgrim is the Catholic baptismal vow. It stands for renewal of innocence and is a usual part of the ritual of Catholic retreats. It is an instance, too, of the birth and rebirth symbolism quite common in ritual liminality everywhere. But here the immediate context must not be neglected, for the vow is made in close association with a typically Celtic saint, and thus may well represent a reaffirmation of ethnic identity.

The pilgrim must then walk around the basilica four times, repeating, as he walks, seven decades of the Rosary Beads (each decade consisting of an Our Father, ten Hail Marys, and a Glory Be to the Father), and one Creed. It should be mentioned that the prescribed number of circuits round the old church was seven; but, since the new basilica is much larger than the old, the number of "rounds" has been accordingly reduced, to fit more closely the duration of the required prayers. Most of this circuit is on the platform built over the water at the back of the church, and gives pilgrims the impression that they are walking on the deck of a huge ship.

If the devotions at the Irish saints' crosses and the basilica suggest a national emphasis, the rituals which follow accentuate even further the archaic Celtic heritage of the Purgatory. The pilgrim has now to go to a craggy knoll in the island's center, "the real holy ground, venerated for immemorial ages" (Curtayne 1944:169). Spread out on its slope are what have always been known as the "beds"—six rings of rough stones and upended boulders which appear to be the remnants of beehive cells, or oratories (similar structures, still complete, may also be seen near the tip of the Dingle Peninsula).[4] It is believed that the cells were once occupied by

---

[4] The structures probably were badly defaced in the seventeenth and early eighteenth centuries. Our contention that the flawed or damaged condition of archaic symbol-vehicles (signifiers) forms an important part of their "orectic pole" of meaning is supported by a footnote in Canon O'Connor's St. Patrick's Purgatory (1903:13). In 1857 an American Catholic gentleman suggested that the beds be restored in "first-class masonry," and he offered the curator (who looked after the island in the off-season) a thousand dollars for that purpose. When the bishop of Clogher heard of this, he said, 'The project could not be entertained for a moment. These cells, venerable for their antiquity, speak trumpet-tongued of the glorious past. They shall never be altered or repaired by human hands."

Christian monks of the Celtic dispensation who guarded the sanctuary. By ancient tradition, the "beds" are associated with SS. Brigid, Brendan, Catherine, Columcille, Molaise, and Dabheoc, but the association is honorific only. With the possible exception of Dabheoc (there may have been two saints of that name, one in the late fifth, the other in the early seventh, centuries), no claim is now made that any of these saints visited Lough Derg.

St. Catherine is the only foreign saint to whom a "bed" is dedicated. Some authorities believe that she was St. Catherine of Bologna, whose devotion was brought to Lough Derg by the Franciscans, who took charge of the pilgrimage from 1638 to 1780. Our view is that she was probably the fourth-century Alexandrian saint miraculously saved from execution on a spiked wheel (or wheels)— as her legend relates—but later martyred by being beheaded. According to tradition, her body was conveyed to the top of Mount Sinai, where there is still a famous monastery dedicated to her. Catherine of Alexandria is not only the patroness of Christian philosophers but also of pilgrims (possibly because of her posthumous connection with the Holy Land). Little is known of her life, except for a few lines in Eusebius. Felix Fabri (Palestine Pilgrims' Text Society, vol. 10, p. 570), describes a stone "bed," on the top of Mount Sinai, on which the saint's body was supposed to have been deposited by angels: "There is a place hollowed out for the reception of a human body lying at full length." Is this perhaps the origin of St. Catherine's bed in Lough Derg?

The other beds are dedicated to very early local saints, yet pilgrims from outside Ireland must visit them and perform the rituals there. Brigid, Columcille, and Brendan were energetic missionaries and travelers. Brigid, born in Louth, was a famed abbess and founder of convents, the "Mary of the Gael," a thaumaturge, and patroness of all those engaged in dairy work; Columcille, or Columba, was born in Donegal, later became abbot of Iona, and was among the great missionaries of the Western Church in the sixth century. Founder of a hundred monasteries, he was the Apostle of Caledonia. Patrick, Brigid, and Columcille make up the Thaumaturgic Triad, which Irish-Norman clergymen and writers celebrated throughout medieval Christendom. While these saints achieved national, even international, recognition, Molaise (or Laserian), anchorite of Devenish and bishop of Leighlin (within whose jurisdiction Station Island then lay), is a specifically local saint, though he firmly upheld the Roman practice in regard to the date of Easter—as are Dabheoc the Elder (by tradition the first abbot of Lough Derg) and Dabheoc the Younger, now regarded as the special patron of Lough Derg.

In the center of each stone circle stands a bronze crucifix. The crucifixes, of twentieth-century manufacture, are numbered and inscribed with the name of the saint, to guide the novice pilgrim. At each of the beds the same ritual is performed. Three Our Fathers, three Hail Marys, and the Creed are said during three circuits round the outside of the bed. The same prayers are then repeated while the pilgrim kneels outside the entrance of the bed. They are again repeated during three circuits inside, and yet again while the pilgrim kneels at the crucifix in the center of the bed. The order of visitation is Brigid, Brendan, Catherine, Columcille, and ends with the "large penitential bed," a double circle dedicated to SS. Dabheoc and Molaise. Six circuits are made around the outside of this double circle, while the pilgrim repeats nine Our Fathers, nine Hail Marys, and the Creed. The same prayers are repeated during six inside circuits, and again while the pilgrim kneels in the center of the bed. After this he proceeds to the second entrance to the bed or stone circle and, kneeling, says three Our Fathers, three Hail Marys and the Creed, repeating these devotions whilst making the inside circuit, and again kneeling in the center of the bed. When one realizes that the stone circles are small and the slope steep, with sharp stones protruding from the ground (foundation stones left by the seventeenth-century despoilers), it becomes clear that penitence is no idle word here, especially when one considers, too, the large numbers of pilgrims pressing to do their devoirs, and the frequent westerly rains which drench the island.

But the first station is not yet over! The pilgrim has to go to the water's edge at the east and say five Our Fathers, five Hail Marys, and the Creed; first standing, then kneeling. Even this is some relief from what Curtayne calls "those terrible and remorseless circles of stone" (p. 171). The pilgrim then returns to the St. Patrick's

Cross, where the round began; kneeling, he says one Our Father, one Hail Mary, and the Creed. The first station is concluded by the recitation of five Our Fathers, five Hail Marys, and the Creed for the pope's intention (for the object of his prayers), in the basilica. It is reckoned that one station takes about an hour and a quarter to complete.[5]

The pilgrim may now break his fast. He eats in the hostel, seated on a long bench by a plain table, his bare feet resting on the cold cement floor. He is provided with an oaten biscuit, eaten dry, or dry bread, which may, as a concession to the gourmet in all of us, be toasted! In drinks he has a choice: cold or hot water (drawn from the lake and ironically called Lough Derg wine), flavored with salt and pepper or sweetened; or he may have tea, without milk but sweetened if he wishes.

On the first day, two more stations, identical to the first, are obligatory; pilgrims have to make nine stations in their three days on the island. Formerly, the rule was to make three rounds per day; but the railway timetable now determines that the pilgrim must leave at about eleven on the morning of the third day to catch the train from Pettigo. Consequently, he makes three stations the first day, four stations during the all-night vigil which begins the second day, and two hurried stations on the morning of the third day. In addition, he must attend two church services each evening, one at six, the other at nine. He may indulge the flesh to the extent of resting by the turf fire in the hostel for a smoke and a chat. He is also free to drink hot or cold water, salted, peppered, or sweetened, according to taste.

The stations of the first day are only the aperitif, so to speak. The main course is the all-night vigil in the basilica, when four Stations of the Cross are recited aloud, led by a pilgrim priest or by a senior pilgrim. (The "Stations of the Cross" comprise a rite of the universal Church in which the priest leads the congregation around fourteen depictions, set up within the church, of the fourteen major incidents during the sufferings of Jesus, from his condemnation by Pilate to the descent from the Cross.) Between succeeding perfor-

[5] According to a guide to "authorized devotional exercises" printed in 1876, cited by O'Connor (1903:210–11).

mances of a set of Stations, a fifteen-minute intermission is allowed, during which pilgrims often walk around outside to keep themselves awake. A good deal of Lough Derg folklore has been inspired by the need to keep awake. It used to be said that a pilgrim was in danger of damnation if he dozed off during the vigil; now the threat, considerably mitigated, is that the pilgrim who succumbs to sleep will receive no indulgences for the pilgrimage. Although the notion of indulgences has generally slipped into the background of Catholic thought since Vatican II, it still thrives among Irish pilgrims, who strongly believe that prelates of the Church may grant them remission before God of the temporal punishment due for sins whose guilt has been forgiven. Rome has been well aware for many centuries of the importance of St. Patrick's Purgatory, not only as a cohesive force among Irish Catholics but as a link with the universal Church. Successive popes have therefore granted indulgences to different components of the pilgrimage ritual at Lough Derg. From time to time cardinals and papal nuncios have visited the pilgrimage and reported back to the pope; favorable reports have been followed by the granting of further indulgences. The doctrine of indulgences has a special emphasis in Ireland, as in other Celtic lands (such as Brittany, Cornwall, Galicia, Wales, and the Western Isles of Scotland), where a penumbra of animistic ideas surrounds Christian beliefs about death and the fate of the soul. According to universal Catholic teaching, all papal indulgences may be applied to the souls in purgatory (known in Ireland as "the holy souls"), though no one may apply indulgences to other living persons, since each living person must exercise his free will to effect his own salvation. This means that a pilgrim can shorten or even terminate the purgatory of a dead relative or friend by obtaining a papal indulgence for performing the stations at Lough Derg and then applying the remission of temporal punishment—here the pains of purgatory—to the loved one. The alleged origin and the very name of St. Patrick's Purgatory link it with the doctrine of purgation after death. Many pilgrims believe that the more they suffer deprivation on Station Island, the more they are easing the torment of their beloved dead in purgatory. "The pilgrimage joins the living and the dead in a chain of love and suffering," as an Irish priest once put it in a sermon we heard at Knock.

In any event, the night vigil is surely purgatorial. Curtayne describes the scene (p. 173):

The average man usually finds himself being tortured with the desire for sleep about 2 A.M. There is a leaden weight on his eyelids and he moves and prays like a somnambulist. The choice of prayers seems at first sight to make the vigil still harder. There seems to be never any respite from that terrific iteration of *Paters*, *Aves*, Creeds. During this night of vigil he has to say aloud three hundred and ninety-six *Paters*, six hundred and forty-eight *Aves*, and one hundred and twenty-four Creeds.

The simplicity of the three reiterated prayers is dwelt upon by Irish commentators (Curtayne 1944:174; Carey 1939:19), who also note that the same prayers must have been said by the seven saints venerated during the rounds (the saints of the "beds" and St. Patrick himself). Some say that the mantralike repetition, far from dulling the mind, eventually makes the pilgrim realize the true meaning of the words (Curtayne 1944:173). Repetition as a "frame" for "flow," that intrinsically regarding experience discussed by Csikszentmihalyi, will be considered at the end of this chapter.

The day after the vigil is the pilgrim's own; he has no stations of obligation. But he spends most of it fighting sleep, for he must not go to bed until half past nine at night. Pilgrims say that when they finally sink onto the spring mattresses under Irish linen in the hospice cubicles, they experience sleep's plenitude, plummeting into abysses of repose unknown to mundane life (Curtayne 1944:176). But a bell wakes them at six in the morning, and they must crowd two stations—two and a half hours of obligatory prayer—into the next five hours before the boat leaves, if they are to fulfill the pilgrimage. Everyone on the island gathers at the landing stage to watch the boat depart, for it is the day's big nonspiritual event. The ferryman dons a peaked cap and sounds a long warning note on a bugle, following ancient custom. When everyone is finally embarked—and there are always a few feckless latecomers—the heavy oars dip, and the "bulging amplitude" of the barque (to borrow a phrase from a poem by Wilfred Owen), like the boat which carried King Arthur to Avalon, "budges the ripples" as it moves slowly away. Veteran pilgrims may break into the traditional farewell hymn to Lough Derg:

> *Oh! fare thee well, Lough Derg,*
> *Shall I ever see you more?*
> *My heart is filled with sorrow*
> *To leave thy sainted shore. . . .*

and so on for six stanzas replete with reference to St. Patrick and St. Dabheoc, "without guile."

THE MEANING OF LOUGH DERG FOR THE IRISH

It is most probable that Lough Derg and its islands were sacred places, perhaps even pilgrimage centers, before the coming of Christianity. Máire MacNeill (1962:75,400,503–8,525,530–1) has compiled a large number of folk tales in which St. Patrick is reported to have fought a female fiend called the Caorthannach, or Corra—the Devil's mother, in the form of a snake, eel, or dragon. The struggle usually begins on Croagh Patrick and ends when Patrick destroys the beast with his crozier in Lough Derg (as we have already mentioned, the lake is said to have got its name from the serpent's blood; MacNeil 1962:505). It is perhaps interesting to note that in the southern gable of the old St. Patrick's Church on Station Island is an ancient stone figure resembling a wolf with a serpent's tail. This is alleged to be a representation of the monster killed by St. Patrick when he visited Lough Derg. Máire MacNeill believes that the serpent-slaying legend is the source of the tradition that St. Patrick destroyed or banished all the snakes in Ireland. Tales of this mythemic type, saint overcoming serpent or fiend, often refer to the displacement of one religious tradition by another. Whether this is the case here or not, folk tradition places the origin of the pilgrimage in the epoch of contestation between the old Celtic religion and St. Patrick's brand of Romano-British Christianity.

Archaism is the cement which keeps the Lough Derg pilgrimage together and makes of it a symbol of Irish nationalism. In the words of one Irish poet, it is "a fragment fallen from ancient times,/that floateth there unchanged" (cited in Curtayne, p. 121). Nationalism is a potent force at Lough Derg. This extends to the overseas Irish, many of whom make the pilgrimage. The majority are from British centers of Irish settlement, especially Glasgow and Liverpool. Indeed it was from a Manchester Irishman, three generations removed from the homeland, that we first heard of St. Patrick's Purgatory. Irish-Americans and Irish-Australians are frequently found in the pilgrim throngs. The devotion is everywhere regarded as peculiarly Irish, though, as we shall see, it was one of the great international pilgrimages in the Middle Ages. Careful observers will note that few English Catholics visit the holy isle. Those who do go are either aristocratic "Old Catholics" or intellectuals.

An interesting incident pertaining to English Catholics is related by Curtayne (pp. 142–43). Earlier in this century the secretary of the Catholic Truth Society of England wrote to the prior of Lough Derg to make arrangements for an English pilgrimage of five hundred persons. The prior replied that it might be difficult to house all of them at one time, together with the usual Irish contingent. We should point out here that the pilgrimage season lasts for only ten weeks each year, from June 1 to August 15, and that 15,000 people, on average, come each year to Station Island, where they are housed in the two large hospices, one for men, the other for women. Since each group remains for three days, approximately twenty-five groups of six hundred pilgrims each make the pilgrimage every summer. The hospices can just accommodate them. Thus the prior had good reason for requesting that the English pilgrims come in two groups, some time apart. But the English pilgrims seems to have experienced a failure of nerve at the thought of being crowded together with so many turbulent Irish. At any rate, the secretary answered the prior that the proposed pilgrimage would be represented "by one gentleman."

Curtayne gives us an inside view of the pilgrimage when she writes (p. 143): Most pilgrims develop for this rocky island and its harsh routine an affection that really defies explanation. Again and again they return to it with a gaeity, an uplifting of the heart, a profound sense of relief, in short the very sentiments proper to homecoming after life-long exile. That which speaks to them at Lough Derg is *race*. In going there they are answering the call of the blood.

One is strongly reminded of the Mexican devotion to the Guadalupe pilgrimage, which is for Mexicans the central symbol of their race. The paradigmatic character of Lough Derg was strikingly attested by 264 political prisoners interned by the British at Ballykinlar in County Down during "the Trouble" of 1921. They conceived the idea of performing the Lough Derg pilgrimage, in facsimile as it were, in their prison camp. In keeping with the pilgrimage's populist style through the ages, no priest or chaplain took the initiative here. The few prisoners who had been to Lough Derg explained the whole routine of the stations to the rest. The prior was written to for permission, which he granted to the prisoners as if their British guards were nonexistent, though he instructed them to omit the all-night vigil and substitute a fourth station each day for it. From the eleventh to the fifteenth of August, the last days of the pilgrimage season, the prisoners performed the devotions and went on a strict fast (Curtayne, p. 144).

The pilgrimage to Lough Derg has often been assailed by foes of the "great Irishry" (the *magna Irecheria* mentioned in thirteenth-century records such as the *Annals of Ulster*). There is an ancient tradition that in A.D. 836, the abbey that stood on Saints' Island was plundered by the Danes. At that time the pilgrimage must have been to Saints' Island, where traditionally each pilgrim spent twenty-four hours alone in the penitential cave. As mentioned earlier, the Borgia pope Alexander VI closed the cave in 1497, and banned the pilgrimage, but his decree was disregarded by the Irish. In 1503 Pius III officially removed the ban, and in the sixteenth and seventeenth centuries phenomenal numbers of foreign pilgrims swarmed to Lough Derg, sometimes impelled by fantastic, romantic notions of the visions and dreams of hell, purgatory, and earthly paradise to be experienced in the cave. In May, 1632, as mentioned, the structures on Station Island were destroyed by order of the British Government under the direction of Spottiswood, the Protestant bishop of Clogher, and the Augustinian canons were ejected and deported (yet pilgrims continued to come as before). This assault had been preceded by a propaganda campaign alleging that the legends and romances about St. Patrick's Purgatory were held by the people to be articles of faith, and that Catholics really believed there to be a passage from the island into the realms of purgatory, and thus ultimately to heaven.

Many writers had helped to weave this tissue of somber romance. The earliest extant account of a miraculous vision in the cave of St. Patrick's Purgatory is preserved in the Saltrey manuscript of the tale of the Knight Owen, who was said to have visited Lough Derg in 1147, and in the cave there to have had a vision of the afterlife, fought with demons, been comforted by angels, and to have passed through hell and the portals of paradise. The Saltrey monk's account of what seems to have been quite a "trip," in the modern idiom, generated many versions, seventy-four in Latin by the year 1500, as well as innumerable versions in English, French, Italian, German and Bohemian. The famous poetess Marie de France produced a poetical rendering in Old French; the Italian chronicler Jacobus de Voragine included the tale in his celebrated *Golden Legend;* Ralph Higden inserted it in his *Polychronicon.* Many Irish writers, among them Shane Leslie, even insist that Dante was indebted to the Saltrey manuscript for certain ideas and images in the *Divine Comedy.* It is hard to sort out, however, what is specific to the Knight Owen's tale as compared with other accounts of fiery pits, pools of ice, rivers of fire, and perilous bridges, all of which were regular motifs of medieval vision cycles such as those associated with SS. Brendan, Fursey, and Adamnan of Iona. Each and all of these might have provided Dante with material. One major difference is that the Saltrey manuscript's account tends to confuse hell with purgatory, and opposes both to a terrestrial Eden; such a theological blunder would not have been made by a contemporary Irish writer, and was certainly not made by Dante! Ariosto in *Orlando Furioso* mentions the fabulous cave in Ireland, listing the pilgrimage among the "deeds of daring" (*l'audac imprese*) which a knight of that chivalrous epoch should undertake. Calderón, the seventeenth-century Spanish dramatist, wrote a religious verse-play, *El Purgatorio de San Patricio,* which was performed in the Royal Theater of Madrid. One could extend this list considerably, and add to it accounts of and by pilgrims from as far to the east as Hungary; among them was Laurence Rathold de Pasztho, whose visit to Lough Derg in 1411 is recorded in a narrative given in a manuscript account composed by Jacobus Yonge, notary of Dublin, and is now in the Royal Collection at the British Museum, catalogued W.B. IX. Laurence relates that, according to custom, the Augustinian monks recited over him the office of the dead, sprinkled him with holy water, and locked him in the cave, where he dreamed of imps (put to flight by the sign of the cross, of disguised demons, and finally of the archangel Michael, his patron, who conducted him through purgatory, where he saw many of his friends being tormented, and at last back to the entrance, which the prior opened to him at six in the morning (O'Connor 1903:253).

Accounts such as these were utilized by British Protestants to support their contention that the Catholic Church not only condoned animistic superstitions but actually promoted them as Christian truth. Again, as has so often been the case in the ancient struggle between dedicated iconoclasts and dedicated iconophiles, the former took literally what the latter took metaphorically and symbolically. Confusion was compounded by a failure to distinguish the Irish conception of Lough Derg from the alien, even exotic, view. The Irish attitude, as expressed in Irish bardic poetry, was severe, ascetic, realistic. The foreign view, we have just seen, was romantic, naive, colorful, imaginative. In the Irish literary tradition there is no reference to visions, to conversations with the dead, to paradise or hell. For instance, Donnchad Mor O Dálaig, who died in 1244, when the romantic view of Lough Derg was prevalent overseas, wrote a poem lamenting that he had gone to Lough Derg to weep over the Passion of Christ but his eyes were tearless. He begs God for the gift of tears, for sorrow like Patrick's. He confesses that the cold and the fasting of the pilgrimage are really too good for his body, hardened in its sinfulness; that he is deeply ashamed of performing the pilgrimage rite with a heart as hard as stone (as summarized by Curtayne, pp. 56–57).

Oh misery me on my pilgrimage to Lough Dearg!
Oh King of Belfries and bells.
For keening thy woes and thy wounds

Not a tear can I drag from my eyes
[cited in Shane Leslie, *St. Patrick's Purgatory* 1961:10].

O Dálaig's successors—Feargal O'Higinn (1550–91), Feargal Mac Ward (late sixteenth century), and many more—wrote in the same strain, of spiritual aridity, of the apparent desertion of God, the need for penance, the stoniness of the heart requiring the rough medicine of the flinty island, the painful beds which the poet is yet sorry to leave. The ascetic attitude of these writers was traditional to Ireland. John Ryan (*Irish Monasticism* 1972:vii) is representative of innumerable scholars in the field of Irish ecclesiology when he argues that the Irish Church had been "markedly 'monastic' in character," since the time of St. Patrick and his immediate missionary successors, and that the austerer ritual modes of the cloister had pervaded Irish religious life generally. St. Patrick's Purgatory is a survival of that archaic Celtic spirit, a monastery for laymen. We stress the laity, for even though Augustinian canons took charge of the pilgrimage for five centuries, and Franciscan friars did so for a century and a half, the ordinary Irish kept the pilgrimage going during the years of ban and persecution. When the purgatorial cave (even caves, for extra caves were opened in the eighteenth century) was closed up by the pilgrimage authorities themselves in 1780, and the vigil was decreed to be held in church, there was no decline in the popularity of pilgrimage. For its prime function was penitence, not the seeking of weird visions.

The social anthropologist may well inquire if St. Patrick's Purgatory has some social function, even a covert one. It has been suggested (most recently perhaps by Daniel Gross 1971:139) that Latin European and Latin American pilgrimages to the shrines of miracle-working images of Christ, the Virgin, or a saint, have the function of maintaining an important aspect of the social structure; that is, the asymmetrical relationship between patron and client, which exists both in the quasi-feudal property relationship between landowner and peon and in the economic relationship between merchant and farmer. Here the essence of the pilgrimage is in the promise or vow: if you, the powerful one, help me in my weakness and affliction, I will later obey you and do what you require of me.

128

There is reciprocity of service between unequals. Many pilgrimages maintain this feudal, or feudalized, paradigm. But such a characterization hardly applies to Lough Derg, which is clearly homologous to the Pan-Hindu pilgrimage centers (described by S. H. Bhardwaj 1973), frequented by those who come to worship and do spiritual penance, rather than to seek material favors. For though St. Patrick is considered the patron of Lough Derg, pilgrims rarely come to fulfill a particular vow to him. The main outward purpose of the pilgrimage is to do penance by following the general *via crucis* model, represented in particular in the universal Church by the fourteen Stations of the Cross (in symbolic imitation of the route taken by Jesus through Jerusalem to Calvary, a route still followed by Christian pilgrims to Jerusalem, especially on Good Friday). As we have mentioned earlier, the fourteen Stations are represented on the stained-glass windows of the Basilica of St. Patrick. Each window depicts a saint bearing a plaque on which is shown one of the stations; the plaques are of lighter glass, so that they stand out in considerable relief. Thus the Station of the Cross is the focus of attention, while the saint is, as it were, its servitor. The fourteen Stations are (1) the condemnation by Pilate, (2) the reception of the cross, (3) Christ's first fall, (4) his meeting with his mother, (5) Simon of Cyrene carrying the cross, (6) Veronica wiping the face of Jesus, (7) the second fall, (8) the exhortation to the women of Jerusalem, (9) the third fall, (10) the stripping of the clothes, (11) the crucifixion, (12) the death, (13) the descent from the cross, (14) the burial. The fourteen saints bearing the plaques begin with the twelve apostles—ranged in the order given in the tenth chapter of the Gospel of Matthew: (1) Simon Peter, (2) Andrew, (3) James, (4) John, (5) Philip, (6) Bartholomew, (7) Thomas, (8) Matthew, (9) James son of Alpheus, (10) Thaddeus, (11) Simon the Cananean, and (12) Matthias (in place of Judas)—and end with (13) the Virgin Mary and (14) St. Paul. Thus the themes of the *via crucis*, or Christ's Passion, and the apostolic mission are here combined and related to the beginnings of Christianity as an organized religion.

But the stations outside the basilica—the crosses and the beds—refer to Celtic saints, with the possible exception of St. Catherine, as we have noted above. If we add St. Patrick to the five Celtic saints Brigid, Columcille, Brendan, Dabheoc, and Molaise, we have six Irish saints to match with the twelve apostles. According to tradition, Dabheoc was a disciple of St. Patrick and came from Wales; he may have been the son of a British lesser king. He is said to have been the first abbot in charge of the monastic settlement on Saints' Island, from which his monks took over the care of the penitential cave on Station Island, where a few of them also lived. Dabheoc is listed as one of the Twelve Apostles of Ireland in a legend which describes St. Patrick's cursing of the pagan sanctuary of Tara. If we pursue a Lévi-Straussian structuralist course here, we may regard St. Catherine as being structurally homologous in the exterior set of saints to the Virgin Mary and St. Paul among the saints represented in the basilica windows. The twelve original Christian apostles plus two other holy persons—one a Virgin, the other a martyred adjunct apostle—correspond, in a sense, to the six Irish apostles, plus the virgin-martyr Catherine.

It may also be noted that all the Irish saints venerated at Lough Derg are monastic; some were the founders of monasteries and convents. Four were missionaries and formidable travelers. Their disciples did much of the missionizing of Western Europe. Here we should once more point out the special importance of monasticism in the Celtic West. From the sixth century on, Ireland was the home of a vigorous monasticism, for the most part unaffected by the invasions which caused such suffering in mainland Europe during the sixth, seventh, and eighth centuries. For a long while in Ireland, the church was not organized into territorial dioceses under the administration of bishops, as it was in areas that had been firmly under the Roman Empire. Instead, it was organized around the monastery—perhaps because the tribe (*tuath*) was reproduced in the Irish Church, in which the abbots, like clan heads, were paramount. Unless a bishop was also an abbot, his only distinctive function was that of ordaining priests.

Irish monasteries were centers of learning, mainly in Latin—and much attention was paid to the marvelously colorful illumination of manuscripts. Irish monks frequently migrated to other countries.

They called themselves in this missionary role, *peregrini*, "pilgrims." They went to the Orkneys, the Faroes, the rough coasts of Caledonia, even to Iceland; to the forests of the Rhine and the Danube, the rugged hills of Gaul, the foothills of the Alps, the cities and remote valleys of Italy. This combination of monasticism and eastward missionary migration was peculiarly Celtic at that time, countering the previous trend of peoples to the West. Our contention here is that the archaic, unfettered monasticism intrinsic to old Ireland was accessible to the often persecuted Irish Catholic laity in the Lough Derg pilgrimage, and became one of the important "signifieds," at both the orectic and the normative pole of meaning, of the pilgrimage. Irishness was, in part, monastic and ascetic—characterized by the self-abnegation both of the contemplative in the mode of peace and recollection and of the patriot in the mode of violence and rebellion. But the two modes converge. The notion that a monk does penance not only for his own sins but for those of others, may be important in this connection also. For it is this point which least supports a Durkheimian explanation of Lough Derg as a kind of national totemic center, where the Irish periodically reaffirm and strengthen their sentiments of solidarity. The fact is that the whole unhappy island never did enjoy true solidarity—nor even a single indigenous government. The people, united in religious belief but divided by loyalty to local chiefs and clan heads, were an easy prey, first to the Vikings, then to the Norman English, beginning with Strongbow's conquests in 1172. The past eight centuries of Irish history have been punctuated by uprisings and rebellion against the British and by conflicts with the settlers whom the British have sponsored. Yet disunity among the Irish themselves has persisted. Though persecution strengthened their common religion, it weakened their capacity for united, organized, effective resistance.

The perennial divisiveness in Irish politics has been lamented by many Irish writers, among them Shane Leslie in his *Story of St. Patrick's Purgatory* (1917), a reconstructed chronicle of Lough Derg, based on history and legend. Referring to the end of the peaceful period known as Ireland's Golden Age (between the apostolic era of

St. Patrick and the invasions of the Norsemen and Danes), Leslie describes (pp. 23–24) what became a continuing theme in Irish political culture:

Years slipt by and the unwonted calm had begun to break. The joy of battle had mingled too often in the blood of the people for them to live at peace forever. Old jealousies were wrapt, like fat, round their hearts, and the waters of baptism had not washed away the feuds that lay among the royal clans of Ireland. Old stirrings were about in the country, signals passing from mouth to mouth. Men began to remember they owed duties to their Kings as well as to their God. Once again the reaping hooks were hammered into blades. The houses of religion alone took no part in the strife. They had a warfare of their own. All the country about Derg was at war. Tribe had risen against tribe. The same sunlight that lit the bronze cross in the monastery would be twinkling the other side of the mountains on the spears' points of the O'Donnells marching to war.

It is in this context—which, *mutatis mutandis,* has prevailed in Ireland since time immemorial—that we must consider that only a few self-selected persons go annually to Lough Derg, as compared to the large numbers who make the modern pilgrimage to the Shrine of the Apparitions at Knock (Cnoc Mhuire) in County Mayo. It has been calculated, not too wildly we think, that 700,000 pilgrims visit Knock annually,[6] as contrasted with 12,000 to 15,000 at Lough Derg (the average number was about 3,000 in the mid-nineteenth century; O'Connor 1903:196–97). Knock is known as the national shrine, and in some respects might indeed be described, in Durkheimian or Radcliffe-Brownian terms, as a kind of totemic center. Lough Derg represents, in its social dimension, penance and self-punishment for Irish cultural and political divisiveness. If anything, Lough Derg is the structural inverse of Knock. (All of this reinforces the need to study any particular pilgrimage as part of a *field* of pilgrimages, rather than as an isolate.) Those who feel bitterly the divisions of the present and know, not only through books but by oral tradition in family and village, the bitter fruits of past internal conflict, forsake the arenas of political and social conflict, and

6 "In 1972 the number of pilgrims was well over three-quarters of a million" (*Knock Shrine Annual* 1973:19).

journey to a liminal island crowded with symbols of what is for them a universal religion, symbols of the pristine essence of that religion's encounter with the preexisting Celtic culture. There they do penance and atone for sins, both personal and collective, committed in the realm of social structure. One major bonus of the penitential exercises is the brief revelation of an atemporal world of communitas, a community of sufferers—a purgatory full of hope, since such annealing suffering is thought to be the way to blessedness.

Irish Catholic writers themselves continually pose the question, How can human beings endure the severe ordeal of the Lough Derg exercises, upon the simple fare allowed? (see Carey 1939:20; also O'Connor 1903:237). They usually answer in religious terms, pointing to the special graces flowing from the exercises and from the spirit in which they are undertaken. But other explanations are given, too. Carey calls attention to the possible strengthening effect of minerals in the water, the "Lough Derg wine"; and the beneficial effect of a sparse diet, "particularly upon people who had indulged too freely in the pleasures of the table" (1939:20). Yet he seems to realize that these are hardly valid explanations,[7] and marvels that "the most fragile persons have been known to sustain the exercises, and in many cases to emerge from the experience feeling even stronger than before" (p. 20). All the writers agree that there is a connection between the pilgrims' discipline and privations and their sense of existential communitas, which we have defined elsewhere as "the direct, immediate, and total confrontation of human identities" (V. Turner 1973:193). For example, O'Connor wrote in 1930 (pp. 237–38): "At this shrine a true spirit of fraternity and equality prevails. Dignities, honours, wealth, education, and social position find here no special distinction or acknowledgment. The prince and the peasant, the highborn dame and the lowly cottage maiden (cailin) must here alike submit to the Station discipline, which knows no relaxation, except for sufficient cause submitted to and approved

[7] Especially in view of the fact that there was an outbreak of typhoid fever in 1912, due to the drinking of unboiled water from a lake polluted by sewage! Since that time water has been piped to Station Island from Lake Caricknamaddy, nearly two miles away (Curtayne 1944:138).

by the prior." Curtayne has an eloquent passage expressing this view (1944:177–79):

Every boatload of pilgrims contains a cross-section of human society that has a special interest. Sharp contrasts in age are frequent: two men of ninety have been known to have made the pilgrimage in recent years, while girls and boys in their very early teens are always among the crowd. The pilgrims also exhibit marked contrasts in type and condition: women whose clothes, though carefully chosen with a view to simplicity, nevertheless bear the stamp of wealth, are side by side with others clearly on the outermost edge of what is known as decent poverty; extremely sophisticated city people are thrown into the company of very simple country folk and appear to enjoy it; on this island, men of genius and learning find common ground with those who are totally illiterate. . . . When the newcomer casts off his footwear it is a symbol that he is shedding at the same time all those externals that make up status and lend importance to the individual: house, family and dependents, atmosphere, daily occupation. If he is a personage in his ordinary life, he here undergoes an immense levelling and becomes just one of the crowd.

Though class and status are here in abeyance, Irishness is not. We have seen that the sacra of Irish culture, the symbols of its most powerful self-image, are displayed in concentrated form on the tiny island. As Cardinal Logue said in his 1913 address (quoted in Gibbons 1937:69–70):

I have no doubt that whatever else changes in Ireland, Lough Derg will never change. It is as unchangeable as the hills by which we are surrounded. . . . It is as undying as the Faith of Ireland itself. (Applause.) There is nothing to which St. Patrick ever set his hand that did not prosper in this country. He established this Pilgrimage, this place of penance and prayer, and what it was in his own day, it has continued to be since. In making your stations and going round the beds of this small Island, you are walking in the footsteps of saints, not merely the religious who sanctified themselves and acquired perfection on this lone island.

That there is no sound documentary evidence of St. Patrick's ever having visited Lough Derg, does not diminish the force of Cardinal Logue's statement.

At this point we should like to extend and qualify our notion of communitas. In *The Ritual Process* (V. Turner 1969:132) existential communitas was distinguished from normative communitas and ideological communitas. Normative communitas derives from existential communitas: out of the human need to mobilize and organize resources, and to maintain social control, existential communitas eventually ceases to be spontaneous, becomes organized into a perduring social system; in other words, comes to terms with its social structural environment, mimics it in self-defense as it were. Religious systems and pilgrimage systems are examples of normative communitas, each originating in a nonutilitarian experience of brotherhood and fellowship, which the participating group attempts to preserve, in and by its religious, moral, and legal codes, and its religious and civil ceremonies. "Ideological communitas" refers to a wide variety of ideal, utopian models for societies which are conceived to exemplify or supply the optimal conditions for existential communitas. The pilgrimage to Lough Derg, its social organization, and its ritual process are all expressions of normative communitas. The symbol vehicles—the images, the saints' beds, the sentiments expressed and metaphors elaborated in sermons and devotional literature about St. Patrick's Purgatory—belong to the realm of ideological communitas, which is equivalent in culture to normative communitas in social structure. Ideological communitas's most distinctive feature is the way in which it polarizes the general and the particular, the universal and the local. Dominant ritual symbols possess this semantic polarity. At one pole they refer to ideals, values, legal principles, norms of social structure, theological doctrines, and the like; this we term the normative pole. At the other, they represent objects, activities, relationships, and ideas which, in the relevant culture, may be expected to arouse emotion and desire, feeling and willing; this we call the orectic pole. In the pilgrimage process, we maintain, the sacra found in the innermost shrine are semantically polarized between, on one hand, theological doctrines and ethical imperatives of a general kind, of the Great Tradition—and, on the other, highly localized, culturally specific objects and ideas, the orectic pole always being more closely related to the outward, sensorily perceptible form of the symbol than is the normative pole. At Lough Derg, the circular, stony saints' beds replicate ruins found in many parts of Ireland, going back to the beginnings of Christianity and even before. Every Catholic Irish child is taught the stories and traditions of the Celtic saints associated with the beds. Though they were celibates, Patrick and Brigid achieve symbolic parenthood with reference to the Christian culture they begot and bore. The church, called a "prison" during the all-night vigil, is both a tomb and a womb of rebirth. Strong emotions going back to childhood are generated by these symbols, indeed by their very archaism, to which may respond archaic physiological processes of the human psychobiological organism. We have argued elsewhere (*The Forest of Symbols* 1967:28; *The Drums of Affliction* 1968:18) that through the controlled, systematic, repetitive activity of ritual a transference may well be effected between semantic values of the two poles in the psyche of the actor, depending on how completely he enters the "flow" of the ritual process. At Lough Derg, it is entirely probable that Catholic ideas and doctrines become impregnated with Irish experiences, not only personal experiences but communitas experiences in an Irish landscape and culture setting, while the specific symbols and ideas of Irishness, including that of being a persecuted people, are correspondingly Catholicized, "elevated to the altars of the Church," so to speak, where Ireland becomes "the martyr nation." In other words, Irishness is raised to a more abstract plane of generalization and normativeness. Hence the generation of a dual loyalty to pope and people. Pilgrim symbology provides a clue to the dynamic interaction of the emotion-laden particular with the cognitive general. It may also provide a clue to the iconoclastic passion of the English assailants of the Lough Derg pilgrimage, who wished both to crush the spirit of Irish independence and to break the Roman link. The symbols they attacked had played a part in the formation of an Irish nationalist elite, and many are the tales directly relating Lough Derg to moments in the national struggle for independence. Penitence for Irish disunity may serve to create unity, which may go hand in hand with militant political action. Far from being an opiate for the people, Lough Derg and other pilgrimage shrines in Ireland—as in Mexico, Poland, and elsewhere—may have kept alive the cultural basis for national political struggle, providing it with its root paradigm: that martyrdom should be embraced, if necessary, for the good of the people. In such wise we may partially account for the tenacity and obstinacy of Irish resistance over the centuries of foreign occupation, what opponents call its "fanaticism," and partisans its "stubborn courage." Normative and ideological communitas owe their power to survive (as against the potent, memorable evanescence of existential communitas) precisely to this harnessing of the *gemeinschaft* of locality and kin to the service of wider, more abstract purposes. But the purity of existential communitas has now become polluted by the seven deadly sins of social structure, against which the Ten Commandments were directed. "Our" community becomes a structured cell opposed to "their" community, and the sentiment of humankindness at the heart of communitas vanishes as though it had never been.

Something should be said, in conclusion, about the relationship at Lough Derg between normative communitas and "flow," (to repeat MacAloon and Csikszentmihalyi's definition, "the holistic sensation when we act with total involvement"). It is obvious from many reports about the pilgrimage that many of the pilgrims are "repeaters," and that the sadness of their fairwell songs as they leave Station Island is genuine. Clearly, the ascetic exercises are, in a sense, enjoyable. Indeed, it is partly to account for the pleasurable component in rigorously "framed" activities that Csikszentmihalyi undertook the comprehensive investigation, reported in his *Beyond Boredom and Anxiety* (1975b), of "play-forms" and art-forms. Although he analyzed nonreligious activities such as rock-climbing, chess, basketball, music composition, and surgery, his conclusions seem to us to be strikingly applicable to the experience of Lough Derg pilgrims. In his recent article "Play and Intrinsic Rewards" (1975a), Csikszentmihalyi summarizes (p. 41) the essential qualities of such activities thus: "(a) a person is able to concentrate on a limited stimulus field, (b) in which he or she can use his or her skills to meet clear demands (c) thereby forgetting his or her own problems, and (d) his or her own separate identity, (e) at the same time obtaining a feeling of control over the environment, (f) which may result in a transcendence of ego-boundaries and consequent psychic integration with metapersonal systems." He applies the generic term "flow" to the common experiential state underlying various forms not only of "play" but of other "framed" activities as well.

137

In Csikszentmihalyi's words (p. 42), the "intrinsically rewarding" experience of flow is dependent on certain activities. The Lough Derg pilgrimage surely provides "clearly detailed activities in which the faithful can participate with the understanding that in so doing they are meeting the challenges of life" (p. 61). The sequential order of the station devotions; the numbered reiteration of Our Fathers, Hail Marys, and the Creed; the limits set by the island itself and by its sacred topography—all these enable pilgrims "to concentrate on a limited stimulus field," which screens out the "noise" of the mundane world and exacts from them patient attention to the tasks at hand. In chanting groups, they truly forget their own problems and even separate identities in the great collective trance of the night stations in the basilica. Ego-boundaries are transcended, if one can believe the many accounts by pilgrims; and there is a consequent integration with metapersonal systems— specifically, we have suggested, with a sort of mystical nationalism, which unites, in a single symbolic field, universal-Catholic and traditional-Irish norms and sentiments. All this is clearly indicated in O'Connor's impassioned prose (1903:241):

Seeing the peculiar efficacy of the exercises of this pilgrimage towards renewing and increasing the spiritual life, the sanctity of the place, and the graces and indulgences there received, what wonder is it that the eye of the pilgrim is charmed, his heart elevated, his faith enlivened, nay, even his love for holy Ireland increased, when first the Island of Lough Derg meets his view? And what wonder is it that the Irish people should so love this Sanctuary? We love it on account of its association with the name of our National Apostle; on account of the number of saints, who here practised the Gospel counsels of perfection, and whose names are in benediction in the Irish Church; we love it because of the traditions, which enshrine it in the Irish heart; because of the numberless sinners here reconciled to God, and who here "chose the better part"; and finally, we love it for the numberless graces here received, and the blessings it is the means of obtaining for its numerous votaries, and because it invites in us lofty desires of becoming more holy.

We can well understand Csikszentmihalyi's comment (p. 61) that the effectiveness of political, religious, and cultural movements may depend in part on the flow experiences they make possible.

138

Here, too, we should distinguish the orderly "normative communitas" of Lough Derg and other archaic pilgrimages from the "spontaneous communitas" of a pilgrimage's genesis following the first report of apparitions or miracles at some favored site. Flow is most often the effect of persons acting on a limited area of their environment (Csikszentmihalyi 1975a:43), of a narrowing of consciousness provided by rules and procedures, but only if these are reinforced by motivations. In pilgrimage, motivations are the need for penance, the vow to endure suffering for the sake of another, and the desire for salvation. More materialistic motivations—the desire for health, strength, longevity, and fertility, which ordinary men and women have always sought from their deities—must also be reckoned among the perennial incentives of pilgrimage. Whatever the motivational "trigger" may be, the rigorous routines of the devotional exercises frame the pilgrims' activities and lead to the loss of that "self-construct, the intermediary which one learns to interpose between stimulus and response" in everyday, mundane social life (p. 49). This egoless state, Csikszentmihalyi considers, is intrinsic to the "enjoyment" experienced when action and awareness are merged, and accounts for the autotelic nature of flow (p. 53). One might therefore hazard the suggestion that pilgrimage as a cultural form, and particular pilgrimages as historical institutions, have survived so long and in the face of so many countervailing pressures (antireligious and iconoclastic movements), precisely because they provide eminently satisfactory frames for the flow experience, in both the journey to and the exercises at the pilgrimage center. Asceticism has its joys—the joys of flow. And flow can serve to reinforce the symbols and values with which its frames are associated.

CHAPTER FOUR

Iconophily and Iconoclasm in Marian Pilgrimage

IN THE COURSE of this study, we have seen that pilgrimage shrines, in principal centers of peace and communitas, are often involved in social and political conflicts of great vehemence and intensity. This paradox has particularly marked the famous Marian shrines; the flux of Marian devotions has indeed been related to some of the major political and theological changes in Western History.

Let us begin *in medias res*, with an event which vividly illustrates the issue of iconophobia versus iconophily, which in a more general sense is a pervasive theme of this chapter. The event was the burning of certain statues of the Virgin in London in 1538, by order of Henry VIII's vicar general Thomas Cromwell, at the instigation of Bishop Hugh Latimer of Worcester. Earlier Latimer had asked in a sermon:

What thinke ye of these images that are had more than their felowes in reputation? that are gone into with such labour and werines of the body, frequented with such our cost, sought out and visited

STATION ISLAND, LOUGH DERG, IRELAND. THE PRESENT-DAY SITE OF ST. PATRICK'S PURGATORY AS SEEN FROM THE MAINLAND JETTY.

MASS AT THE GABLE OF THE APPARITION, KNOCK, IRELAND. ON THIS SPOT, IN 1879, APPEARED A GLOWING TABLEAU OF THE VIRGIN, ST. JO-SEPH, ST. JOHN, AND THE LAMB ON THE ALTAR. THE APPARITION WAS TAKEN AS A SIGN OF ENCOURAGEMENT TO THE IRISH.

PLATE 9

OUR LADY OF WALSINGHAM, ENGLAND. THIS LITTLE STATUE (NOW IN THE SLIPPER CHAPEL AT NEARBY HOUGHTON-IN-THE-DALE), ONLY ABOUT EIGHTEEN INCHES IN HEIGHT AND OF RELATIVELY RECENT DATE, WAS COPIED FROM THE THIRTEENTH-CENTURY SEAL OF THE PRIORY OF WALSINGHAM.

PILGRIMAGE PLAQUE AT WALSINGHAM, ENGLAND. COMMEMORATING THE FIRST MODERN NATIONAL PILGRIMAGE, MADE IN 1948, TO THE SHRINE OF WALSINGHAM.

PLATE 10

THE SANTISSIMO BAMBINO D'ARACOELI, ROME. THIS JEWEL-
ENCRUSTED FIGURE OF THE HOLY CHILD IS BELIEVED TO HAVE BEEN CARVED OF
OLIVE WOOD FROM THE GARDEN OF GETHSEMANE. LETTERS PETITIONING HIS
INTERCESSION ARE PILED UP BEFORE HIM.

PLATE 11

GROTTO OF MASSABIELLE, NEAR LOURDES. THE PRECISE SITE OF THE VIRGIN'S APPARITION TO BERNADETTE SOUBIROUS IS MARKED BY THE STATUE OF OUR LADY, WHICH BEARS THE INSCRIPTION "I AM THE IMMACULATE CONCEPTION." THE HEALING WATERS HAVE THEIR SOURCE BEHIND THE ALTAR. PILGRIMS DEPOSIT LETTERS OF PETITION TO THE VIRGIN IN A CONTAINER BEHIND THE ALTAR.

BENEDICTION OF PILGRIMS, LOURDES. PART OF THE LOWER BASILICA AND ONE OF THE GREAT ARCHED RAMPS USED FOR WHEELCHAIRS CAN BE SEEN IN THE BACKGROUND.

PLATE 12

with such confidence? what say ye by such images, that are so famous, so noble, so noted, beying of them so many and so diuers in England. Do you think that this preferryng of picture to picture, image to image, is the right vse, and not rather the abuse of images? [Quoted in Jusserand 1891:355.]

In the political climate of the 1530s these comments stood every chance of being translated into violent action. Indeed, in 1538 Latimer wrote to Cromwell: "I trust your Lordship will bestow our great sibyll [the image of Our Lady of Worcester] to some purpose. . . . She herself with her older sister of Walsingham, her younger sister of Ipswich, with their other two sisters of Doncaster and Pen-Rhys, would make a jolly muster in Smithfield. They would not be all day burning." The last comment was not only a sardonic reference to the slow combustion of the Franciscan friar John Forrest, recently executed by Cromwell's men, but ironically, an unwitting prophecy of Latimer's own end, at the hands of Queen Mary's men. Cromwell, at any rate, was not slow in responding to Latimer. According to Hall, in his *Chronicles*, at Chelsea, in September, 1538, "by the special motion of the Lord Cromwell, all the notable images unto the which there were made any special pilgrimages and offerings were utterly taken away, as the images of Walsingham, Ipswich, Worcester, the Lady of Willesden, with many other" (quoted in H. M. Gillett 1957:375).

Latimer's communications could involve us in the study of con turies of Christian infighting, but we wish to call attention only to his central argument against the images at pilgrimage shrines; namely, that the excess of public devotion to them was an abuse of the Church's directives. The Second Council of Nicaea (the seventh ecumenical council, A.D. 787) had decreed that both "the figure of the sacred and life-giving cross" and "the venerated and holy images" were to be "placed suitably in the holy churches of God," but that the honor paid to them was to be "only relative for the sake of their prototypes"; they were to receive "veneration, not adoration." The council's definition was itself a response to the first great wave of iconoclasm in Christian history. About A.D. 726 the Byzantine emperor Leo the Isaurian had published an edict which led to the destruction of images and the persecution of their defenders.

141

After the Second Council of Nicaea, iconoclasm erupted afresh in the Byzantine Empire, and the destruction of monasteries and images went on until 843, when the policy was reversed by the empress Theodora. An interesting aspect of the history of iconoclasm in the East is that the term "icon" (from the Greek), which simply means an image, even an image in the round, has come to be used specifically for the flat paintings and mosaics employed in the Eastern Church, as opposed to the three-dimensional images permitted in the Catholic West. As so often happens, political history has here altered the usage of a common term. A Greek or Russian "icon" is a compromise between the use of statues and the total absence of imagery. Icons are operationally more important in the East, however, than statues are in the West. Incense is regularly burned before icons, they are kissed and carried in procession; but most Western images (with the exception of those few which become objects of special devotion) are regarded as part of the furniture or background, and are not usually thought of as naturalistic portraits or representations, rather as heraldic or conventional emblems.

Bishop Latimer was not a complete iconoclast like Leo the Isaurian before him, or Oliver Cromwell after. His argument was directed against the *abuse* of images, and could claim the Nicene declaration itself as its precedent. The abuse, he held, was most prevalent at the great Marian shrines, such as Walsingham, England's senior pilgrimage, and Willesden, whose Lady was then patroness of London. Behind this criticism was the political consideration, well appreciated by Thomas Cromwell, that certain centers of devotion were likely to foster resistance to Henry VIII's schemes for breaking the influence of the Roman Church and securing its valuable properties for the Crown.

The general intent of the Church's recommendation was that sacred images were not to be particularized, "realistic" representations, but should have a semiheraldic, stereotyped character befitting their function as collective representations. They were not to be taken as "natural symbols," but as "conventional signs." Yet since they represented human beings (in however conventional a way), and were objects of private devotion in side-chapels and niches, as well as serving as architectural and liturgical elements (for instance, the crucifix on the altar), it was inevitable that certain individual images would become personified. This tendency was reinforced by the use of images as sacramentals in the home—material objects (such as crucifixes and pictures of saints) signifying spiritual truths and processes.

As all know, every symbol has a signifier and a signified. The signifier is the sensorily perceptible vehicle of a conception. The personifying process here involves a changing relation between signifier and signified. For example, a specific image of the Virgin Mary is a signifier meant to represent not only the historical woman who once lived in Galilee but the sacred person who resides in heaven, appears at times to living persons, and intercedes with God for the salvation of mankind. The popular tendency is to see the Virgin's supernatural power as intimately bound up with the particular image, rather than to see the image as just another symbol of that power. The signifier's connection with the theological signified thus becomes greatly attenuated. As we have seen in earlier chapters, the outward form of a symbol is connected more closely with its orectic (or emotional/volitional) pole of significance than with its normative (or ideological) pole. Association and analogy connect the sensorily perceived symbol-vehicle, or image, to referents of a dominantly emotional or wishful character. Images, if not idiosyncratic in form to begin with (for example, as the individualized products of a particular artist), often acquire, in the course of time, idiosyncratic physical features, due to discoloration of the original materials (numerous "black" Madonnas, such as the one at Montserrat in Spain, are the result of exposure to the sooty smoke of candles, for instance; others, of the oxidization of silver, as at Rocamadour), or accidental defacement, or due to their being traditionally vested in clothes of a particular period or region. The more particular the form of the symbol-vehicle (and the more attention is paid to its form), the likelier the signifier is to take on a life of its own, apart from its intended or original meaning, or "signified." New significance may then be generated as devotees associate the particularized, personalized image with their own hopes and sorrows as members of a particular community with a specific history.

The original intended signified, related to universally accepted theological principles, may be partially replaced by a new signified, derived from some critical historical event in the community. The original signified is not completely replaced, but rather fused with and partially altered by the new signified; or it may coexist with the new as part of a mosaic of meaning. The "new" signified may not in fact be historically new, but may represent a resurgence of archaic ideas and beliefs. It is not idolatrous worship of the signifier, at the expense of the signified, that is here in question—as theological polemic has too often asserted. Rather is it the creation of a semantic arena in which a multiplicity of signifieds—original, new, archaic—are for a time in conflict. By "original" we here mean theologically primary, which we distinguish from the "archaic," relating to an earlier, suppressed religion. The conflict is between what is often called the instinct of the masses—that is, the deep patterns of the people's cultural tradition—and the conscious efforts of agents of religious orthodoxy to purify the signified of "folk" ideas that are heterodox or theologically irrelevant. Iconoclasm is the simplest, if most draconic, solution; to purify the meaning, it destroys the vehicle. It does not recognize any *necessary* linkage between signifier and signified. It denies that there are "natural symbols." But it has the major, long-term disadvantage of destroying a public center of social and cultural integration. In the short term, this may be precisely what the iconoclasts desire: to destroy the integration provided by a rival world view. But they have then the problem of devising a religious system without visible, tactile signifiers, or of developing signifiers of an impersonal, neutral, or abstract type. Mass literacy is propitious for such a development, for the signs of written language have a less immediate emotional impact than do symbolic objects, gestures, sounds, and actions, which are like the books of the illiterate.

Johan Huizinga, Émile Mâle, and many other scholars have described the propensity of the late Middle Ages to crystallize its religious thought into images. For anthropologists, of course, this propensity is not confined to the European Middle Ages, but is found in innumerable tribal religions, as well as in the folk practices of the other great historical religions, even where "idolatry" is forbidden or discouraged by the orthodox establishment. But Huizinga took too simple a view of the relation between signifier and signified when he wrote the following (*The Waning of the Middle Ages* 1924; 1954:165):

The naïve religious conscience of the multitude had no need of intellectual proofs in matters of faith. The mere presence of a visible image of things holy sufficed to establish their truth. No doubts intervened between the sight of all those pictures and statues—the persons of the Trinity, the flames of hell, the innumerable saints—and belief in their reality. All these conceptions became matters of faith in the most direct manner; they passed straight from the state of images to that of convictions, taking root in the mind as pictures clearly outlined and vividly coloured, possessing all the reality claimed for them by the Church, and even a little more.

What Huizinga did not see was that behind the visible image stood not a single significatum with which it was immediately identified, but an entire semantic field, an area of multivocality, the "referents" of which were drawn from the most disparate sources. First, there was the system of theological doctrines on which the Church insisted. Though Huizinga conceded "the Church did not fail to teach that all honours rendered to the saints, to relics, to holy places, should have God for their object" (p. 165), he did not realize how much this doctrine and others, such as the communion of saints, have influenced the development of the cultuses of Mary and the saints, and how completely they are comprehended by peasants and proletarians. We have been astonished, in places as far removed as the cities of Stockport, in Cheshire, England, and Izamal, in Yucatán, to find how well the poor and unlettered know their basic theology, where pilgrimage is concerned. Sermons, homilies, tracts, advice in the confessional, discussions among the laity on religious and ethnic questions, keep fundamental doctrines alive, doctrines which are indeed embedded in the very rituals of the liturgy. But, of course, the doctrinal ideas share the semantic field with derivatives from archaic, even pre-Christian ritual traditions, as we have seen with the pilgrimages to the Guadalupe and Los Remedios shrines in Mexico, and to St. Patrick's Purgatory in Ireland. But the archaic notions do not belong to the normative pole of the symbol's meaning. Rather do they supply vivid pictures, or "images" if you like, which give emotional coloring to the symbol, and root it deeply in the past of the group's social experience. As a devotional image continues to be venerated over the years, its semantic field incorporates further significata, some resulting from the "development of doctrine," others from historical experience. For example, the belief that on several occasions the Remedios and Guadalupe Virgins saved Mexico City from plague, floods, and drought now forms part of the "meaning" of these images, particularly at their orectic pole. Guadalupe's meaning also encompasses the times when her banner was associated with the struggles for national independence and peasant rights. For the cultural anthropologist, a symbol's meaning is much more than its legitimated interpretation (see V. Turner 1967a: chs. 1 and 2). Beyond the *exegetic meaning*, there are other levels. The *operational meaning* concerns not what people say about a symbol but how they act with reference to it, who so acts, and the social structural context of such action—we also include here the symbol's "social history"; that is, the stereotyped memories of great events with which the symbol has been connected. Symbols also have *positional meaning*, for they are rarely isolated units; they enter into relations with other symbols in clusters and systems of signifiers and signifieds. Some symbols are dominant, others ancillary, in these constellations. Symbols may appear in the dyadic relations, or in triadic relations. In the case of an important image of the Virgin, for example, the theological referents of the signified may belong to a subsystem of the total theological system. Similarly, the signifier itself (in this case the image of the Virgin) may form part of a symbolic complex (such as a painting of Virgin and Child), or a set of images, each located in some significant relation to the main altar of the Church. In these instances, the relation between the component symbols would be of key importance. The natural dependence of a child on its mother might be countered by the Child's standing on the Madonna's knee and giving a priestly blessing, for example, indicating that the infant is God and, hence, that the mother is the Theotokos, the Mother of God. In the twelfth century, the infant was often portrayed with an adult's face—representing the Divine Word; the doctrines of the hypostatic union and the Incarnation were also implied. To cite another example—Gary Gossen (1972) has shown that the arrangement of saints' images in a church with a Tzotzil congregation in Chiapas, Mexico, is influenced both by pre-Columbian cosmological notions and by Christian doctrine. Eva Hunt has observed (in a personal communication) that pilgrimage shrines among the Cuicatec Indians in Oaxaca tend to be grouped in fives (a quincunx, with a shrine at each cardinal point, east, south, west and north, and one in the center) and have successive feast (and market) days, following a pre-Columbia pattern. All three levels—exegetic, operational, and positional—must be taken into account if we are to form an adequate interpretation of a symbol's meaning.

Huizinga was correct, however, in arguing that in the waning Middle Ages "an ultra-realistic conception of all that related to the saints" developed in the popular faith (1954:166). The relation between signifier and signified had worn thin, and a too literal view of images resulted—a constant danger among all kinds of symbolic forms and actions. But Huizinga exempted from his stricture the devotion centered on Christ and His mother, which he considered was still profound (p. 166). This profundity had marked the pilgrimage devotions of the High Middle Ages, whose zenith was the thirteenth century. A balance seems to have been then attained between the normative and orectic poles of symbolic meaning; the outward form was still translucent to the inner meaning, while archaic customs and Christian theological ideas and imagery interresonated harmoniously. We mention the discrepancy between High and late Middle Ages to emphasize that we are dealing here with dynamic phenomena; it is all too easy to make generalizations about pilgrimages and their symbolism without taking into account major differences between historical periods. Jusserand can hardly escape this charge in his otherwise admirable *English Wayfaring Life in the Middle Ages* (1891:passim). Those who look to Chaucer for light on the pilgrimage process would do well to consider that they are dealing with a world on the wane, one where Huizinga's analysis, as well as the barbed shafts of his earlier compatriot Erasmus, would have found a mark. That world, however, was strongly revived in the nineteenth century in mainland Europe, and has shown signs of reviving in Great Britain, where today thousands of pilgrims annually visit the restored Marian shrines of Walsingham, Willesden, and Pen-Rhys—all of which were doomed to destruction by Bishop Latimer and were razed by Thomas Cromwell.

Though the phenomenon of pilgrimage has a common processual form, each pilgrimage has a particular history, which is affected by world and regional history. The duration of a ritual process— whether a puberty rite, a harvest festival, or a communal pilgrimage process—is defined as being outside the historical timestream; often the ritual is performed in a marginal site: a circumcision lodge, a chapel outside of a town, etc. It has, like music or drama, ahistorical diachrony. But the ritual processes are enacted by groups whose nonritual activities place them firmly within the historical process. Their rituals become subject to political manipulation and pressure, respond to the ecological cycle and to economic factors, and thrive or succumb in relation to currents of secular thought. The symbolism and conceptual structure of ritual processes are by no means immune to these historical and nonritual vicissitudes.

It is, therefore, highly interesting to study the broad lines of change in Marian pilgrimage devotions through the Christian centuries, since of all targets of pilgrim travel, the shrines of the Virgin have always been the most popular. Bede Jarrett (1911:88–96) lists, among a hundred "chief places of Catholic pilgrimage in early days, in the Middle Ages, and in modern times," fifty-eight dominantly Marian shrines. (As for the few saints' shrines which compare in worldwide importance with the Marian ones, we can list the great shrine of St. James at Compostela; that of St. Thomas à Becket at Canterbury; St.-Sulpice-de-Favières, in France; the Three Kings at Cologne, in Germany; the Patrician shrines in Ireland; St. Anne de Beaupré, in Canada; and, of course, St. Peter's in Rome.) The total number of Marian shrines, international, national, and regional, is quite extraordinary. The medieval historian Lionel Rothkrug has collected data on at least a thousand pre-Reformation Marian shrines in Germany alone (personal communication). Moreover, new Marian shrines are constantly being established. Since 1900, Fátima in Portugal, and Beauraing and Banneux in Belgium, have achieved recognition even outside the Catholic Church, and attract hundreds of thousands of pilgrims annually.

Yet only a small percentage of the numerous Marian shrines have become pilgrimage centers. Where this has happened, a vision has often been the precipitating factor—either a vision (or dream) in which the Virgin asked that a shrine be erected to her on a given site (see the discussion of the shepherds' cycle in chapter 2), or one in which she revealed, to some lowly person, a hidden image of herself that later became the center of a new cultus. This pattern has been fairly constant over the Christian centuries, and is not confined to any particular place or time. Apart from pagan prototypes, Mary's association with a supernatural vision has a Christian legitimization in the Annunciation, in which the archangel Gabriel appeared to the Virgin to announce the coming of Christ. In the foundation narratives, of course, the Virgin's role is reversed; it is she who acts as God's messenger, giving advice or warning to the sons of men. Since 1830, as we shall see, there has been a marked increase in reports of Marian apparitions, increasingly associated with warnings of dire calamities to be visited on mankind if it does not repent and mend its ways—a kind of Catholic millenarianism. It is interesting to note here that other religions also have their reports of apparitions of female supernaturals of the highest grade. The Zulu believe that Nomkubulwana, the princess of the heavens, appears to adolescent girls. Appearances of Kuan Yin, the Buddhist goddess of mercy, are frequently mentioned in Indian folk literature. And the nineteenth-century Hindu mystic Rama Krishna vividly described his visions of the Great Mother, Kali or Durga (Yogeshananda 1973:passim). In Jung's archetypal pantheon, the Anima, expressed in the Great Mother and other female forms, plays an active, admonitory role; the Anima represents the collective unconscious, rising up in dreams and in the imagery of art to warn men that they have committed themselves too wholeheartedly to conscious, rational activities, in their urge to subdue external nature to their material interests. Terrifying female archetypes portend the avenging power of inner and outer nature, and indicate that if man loses touch with his collective unconscious he will destroy himself in a sterile desert of rationality, objectivity, and technology. Here the archetypal visions seem not to be psychopathological, but therapeutic, serving to redress an unwholesome imbalance.

The predisposing cause of Marian devotion lies not in individual visions, however, but in the tension between its two sources. The first source is learned theory—a body of deductions from theological doctrines about the role of Mary in the economy of salvation. The second is the practice and experience of the unlearned. Visions appear at the point of major stress between contrary cultures and their major definitions of reality, and may be, as Anthony Wallace has suggested (1956:273), a synthesizing and therapeutic process performed under extreme stress by those already sick.

It has sometimes been suggested that the Marian cultus is a relatively late development in Christianity, as the Great Goddess cultus has been a relative late-comer in Hinduism. This view seems to be refuted, however, by second-century frescoes in the Roman catacombs, notably a painting in the Catacomb of Priscilla. This fresco represents the Virgin Mary seated with the child Jesus on her knee; to her left is a figure generally agreed to be the prophet Isaiah— whose words "The Lord himself shall give you a sign. Behold a Virgin shall conceive and bear a son, and his name shall be called Emmanuel" are regarded by the Church as a prophecy of the Incarnation. A star between Mary and Isaiah stands for the star of Bethlehem. To the prophet's left are branches of a blossoming tree, a motif which became prominent in later Christian iconography; it represents another Old Testament prophecy: "The Rod of Jesse hath blossomed; a Virgin hath brought forth Love and Man." From distinctive features shared with non-Christian Roman paintings, the fresco in the Catacomb of Priscilla has been tentatively dated at around A.D. 170.

In the late fourth century, before the Council of Ephesus defined Mary's role, St. Epiphanius of Salamis apparently found it necessary to denounce an obscure sect known as the Collyridians, or Philomarianites, for their sacrificial offering of cakes to Mary (a practice which indicates that syncretism with a pre-Christian goddess was perhaps at issue here).[1] The Collyridians, like the Montanists, had female priests. There had of course been a formidable number of circum-Mediterranean mother-goddesses— among them, Tiamat, in Babylonia; Hathor, Nut, Isis, and Mehurt,

---

[1] For a full discussion of St. Epiphanius's position, see Jugie (1944:77–81).

in Egypt; Demeter, Agbele, Dindymene, Hecate, and Artemis, in Greece; and Mari, in Syria. Epiphanius laid down the rule which has since prevailed: "Let Mary be held in honor. Let the Father, Son, and Holy Ghost be adored, but let no one adore Mary." The popular cultus of Mary, when first introduced by missionaries, almost always tended to emphasize her aspect as the mother of Jesus. And missionaries encouraged the transfer to her of attitudes and concepts about mother-goddesses who had a similar function in the old religion or who were structurally homologous in the pre-Christian pantheon. The famous Franciscan friar Bernardino de Sahagún, whose *Historia de las Cosas de Nueva España* (1529) is the foundation of Mexican historical and ethnographic studies, applauded the fervent devotion of Aztec converts to Our Lady of Guadalupe on the hill of Tepeyac, where sacrifices had formerly been offered to the Aztec goddess Tonantzin. The Aztec goddess was supposed to have given birth to Teohuitznáhuac without violence to her virginity, and was invoked as a rainmaker (Our Lady of Guadalupe, too, traditionally had a special relationship to water; for example, she is held to have saved Mexico City from floods in 1629). In the classic text of the Lady's appearances to the Aztec commoner Juan Diego, she designated herself as the mother of the Mexicans. Sahagún criticized the adherence to the pagan name. "It is something that should be remedied," he wrote, "because the proper name for the Mother of God and Our Lady is not *Tonantzin* but God-*Nantzin* or *Teonantzin*" (from the Nahuatl, *teo*, "god"; see Sahagún, 1956 ed.: vol. 3, p. 321).

In the early Christian centuries the problem of taming popular cultus to the service of theology must have been more difficult, since Great Goddesses abounded in the primitive Semitic and Indo-European cultures (in addition to the deities already mentioned, there were Al-Uzza in Arabia and Ishtar in Babylonia, the former deity connected with the moon, the latter with the planet Venus; Danu and Brigit in ancient Celtic Ireland; Freya and the Norns in Nordic culture; the Moirai in Hellas). Moreover, it was necessary to avoid deifying Mary in order to preserve the humanity in the person of Jesus Christ; that is, to maintain the dogma of the Incarnation. If Mary were a goddess, Jesus would not have had a human nature; hence the doctrine of the hypostatic union of the divine and human natures of Christ would have been undermined. The Christian theology of the salvific process was initially articulated by a series of general councils, the first eight of which were held in Asia Minor, traditionally a major center of mother-goddess worship. The Third Ecumenical Council, at Ephesus, A.D. 431, defined Mary's role in such a way as to legitimate and foster her already flourishing popular cultus. Ephesus was a peculiarly appropriate choice of locale, for this city had not only been the center of the important cult of Diana of the Ephesians, a many-breasted Magna Mater, but was also, according to Christian oral and apocryphal tradition, the site of Mary's death, or dormition, and Assumption. Here cult, tradition, and theology came together; the Council of Ephesus set the terms for Marian devotion and, more specifically, Marian pilgrimage, for over fifteen centuries.

We have mentioned the shadow of conflict that has dogged the footsteps of the mild Virgin throughout history. The Council of Ephesus was no exception (see Camelot 1962 and 1967). It was an acrimonious occasion full of factional struggles and Machiavellian manipulations. Convoked by the Byzantine emperor Theodosius II and his Western colleague Valentinian III, with the consent of Pope Celestine I, it culminated in the condemnation of Nestorius as a heretic, and in the defeat of his supporters from Antioch, mainly by the Alexandrian faction. This condemnation was closely linked to the enunciation by the council of the doctrine of Mary as Theotokos, which remains central to the dominance of Marian pilgrimage over other forms. It accounts, for example, for her reputed efficacy as the supreme intercessor with God on behalf of sinners and the sick. At the important First Council of Nicaea, A.D. 325 (more than a century before the Council of Ephesus), which gave the Christian world the Nicene Creed, the doctrine of the hypostatic union had been dogmatically defined. This held that in Christ, two natures, the divine and the human, subsist in one Person.

Nestorius had repeatedly opposed this position, however, declaring that Mary did not bring forth the Word of God, the eternal Logos of theology, the Second Person of the Trinity; that she had brought forth instead only the temple or organ of the Godhead, the man Jesus, whom Nestorius went on to describe as "the animated purple of the King"—in no sense, Nestorius held, was Jesus "the King" himself; Mary was mother of one nature only, not of the Person in whom two natures were united; she was not the progenetrix of a divine Person, only of a single material nature. In rejecting this view, the Council of Ephesus defined Mary as mother in the flesh of God's Word made flesh. A son, the council declared, is necessarily a person, not a nature. It further condemned Nestorius's concept of "moral union." By this he meant that the two natures were, as he put it, merely "juxtaposed or joined" in Jesus Christ. The council defined the union as a physical fusion. Nestorius had argued that the Word, the Second Person of the Trinity, coeternal with the Father and the Holy Ghost, dwelt in Jesus in precisely the same way as God indwells in the just, though in a more excellent degree—a matter of quantity, not quality, since the goal of the indwelling of the Word in Jesus is the redemption of all mankind, not a single soul, and is not the most perfect expression or manifestation of the divine activity. Nestorius had deduced from these premises that Mary was the mother of Christ (Christotokos) but could not be the mother of God (Theotokos). The majority of the Ephesian Fathers maintained against this that God, the plenitude of the Second Person made flesh, was born of the Virgin Mary. They thus saved for the Church the doctrine of the Incarnation, the physical union of the two natures in one Divine Person. Nestorius later paid lip-service to this doctrine, but he regularly spoke of the two natures as if they were two persons. In saying "the incarnate God did not suffer and die, but raised up from the dead him in whom He was incarnate," he was clearly referring to two persons. Nestorius also contended that if Mary is called the Mother of God, she will be made into a goddess, and the Gentiles would be scandalized. Actually, the Ephesian definition was partly directed against this very danger. God was born of Mary, but she contributed to him only human nature and nothing of divine nature. She herself was completely human in nature, a created being, not an uncreated being, like God, though her role as Theotokos makes her unique among human beings. Her beauty is precisely in her humanity and in the specific direction of that humanity in the scheme of redemption. As

Epiphanius had pointed out, she should receive veneration, but not adoration or worship (*latria*). But her veneration (*hyperdulia*), though similar in kind to that paid to the saints (*dulia*), is greater in degree; it is the highest degree of veneration. She is not venerated in isolation, however, but always (at least implicitly) on account of her relation to Christ. She incites awe not because of any divinity, but precisely because she is "one of us." She grieves and worries when the boy Jesus is lost in Jerusalem; at Cana she urges him against his better judgment to work the miracle of turning the water into wine—which miracle inaugurated his three years of teaching, leading inevitably to the Crucifixion. Both her worry and her impatience are human, and excite a human response in Jesus, showing him to be her son. Yet she is the channel and instrument of the Incarnation. It is the disparity, not the parity, between mother and Son, which so impressed the early Christians, and continues to impress Catholic and Orthodox believers alike. Mary is a paradigmatic instance of the recurrent Christian theme of the power of the weak; other examples are the Nativity of Christ among animals and shepherds, the Crucifixion, and the martyrdom of the apostles, all of which were simultaneously material failures and spiritual triumphs. She is portrayed as a young female in a strongly patrilineal society, yet she is held to have become Queen of Heaven and spiritual mother of all Catholics. As a woman, Mary was vulnerable to the ills of the human state at all stages of her earthly life: as maiden, young mother, mature woman, and widow bereft of her son. (In recent centuries, the Feast of the Seven Sorrows of Mary has celebrated "the spiritual martyrdom of the Mother of God" and her compassion for her Son's Passion.) Yet hers is the ultimate success story, so to speak; the human being whose griefs were greatest becomes the one whose power to remedy the griefs of others is also greatest. Hence she becomes the greatest pilgrimage saint, whose pleas are most efficacious with God, as they were with Jesus her son at Cana at a crucial point in the narrative of the Incarnation.

It is the doctrine of the Assumption of the Virgin which is probably of the greatest importance in connecting Marian devotion with pilgrimage. This holds that both the body and the soul of Mary were taken into heaven when she died, in anticipation of the universal judgment. Although this dogma was not officially defined until 1950, in the apostolic constitution *Munificentissimus Deus,* by Pope Pius XII, the Feast of the Assumption, on August 15, is perhaps the principal and oldest of all Marian feasts.[2] At many Marian pilgrimage centers it is the best-attended day, even if it is not the date of the shrine's main feast. In accordance with the tendency to seek homologues between events in the lives of Jesus and Mary, missals and prayer books often note that the Assumption was for Mary what the Resurrection was for Jesus. Mary was with her Son in Her sufferings and she is with Him in his triumph: she already has that fullness of glory that we hope to have at the end of time. By "fullness of glory" is meant that reunion of body and soul in heaven which, for all other humankind, must await the Last Judgment. At the folk level, the doctrine of the Assumption underlies the belief that Mary can and does manifest herself to the sensory perceptions of selected mortals in apparitions, defined theologically as certain kinds of supernatural vision; namely, those that are bodily or visible. Her body having disappeared from the world at the Assumption, it is argued that she can reappear in the body, in a more concrete way than a saint whose body remains buried or whose relics are believed scattered in different places. Mary continues to connect earth and heaven in a "bodily" or "visible" way. This and many other beliefs are clearly inferred from doctrine as much as from persistent folk beliefs.

If the Assumption connects Mary with apparitions, the marriage feast at Cana, still a popular theme today in sermons at pilgrimage centers in Ireland and Mexico, connects her scripturally with miracles. The changing of water into wine, Jesus's first miracle, was performed at Mary's intercession, even, it seems, her importunate intercession. From this scriptural episode, ordinary people deduce that she has special access to her divine son, and that pleas to her to intercede on their behalf will be especially efficacious.

Another important scriptural and theological idea in the concep-

[2] If the feast celebrated on August 15 in honor of the Blessed Mother of God at the Jerusalem Church of the Kathisma (meaning "rest" in Greek) may be regarded as its forerunner, the Feast of the Assumption began as early as the beginning of the fifth century. See *The New Catholic Encyclopedia* (1967), s.v. "Dormition of the Virgin."

tual frame of Marian devotion is the view that Mary is core-demptress of mankind, with the Redeemer Jesus Christ. This idea arises from a structuralist reversal of signs which would have delighted Lévi-Strauss. Mary is contrasted with Eve, through whom mankind, represented by Adam, fell into original sin. St. Irenaeus, the second-century Church Father who has been called "the first theologian of the Virgin Mother," was the first to elaborate the theme that Mary cancels in each minute particular the harm done by Eve, each of them acting by the use of her free will. Eve and Mary thus constitute what Lévi-Strauss would call a "binary opposition." St. Iraenaeus wrote (*Adversus Haereses*, III,22,4; V,19,1):

As Eve, who had Adam as her husband but was nevertheless a virgin, was disobedient, and thereby became the cause of death to herself and to the whole of mankind, so also Mary, who had a preordained husband and was still a virgin, by obedience became a cause of her own salvation and the salvation of the whole human race. . . . As Eve was led astray by an angel's [Lucifer's] discourse to fly from God, after transgressing His word, so by an angel's [Gabriel's] discourse Mary had the Gospel preached unto her, that she might bear God, obeying His word.

But Mary is not merely the antithesis of Eve, in Irenaeus's thinking: she is also her advocate, who will restore her to her pristine state. Justin Martyr compared her with Eve immaculate and incorrupt before the Fall. Mary's redemptive role with respect to Eve is structurally homologous with Christ's redemptive role with respect to Adam. Eve and Mary often stand for corporate, collective humanity, Adam and Christ for singular, unique man, in the symbology of Christian theology. Mary is often seen as standing for the Church; Eve, for mankind outside the Church. Thus Eve has physical progeny, the generations of mankind, while Mary has spiritual progeny, regenerated mankind within the Church. Note, in both cases, the hidden metaphor of woman as vessel, container, encloser of a human group. (Here we have the idea that men in groups are bounded by the feminine.) The two characters of the feminine may be termed "elementary" and "transformative." The first is connected with archaic repetitive processes, expressed in pagan mythology by the Moirai, Norns, Fates, and Weavers; the second, with initiation and transformation of state (see Erich Neumann, *The*

Great Mother 1972). Here Eve = the elementary character (Neumann, pp. 25–28, 44–47, 95–98), and Mary = the transformative character (pp. 28–31, 46–48).

All these considerations influence Mary's role in pilgrimage as a healer of ills brought about by sin. In keeping with the extroverted character of pilgrimage, as against the introverted character of mysticism, these "ills" are often taken quite literally to mean bodily disease. A vow to Mary to visit one of her great shrines will, the pilgrim believes, induce her to intercede with God, specifically with her Son, the Second Person of the Divine Trinity, on the pilgrim's behalf, to cure him or his loved ones of illness or to avert imminent death. In theological literature on the concept of intercession, Jesus Christ is often referred to as "mediator," and Mary, the angels, and saints, as "intercessors." Jesus "mediates" because he shares the two natures, divine and human; his office of mediator belongs to him as man, its unique efficacy belongs to him as God. As mediator he is said to restore the friendship between God and man, lost through the Fall. But the need for intercession is not ruled out by Christ's mediation; the best of our fellows speaks for us representatively. The pilgrim must of course undergo due penance for his sins (part of that penance being the hardships and risks of his journey), and must go to confession and Communion shortly after his arrival at the pilgrimage center. It is recourse to these sacraments which relieves the pilgrim of his vow. These are officially regarded as indispensable conditions if a favor or miracle is to be anticipated. Nevertheless, there are many accounts of the cure or conversion of atheists and non-Christians at pilgrimage centers. For the notion that God's grace is unpredictable, is prevalent in pilgrimage centers; the rain (of grace) falls alike on the just and the unjust.

Pilgrimages in general, and Marian pilgrimages in particular, owe much of their theological rationale in Catholic and Orthodox Christendom to the doctrine of the communion of saints. Catholic scholars hold that this doctrine had cultic roots in the veneration paid to the first Christian martyrs.[3] From the first century onward, martyrdom was regarded as a certain sign of election, and martyrs

---

[3] An authoritative account of the growth of the cult of the martyrs and the development of pilgrimages to their tombs is Hippolyte Delahaye's *Les Origines du Culte des Martyrs* (1933).

were believed to pass immediately into God's presence. The sacrifice of the Mass was performed over their tombs. In the early case of St. Polycarp (died c. A.D. 155), his martyrdom, annually commemorated, was referred to as his "birthday"; that is, the date of his "birth" in heaven. Soon it was customary to speak about the "satisfactory" character of the martyrs' sufferings—meaning that by their death they could obtain graces and blessings for others, that they had laid up a store of merit from which others could draw. Tertullian and St. Cyprian were quite explicit about this. Believers visited martyrs' tombs, on their "birthdays" especially, for the purpose of invoking them to intercede directly with God. In the subapostolic age the notion of intercession was reinforced by the popular cult of the angels, pre-Christian in origin but heartily embraced by the early Christian faithful. Angels were invoked to give blessings through the power of God. Marian devotion seems to have been a kind of quintessential expression of the intercessory cult of the martyrs and angels. Mary is regarded as having undergone a "spiritual," if not a corporeal, martyrdom; the Feast of the Seven Sorrows of Mary (September 15) ritualizes this concept. Though the Feast of the Assumption is the homologue of the martyrs' "birthday," Mary once more manifests her special role by having a number of feasts celebrating nodal points in her life, which, like that of Jesus, was for mankind both an instrumentality for salvation and a model for imitation. Her special feasts are the Purification (February 2), coinciding with the Circumcision of Jesus; the Annunciation (March 25); the Assumption (August 15), corresponding to the Ascension of Christ; the Nativity of the Blessed Virgin Mary (September 8); and the Immaculate Conception (December 8). All of these are celebrated with exceptional intensity at Marian pilgrimage centers, though each center normally selects one of them as its principal feast, if that distinction has not been preempted by a Marian apparition which originated the local cultus (at Guadalupe, for example, December 12, the date of the miraculous appearance of Mary's painting on the *tilma*, is held to be more important than December 8, the Feast of the Immaculate Conception).

In its fully developed form, the doctrine of the communion of saints is a sophisticated cultural expression—a "conscious model," perhaps, of ideological communitas. Like tribal religion, it emphasizes the unity of the living and the dead of a given social group. But there is one salient difference. A tribal group or one of its segments (a clan or lineage, say) stresses ties of ascribed *kinship*, which provide *obligatory* links between the living and the dead, with rituals of ancestor veneration used as a means of communication between them. The Church, however, is not, in principle, a kin group, but a group of all those, whether kin or not, who possess the same object of belief. The communion of saints, while stressing the unity under and in Christ of the Church throughout the ages, divides that Church dynamically into three parts: the Church Militant, the Church Suffering, and the Church Triumphant. The Church Militant represents the visible society of the faithful on earth, including sinners as well as the just. The Church Suffering is composed of the souls in purgatory. The Church Triumphant is composed of the saints in heaven, the angels, worthy souls from before the time of Christ, and worthy non-Catholics. These three components communicate directly or indirectly with one another and with God. The living of the Church Militant pray to God and to members of the Church Triumphant on behalf of the members of the Church Suffering, and to God in honor of the saints. The saints intercede with God for the suffering and the living. The suffering, the souls in purgatory, pray to God and the saints for others. It is held, though, that the holy souls of purgatory cannot effectively intercede for the living until their "temporal punishment" is over; this inability is, in fact, regarded as part of their suffering. Christ, the head of the total Church, intercedes continually for the living and the dead. In this system, isolated prayer does not exist; every act of prayer refers to other members. There is, in theological language, a universality of purpose. Every deed of each member is held to affect for good or ill the whole body.

In this system, Mary plays a special role, which gives her a pivotal position in Catholic pilgrimage. She is the first of the blessed, and hence the most efficacious intercessor in relation to God the Father. She is a link binding men to God, since she is the Mother of God. As the "second Eve," she is also, as we have seen, the spiritual mother of all living humankind. Like the other saints, she is no mere model for a virtuous life but is a living and functioning member of the Church. She is liable to put in an appearance, unexpectedly and of her own free will, at any moment and in any place. As regards pilgrimage, the doctrine of the Assumption, while it deprived the Church of her bodily relics,[4] gave her complete mobility through the universal Church, as a potential patron of nations, dioceses, religious societies, and so on. She embodies the communitas of the Church, and is innocent of any blame for sometimes being enlisted by particularistic groups with bloody axes to grind.

This brief sketch must suffice to indicate the central semantic structure of the normative pole of Marian pilgrimage symbols. That pole of meaning has remained remarkably constant throughout history, while there has been much variation at the orectic pole; that is, in the culturally defined feelings and motivations associated with the symbol-vehicles. In this respect, the dominant symbols of Christianity, and indeed those of the other historical relations, which are also maintained by literate specialists, are sharply distinguished from the symbols of tribal societies. In tribal religion there is a high consistency of orectic significance (for instance, in Central Africa the red gum exuded by certain trees stands, in a wide range of societies, for blood and the emotions connected with its shedding), but at the normative pole meanings vary considerably (the red gum stands for matriliny and motherhood in some groups, for patriliny in others, and for hunting cults in yet others). The normative consistency of symbols in the historical religions, in contrast, may be due to the development, in the Western European tradition, of a specialist class of theologians, and to social, political, and cultural centralization; both these developments contribute to uniformity of normative reference and to the generation of universal patterns of doctrine, overriding local differences. Local differences then tend to be expressed at the opposite semantic pole, and to color the ways people feel about the symbols. Such differences also manifest themselves at the level of the signifier; that is, in the form of sensorily perceived symbol-vehicle. Even here, however, theological pressures contribute to the stereotyping of images, attributes of

---

[4] We do not reckon among bodily relics the phials of "Virgin's milk" at Walsingham, or the veils and other items of clothing claimed by other shrines.

saints, and so on, so that they will not be at cross-purposes with dogmas, doctrines, and scriptural models. Local feeling may manifest itself in the materials used—such as the *tilma* on which Our Lady of Guadalupe is painted, the ocote wood from which the image of Our Lady of Octlán is carved, or the *pasta de Michoacán* of which the little figure of the Virgin of Zapopan is made, to cite examples discussed in our chapter on Mexico—or it may be manifested in tales about the origin or history of a given image.

Among the people, Mary has always been something of a wonderworker, and completely "feminine" by the standards of the ancient, entrenched patrilineal societies. She is seen as compassionate, tender, a little capricious perhaps, vulnerable to suffering, infinitely maternal and understanding, and inclined rather to grieve at than to punish the sins of the world. This characterization is consistent with the anthropological theory that, in a patrilineal system, the patriline is the hard jural line of authority and property transmission, while the matriline is the "affectional," soft side, providing sanctuary. We find signs of this attitude with respect to Mary as early as the later part of the fifth century, in the Syriac manuscript known as *Transitus Mariae* (Herbert Thurston 1911), which contains an account (purporting to have been forwarded from the Christians in Rome) of Mary's miracles—among them, the following tale:

Often here in Rome she appears to the people who confess her in prayer, for she has appeared here on the sea when it was troubled and raised itself and was going to destroy the ship in which they were sailing. And the sailors called on the name of the Lady Mary and said: "O Lady Mary, Mother of God, have mercy on us," and straightway she rose upon them like the sun and delivered the ships, ninety-two of them, and rescued them from destruction, and none of them perished.

But, as another tale reveals, Mary could also display a mother's aggression against those who threaten her young: "She appeared by day on the mountain where robbers had fallen upon people and sought to slay them. And these people cried out, saying: 'O Lady Mary, Mother of God, have mercy on us.' And she appeared before them like a flash of lightning, and blinded the eyes of the robbers and they were not seen by them."

Remarkably, these apocryphal texts contained motifs which were to recur frequently in the Marian cultus through the ages. Mary, Star of the Sea, for example, is the object of a widespread devotion. The designation is probably based on a misreading of the Vulgate text of Isaiah 40:15l, in which St. Jerome had translated the Hebrew *mâr* by the Latin *stilla,* a drop (Maas 1907:464). This was misread as *stella,* star, and it influenced later etymological speculation on the Hebrew form of Mary's name, *mâryâm.* Originally thought to be a combination of *mâr* and yâm, meaning "drop of the sea," the name was later taken to mean "star of the sea." Another piece of fanciful folk etymologizing derived the Virgin's Hebrew name from *mâri* (mistress) and *yâm* (sea). Mari was an ancient Syrian goddess, dating back to c. 2500 B.C. (See Frankfort 1955:256, fn. 42). The upshot was that Mary, who has no scriptural association with the sea, became the patroness of sailors. A modern instance of this devotion can be seen at the pilgrimage center of Guadalupe in Mexico: beside the steps leading up to the chapel at the top of the hill of Tepeyac, is a marble image of a boat, presented as an ex-voto to the shrine by sailors from the Philippines who claimed that they had been saved from drowning in a tempest, by the intercession of Our Lady of Guadalupe. Also at Guadalupe, in a room in the basilica filled with ex-votos from grateful petitioners to the Dark Virgin, there is a ceramic plaque showing how a pilgrim was rescued by her from bandits. The two Guadalupe ex-votos have close affinities with the tales in the Syriac manuscript written almost fifteen hundred years earlier. Perhaps this is not surprising, when one looks at the whole span of Marian devotions, for she, of all the saints, has always taken care of people in all their ills and miseries, as a good mother should. While there is a considerable division of labor among the other saints—one caters for headaches, another for financial problems, and so on—Mary has been a protectress of humanity under a wide range of circumstances since the inception of her devotion.

There have been five main stages and types of shrines in the historical development of the popular cultus of the Virgin Mary: (1) the prototypical Palestinian and Roman shrines; (2) post-Islamic, "reduplicative" European shrines; (3) European shrines of the High and late Middle Ages; (4) colonial shrines, which replaced, as it were, the shrines destroyed during the Reformation in Europe; and (5) "apparitional" shrines, which developed during the early Industrial Revolution and have continued throughout the present century with a markedly chiliastic or apocalyptic character.

The Holy Places of Palestine have been visited by pilgrims since the early days of Christianity. The pilgrimage to Palestine belongs to the category of pilgrimage we have called "prototypical," relating directly to the life of the founder and his intimates. Most of the places mentioned in Scripture as the scenes of Jesus's life, mission, and death have become pilgrimage centers; many of them celebrate both Jesus and Mary. Pilgrims to the Holy Land have never gone in expectation of miraculous cures or favors. Rather do they go to make their understanding of Christianity—a faith brought to them from afar—more vivid by immersing themselves in its geographical setting; by restoring their faith's orectic pole, so to speak, in allowing the landscape in which the founder lived to reanimate his message, otherwise received at second or third hand through books, sermons, and so on. More than this, they have sought to imitate Christ by retracing the steps of his life recorded in the Gospels— most potently, by following his last sorrowful journey to Calvary and experiencing in imagination his Resurrection and the birth of the Church. The evangelical route is studded with churches, chapels, and basilicas. Geography is transformed into sacred history by the pilgrim as he reflects upon the sacred texts. The Palestine pilgrimage is the prototype or archparadigm of axiomatic Christian values. For the pilgrim its topography condenses the whole history of man's fall and redemption. Later authors, such as William Blake (in Jerusalem), tried to map that topography on their own homelands, finding point-by-point correlations between sacred Palestinian sites and salient features of their native land.

Palestine of course has many Marian shrines. Two are outstanding: the Church of the Annunciation at Nazareth, and the Church of the Dormition of the Virgin on Mount Zion. At the conclusion of the third session of the Second Vatican Council, on November 21, 1964, the Feast of Our Lady's Presentation at the Temple, Pope Paul VI celebrated Mass together with twenty-four bishops who were the custodians of what the Vatican then regarded as the world's most important Marian shrines. The list of the bishops and their shrines constitutes a virtual "Who's Who" of modern Marian pilgrimage centers. First on the list of shrines is the Church of the Annunciation at Nazareth. The earliest church there was built by the emperor Constantine, A.D. 325, following the famous visit of his mother, St. Helena, to the Holy Land. After the partial destruction of Constantine's church by the Muslims, Tancred the Crusader, prince of Galilee, in 1100 built a new church, which was also later destroyed. The present building dates back to 1730, and is said to include about one-third of the partially ruined original structure. Many other Marian shrines exist in Palestine, and we will not attempt to mention them all. The second outstanding shrine is the Church of the Dormition of the Virgin Mary on Mount Zion, where one tradition holds that she died. Another important shrine is the Church of St. Mary in the Valley of Josaphat (not far from Gethsemane), which is reputed by some to be the place of the Virgin's Assumption, though others claimed that Ephesus was the site of this sacred event. Clearly, theology has retrospectively reinterpreted the cultural landscape described in the Bible.

The earliest known Palestinian pilgrims were, for the most part, devout souls, many of them clergy or in religious orders. (They correspond to the Brahmans and high-caste pilgrims who visit pan-Hindu shrines to seek merit rather than favors or miracles; see p. 238; and Bhardwaj 1973). For example, we know that the great unorthodox theologian Origen went on pilgrimage A.D. 215 and was shown the cave of Christ's nativity; in 382–84, St. Paula and her daughter St. Eustochium, fired by St. Jerome's enthusiastic letters, visited Palestine and left an interesting account; in 385, a certain St. Silvia (who may really have been Etheria, or Egeria) visited the Holy Places and left a lively record in the form of an epistle to her sisters in religion; in 414–16 Paulus Orosius, a disciple of St. Augustine, made the pilgrimage; according to tradition, St. David (died 588?), patron of Wales, also visited the Holy Land; in 570 one Antoninus arrived and left his initials on various holy sites.

By the year 550 there were twenty-six churches in Jerusalem alone. The seventh century brought religious and political conflict to the Holy Land, with decisive consequences for Christian, and a *fortiori* for Marian, pilgrimage, which now began its powerful independent development. The key events were not, as first appeared, the conquest of Palestine in 614 by Khosru II of Persia (during this conquest Golgotha and Joseph of Arimathea's garden were burnt, and the wood of the "True Cross" was stolen in the silver casket made for it by St. Helena, its discoverer), and the reconquest of Jerusalem by the emperor Heraclius, who afterward walked barefoot in mean attire through the city carrying back the recovered relic of the Cross; this day, September 14, 629, is still commemorated annualy in the Catholic Feast of the Exaltation of the Holy Cross. More important for the history of the world was the capitulation of Jerusalem in 637 to the Muslim caliph Omar, after four months of siege. Although Omar's terms were for those days extremely clement, guaranteeing the safety of the Christians and their churches (no new churches were to be built, however, and no bells were to be rung), and though pious Northern European pilgrims intermittently visited the Holy Land (Arculf in 670, St. Willibald in 721, among others), Muslim hegemony over the Holy Land prevented its further development as a place of pilgrimage or monastic retreat. Under the Abbasid caliphate, beginning in 749, Islam became less tolerant, despite the flash of apparent good will which inspired Caliph Harun al-Rashid to allow Charlemagne to endow centers for Latin pilgrims. As the astute caliph intended, this disturbed the Eastern churches, for rivalry between Western and Eastern Christendom was already a doleful factor in Palestine, and was to lead to centuries of bitter struggle over the custodianship of the holy shrines—a struggle fomented by the later Ottomans, whose policy of "divide and rule" was even more successful than that of the ancient Roman and modern British empires. In 937, Muslims burnt the Church of the Holy Sepulcher. This act was a curious result of a Muslim pilgrimage dispute. The Shiite sect had temporarily put a stop to the pilgrimage to Mecca. Consequently, many more pilgrims than usual visited the third most important Muslim shrine, the Dome of the Rock (built between 687 and 691, on the site in Jerusalem from which Muhammad reputedly ascended to heaven). Religious zeal among the pilgrims ran high, and the burning of the neighboring Christian shrine was taken on by them as "The Holy Fire." In the reign of the caliph al-Hakim (Aub 'Ali al-Mansur, died c. 1015) known as "the Mad" or "the Lizard" from his habit of creeping around gazing, all the Christian churches were destroyed. Al-Hakim even attempted to have the rock of the Holy Sepulcher chiseled to pieces, but was foiled by the rock's hardness—this was of course regarded as a miraculous sign by the Christians. Later, when the Seljuk Turks, rebel Muslims, defeated the Fatimid Muslims of Jerusalem, repression was again intensified. This, coupled with certain trends in internal European politics, undoubtedly helped to precipitate the Crusades, the first of which was proclaimed by Pope Urban II in 1095 at the Council of Clermont. As we shall see, the vicissitudes of the Holy Land affected Marian pilgrimage in Europe as well.

The first major Marian shrine in Europe was probably Santa Maria Maggiore in Rome, founded about the year 350, during St. Liberius's pontificate (and thus sometimes called the Basilica Liberiana). With its major altar dedicated to Mary as the "Salus Populi Romani," the Protectress of Rome, Santa Maria Maggiore became the prototype of all the later Marian shrines honoring Mary as protectress of a city or nation. Like most Roman pilgrimage sites, this shrine early came under the control of the organized Church. One of the four major basilicas in Rome,[5] it is a most impressive place—a sort of Marian St. Peter's. As Zsolt Aradi (1954:18) has written: "The history of the city of Rome, the history of the Papacy and the Church are living memories within the walls of this great monument. Popes, kings, prelates, millions of the faithful and many an enemy have all contributed to its atmosphere; wherever

[5] In its broadest sense, "basilica" is an architectural term designating a certain type of rectangular building often used as a public hall in antiquity, and later adopted, with modifications, as the basic form of the early Christian churches. The basilican form is still used in the design of certain Catholic churches today. A canonical distinction is made, within the Church, between major and minor basilicas, in their hierarchical status and liturgical function. Each of the four major basilicas in Rome serves as the seat of one of the patriarchs of the Church when he is in Rome: St. John Lateran (archbasilica for the patriarch of the West, the pope), St. Peter's (for the patriarch of Constantinople), St. Paul's-outside-the-Walls (for the patriarch of Alexandria), and Santa Maria Maggiore (for the patriarch of Antioch). Most basilicas are classed as "minor," including those of Guadalupe, St. Patrick's Purgatory, Loreto, Lourdes, and Padua.

you step, you step on history." Santa Maria Maggiore's foundation legend contains motifs later developed in the foundation myths of other pilgrimage centers. According to Roman tradition, in the year 352 the Virgin appeared in a dream simultaneously to a wealthy, devout Roman and to Pope Liberius, and instructed them to build a church to her on the place where they would find snow (a miraculous sign, for it was then midsummer) the following morning. The next day snow was found on the Esquiline Hill, indicating both the site and the dimensions of the basilica to be built. The church contains a painting of the Madonna and Child, held to have been made by St. Luke the Evangelist and to have been brought to Rome by St. Helena. The reader, now familiar with the Mexican Guadalupe legend, will at once recognize several shared themes: the injunction in a dream or apparition to build a church in honor of Mary; the ritual importance of a hilltop; miraculous unseasonable phenomena as a mark of Our Lady's will (roses in winter at Tepeyac, snow in midsummer at Rome); the presence of a miraculous painting (done by an Apostle from life, according to the Roman tradition; made by Jesus himself in heaven, according to the Mexican tradition portrayed in a mural in the Guadalupe basilica). Another recurrent motif is the specification of a church's dimensions by supernatural means; we shall find this theme again later in connection with the pilgrimage devotion at Walsingham, in Norfolk, England. Owing to the snow in the Roman shrine's foundation legend, the name of the original basilica was Santa Maria ad Nives, "Our Lady of the Snows." To commemorate the decision at Ephesus declaring Mary the Mother of God, Pope Sixtus III rebuilt the basilica in 430–440, and covered its walls with large and elaborate mosaics, commemorating Mary as Theotokos.

Like Our Lady of Guadalupe, Our Lady of the Snows was invoked by the Roman people in times of danger and plague, and her painting was often carried in procession to St. Peter's. One notable occasion was in 597, when the plague was decimating the population of Rome. Gregory the Great led the procession and, just as the prayers were ending—the legend goes—St. Michael the Archangel appeared suddenly over Hadrian's Mausoleum (the present Castel Sant' Angelo), indicating that the pestilence was ended. Mary and

Michael are often associated in legends and in sculpture and paint-ing. There is, for example, a gigantic statue of St. Michael near the shrine of Our Lady of the Remedies near Mexico City. This may be because both are regarded as archenemies of Satan: the Virgin is often portrayed crushing a serpent (the devil) under her heel, recall-ing the text of Genesis 3:15; and pictures of Michael impaling a dragon are also familiar.

Thus Marian pilgrimage was already entrenched in the West when pilgrimage to the Holy Land thinned to a trickle with the rise of the Muslim crescent over Palestine—but only as one of many components in the total pilgrimage system of the Holy City. For Rome, the Holy City of the Church, like Palestine, the Holy Land of the Bible, was not a simple pilgrimage goal, but a pilgrimage com-plex. The Roman pilgrimage was prototypical in that it represented the genesis and first growth, in the apostolic and subapostolic ages, of the Roman structuration of the original Christian message. It thus possesses a certain ambiguity, since the essence of pilgrimage is that it is outside structure, at the opposite social and cultural pole to it. Nevertheless, Rome, like Mecca, remains fundamentally li-minal to the entire world of political organization, for it ideally rep-resents, in however ordered and legalistic a way, God and com-munitas, as against Caesar and political power and authority. Indeed, ecclesiastical "structure" is only a liminal, even "ludic," structure—a play of symbols and masks, like the maskings of tribal initiation—rather than a positive structure based on control over economic resources and organized force. As Stalin once said, how many battalions has the pope? It is, therefore, in various senses that the pilgrimage to Rome (and the journeys obligatorily undertaken thither by all Catholic bishops at stated intervals) should be termed *ad limina*. This term means "to the thresholds"—traditionally, of the Apostles' tombs; but in a wider sense it may mean the pilgrimage to the major *limen* of Western civilization, the "center out there" (see V. Turner 1973:191–230).

When access to the Holy Places was blocked for a time by Islam, there developed a tendency to "reduplicate" the Palestinian shrines in the Christian countries of Europe, either by imitation or through claim to a direct, supernatural translation of material relics from Palestine to Europe. We shall discuss only one early example of this pilgrim genre here—the Spanish shrine of the Virgin of the Pillar (Virgen del Pilar), whose bishop was among the twenty-four who concelebrated Mass at St. Peter's in 1964 with Pope Paul. Zaragozans say that the Basilica of the Virgen del Pilar was the first church raised in Mary's honor and will last as long as the faith endures (Aradi 1954:24). Their local tradition is that St. James the Apostle came to Spain as a missionary, A.D. 40, and that on January 2 he was walking along the Ebro River with seven disciples. At the same time, Mary, then still alive, was in Jerusalem, praying for his success. Jesus appeared to her, and told her that angels would convey her to Spain to encourage the apostle. James and his disciples, kneeling by the river, looked up, saw a radiant light, and heard seraphic music. Mary, seated on a throne borne by angels, appeared to the group and asked that a church be erected on the spot. She then took from an angel a small pillar of jasper topped with a small statue of herself. The apparition then faded, leaving the pillar with the statue as a token of Our Lady's help to St. James. As often happens, the original chapel in which the statue was housed was destroyed, as were many subsequent churches and chapels (the present church was built in 1686 by Charles II of Spain). But Romans, Goths, Vandals, Moors, and other invaders, so it is said, never succeeded in destroying the miraculous statue, which was defended by the Zaragozans with fierce heroism.

As for St. James himself, the patron of Spain, there is a rich literature, both folk and learned.[6] His own remains, according to several accounts, were miraculously conveyed to Spain (some said in a stone boat) from the Holy Land, and his cathedral at Santiago de Compostela is the principal pilgrimage shrine of Spain. From Gali-

[6] Bibliographies may be found in G. G. King (1920), J. S. Stone (1927), W. Starkie (1965), and A. Castro (1954).

Américo Castro (1954:70) admirably assesses the cultus of St. James as follows: "The importance of Santiago as the brother of Christ and as a supernatural force, 'invincible and victorious,' served as a point of support for the impetus of the Reconquest. The course of life intensified the belief . . . and it gave rise to forms of worship which today would be judged heterodox. . . . This cult is an 'axis' of Spanish history, because the shrine at Compostella not only *opened up* Spain by bringing pilgrims from all over Europe, but also gave it an identity as a nation."

lean fisherman he became a hero-knight, turning up when the need was greatest in several decisive battles against the Moors in the Christian reconquest of Spain. Later, he was seen once more in Mexico, where he helped the conquistadors subdue the native inhabitants—thus reversing his role of liberator, though retaining that of patron of Spain.

El Pilar was not the only image of the Madonna believed to have been transported to Europe from an Eastern holy place. Another is Our Lady of Montserrat, whose shrine not far from Barcelona, in an "enormous and fantastic block of mountains 4,000 feet high" (Gillett 1953:70), is of great antiquity. Tradition holds that at some time before the year 888, the image of Our Lady was miraculously found among the rocks of Montserrat. According to Gillett (p. 71): "Ancient chronicles claim that the figure was brought from Jerusalem by way of Egypt to Barcelona, and thence to the mountain to escape Saracen profanation. There is a similar tradition that the ancient figure at Loreto [the shrine of Our Lady of Loreto at the Holy House of Loreto in Italy] was of Egyptian origin."

The Spanish traditions—and, indeed, traditions in England and Italy as well—express the folk belief that if Europe could not go to the Holy Places, the Holy Places, or material tokens of them, could come to Europe. In the case of Loreto, it was believed that the house in which Mary, Joseph, and Jesus had lived in Nazareth flew, quite literally, first to Tersatto (close to present-day Fiume in Yugoslavia); then, three and a half years later, to Loreto on the other side of the Adriatic. Teleportation is no recent artifact of parapsychology! The Holy House, incidentally, is now patron of the modern means of mass communication, such as radio, television, and aviation!

Catholic Spain, in opposition to iconoclastic Islam, used icons and images as mobilizing points. In rivalry with Rome for the leadership of Christendom's struggle with Islam, Spain miraculously imported an apostle of her own, St. James, to counterpose SS. Peter and Paul, and in her traditions linked him with her own major Marian shrine, that of the Virgen del Pilar. History was beginning to give way to miracle in the genesis of pilgrimages. In later chapters, we shall discuss the further development of this trend in successive periods of European and colonial history.

In summary, pilgrimage in the normative frame of the total medieval ecclesia stands at the communitas pole and not initially at the social structural pole of the sacred system. Marian devotions cluster at each pole but it is not without significance that Mary has become easily the foremost saint venerated at the great international, national, and supraregional shrines. For she is the great vessel, the *vas*, of salvation, through whose motherhood the doomed children of the fallen Eve are reborn, transformed—ideally as the result of free will responding to heavenly grace. Mary is not only—in the words of Gabriel's greeting, endlessly repeated in the Rosary down through the ages—"full of grace," but is also to be regarded as a personification of the Church in its nonlegalistic aspect, a collective mother in the order of freedom. It used to be said among Catholics: As Mary goes, so goes the Church. We would qualify this to mean: As communitas goes, so goes the Church. The huge crowds that still frequent the Marian shrines of Lourdes, Guadalupe, Fátima, Knock, Einsiedeln, and Czestochowa—to name but a few—testify to the endurance of this belief. The danger is, of course, that Mary, in principle representing global communitas, has in practice become, in each of her numerous images, exclusive patroness of a given community, region, city, or nation. Wherever she has become such a symbol of xenophobic localism, political structure has subverted communitas.

CHAPTER FIVE
Locality and Universality in Medieval Pilgrimages

IN THE High Middle Ages pilgrimages throve, especially those to Marian shrines. Though they started as local, regional, or patriotic devotions to Our Lady, they were theologically orthodox. In this chapter, we shall trace how several medieval devotions grew into universal pilgrimages, and we shall conflate, for the purpose, the many interesting variations found in this period, roughly from the Muslim invasions of North Africa and Spain to the Reformation. By way of contrast, in chapter 6 we shall turn to modern, or post-Napoleonic, pilgrimages, usually founded in response to a vision or apparition of the Virgin Mary, and increasingly associated with millenarian ideas and predictions of impending doom for an areligious, unrepentant mankind. Both major genres of pilgrimage share many features, of course. But between them lies the industrial revolution, whose effects have transformed the whole of human society and culture radically, and Marian pilgrimage no less.

Apparitions have always been involved in Marian pilgrimage, but there are spectacular differences between the medieval and the modern form and content of such apparitions. Thus it is important to explain at this point what Catholic theologians mean by the terms "apparition," "vision," and "dream." As an institution committed by Scripture to belief in the reality of a supernatural order, the Church cannot ignore phenomena which a substantial number of Catholics believe to be supernatural in essence. In the examination of such phenomena, the Church applies a critical apparatus of considerable analytical power, derived from secular philosophical traditions and not very dissimilar to the procedures of scientific inquiry. It makes the initial assumption that God exists and can intervene in the operation of "scientific laws" to produce effects entirely beyond the power of natural causes. Essential to the Christian faith, of course, is the belief that God has intervened in the past, and implicit is the idea that he may intervene again. On the other hand, a supernatural cause will be officially admitted as the explanation of an event only when all other possible explanations have been tested and found wanting by the Church. Varying degrees of certitude are recognized, short of that complete certitude which is seldom attainable in any domain of human inquiry. Technically, an "apparition" is not the "specter" or "ghost" of popular speech—Hamlet's father's shade or Banquo's ghost, for example—but refers to a supernatural vision that is bodily, or visible. The generic term "vision" includes not only apparitions but also "imaginative visions," usually produced in the imagination during sleep. There is also the category of "intellectual visions," in which the mind perceives a spiritual truth, without any sensory image—for example, St. Theresa of Ávila's vision of the Trinity. The theologians of the Church do not regard visions or apparitions as necessary for spiritual or moral perfection, but as special graces, or charisms, granted by God for the good of others, rather than for the good of the recipient. The danger that imaginative and sensible visions may be the product of abnormal psychological states is fully recognized and is usually carefully inquired into. And since the supernatural realm may contain beings other than God and the saints, the Church is mindful that apparitions and visions may be counterfeited by inimical supernatural agents like the devil. The ecclesiastical commissions appointed to investigate reported visions take all these possibilities into account.

Since Vatican II, there has been a significant decline, perhaps for ecumenical reasons, in official interest in apparitional phenomena, but this decline may have been amply compensated for by the sharply increased interest the counter culture has manifested in the supernatural realm.

In medieval times, apparitions seem to have been regarded as an accepted, if rather rare, feature of human life. Yet it seems that in many cases accounts of the apparitions associated with the important medieval centers were not circulated until many years after the pilgrimages themselves were well established. In contrast, modern Marian pilgrimages begin quite explicitly with contemporary apparitions or other kinds of visions, and are subjected to close inquiry by the Church—and to ridicule by nonbelievers. The rhetoric of both inquiry and skepticism has been, since the mid-nineteenth century, that of the scientific realm. Medicine, biology, psychology, and latterly the social sciences, have been ransacked for scientific explanations of those "supernatural" phenomena which have sufficiently impressed the masses to start the pilgrimage stream moving. Undoubtedly, in an age of rationalized industry, bureaucracy, and the "cult of every technical excellence" (in the words of W. H. Auden), there must be an aspiration toward the irrational, the miraculous, the nontechnical. For every structure there is an antistructure. Besides, the rationalizing of production and exchange at every level, in a total context of competitive nationalism, itself has nonrational consequences: slumps, unemployment, maldistribution of income, monopoly and totalitarianism, war, and similar scourges of the ordinary individual in an industrialized land or its colonial backwaters. These consequences increase the pervasive sense of anxiety, and foster tendencies to become dependent on powerful and (it is to be hoped) benevolent figures (charisma, communitas, and healing form a specifically modern triad, as Richard Almond points out in his book *The Healing Community: Dynamics of the Therapeutic Milieu*, 1974). In this climate, what is more natural than to turn for help and guidance once more to the Theotokos, Mother of God and spiritual mother of humanity, if one is already steeped in the theology and tradition of the Church—the structured guardian of Western antistructure, at least in its pilgrimage aspect? The genesis and growth of two important medieval apparitional pilgrimages is illuminating in this connection.

WALSINGHAM AND LORETO

Early medieval Marian pilgrimages continued the post-Islamic trend of replicating or "replacing" the lost shrines of Palestine and other parts of the Near East. We have already mentioned, as Spanish shrines with supposedly miraculous Palestinian connection, Compostela, and the shrine of Our Lady of the Pillar at Zaragoza. Another example, from England, is the shrine of Our Lady of Walsingham by the river Stiffkey in Norfolk.[1] We visited the town of Little Walsingham—once famous for the principal shrine of Our Lady in medieval England—in the summer of 1971. It was once more a thriving place of pilgrimage. Before arriving at Walsingham, we passed, a mile and a half from the town, the ancient Slipper Chapel (now the Catholic pilgrimage center)—at Houghton-in-the-Dale—which signified we were reaching holy ground. In the town of Walsingham itself we were shown a small rectangle of foundation stones, the much disputed site of the early shrine, which was a "Holy House," a replica (built c. 1061) of Mary's house at Nazareth. During the Middle Ages a great priory had been established beside the Holy House. Scarcely anything remains of either the priory or the early Holy House except one high arch on the priory lawns. On the other side of the main street stands a new Holy House, built by the Anglicans in 1921, on a site which they believe to be the true position of the original Holy House. Thus, like Jerusalem's shrines, Walsingham is divided between different groups of Christians.

Walsingham has clearly had a stormy history, one phase of which culminated in the destruction of the priory and the Holy House by Henry VIII in 1538, while another began on August 20, 1897, when the first official Catholic pilgrimage since the Reformation wended its way down the brambled lanes to the Slipper Chapel, purchased by a pious lady, Miss Charlotte Boyde, a recent convert from Anglicanism. The Slipper Chapel, built in the fourteenth century and

---

[1] Good accounts of the history of the Walsingham pilgrimge may be found in J. C. Dickinson (1956) and H. M. Gillett (1946).

dedicated to St. Catherine (of Alexandria—patroness of pilgrims and of those who guarded the Holy Places in Palestine), is the place where, according to tradition, pilgrims to Walsingham removed their shoes and made confession before proceeding to the main shrine. Henry VIII himself, when he was still married to Katharine of Aragon, walked barefoot from the Slipper Chapel to the shrine of Our Lady, there to pray to the Virgin for a male heir. Some historians have in fact speculated that Henry's later very special animus against Marian shrines may have been partly due to his disappointment at not siring a healthy son, despite his lighting of innumerable votive candles and his gifts to shrine custodians. However that may be, Walsingham Priory was destroyed at the dissolution of the monasteries; Richard Vowell, the nineteenth and last Augustinian prior, was pensioned off as vicar of nearby South Creake; and the Slipper Chapel, though not destroyed, fell on hard times, becoming a forge, a poor house, and finally a byre (cow barn). After the Catholic revival of the pilgrimage, now centered on the Slipper Chapel, this building was restored in 1934.

An entire book would not be enough to discuss the Walsingham pilgrimage and all the extraordinary people who have been associated with it—not the least among these being the eccentric Anglican vicar of Walsingham, Father Hope Patten (1885–1958), known to his less "High Church" colleagues as Pope Hatten,[2] who almost single-handedly created the Anglican pilgrimage in 1923, and thus spurred on the revival of the rival Catholic one. Little Walsingham, like many other famous pilgrimage centers, is today swarming with pilgrims, a phenomenon all the more remarkable in view of the isolation of this small village from the main lines of communication by road or rail. Once a place has been a focus of pilgrimage communitas, as we have seen, it is likely to revive after destruction, as long as tradition keeps its memory green.

As to Walsingham's foundation, H. M. Gillett has presented evidence (1957:293–95) from the Augustinian priory cartulary and other sources indicating that a certain Geoffrey de Faveraches (or Faverches), a Norman lord, established a priory of Augustinian canons

[2] Colin Stephenson has written a genial biography of Father Patton in *Walsingham Way* (1970).

early in the twelfth century and entrusted it with the care of the Holy House, which had been built by his mother, the widow Richeldis. A Book of Hours from the late fifteenth century, now in the University Library, Cambridge, however, mentions 1061 as the date of the founding of the Holy House, known as St. Mary's Chapel. (It must be remembered that Normans like Richeldis held land in England before the Conquest, having been especially encouraged to settle there by Edward the Confessor.) The date 1061 had clearly become traditional, for it is also found in the famous Pynson ballad containing the popular legend. Printed by Richard Pynson about 1495, the ballad is dated 1461 by means of internal evidence. According to the ballad, in twenty-one verses, "the widow, Richeldis de Faveraches, had been accorded a thrice-repeated vision of Our Lady at Walsingham" (Gillett 1957:295). Richeldis had begged of the Virgin to be allowed to honor her in some outstanding work. Mary then led her, "in spirit," to Nazareth, and showed her the little house wherein "Gabriel her greeted" (that is, the House of the Annunciation, then incorporated within the precincts of the Basilica of the Annunciation). There the Virgin commanded Richeldis to make another house like it at Walsingham. The Pynson ballad clearly expresses the reduplication theme:

> O England great cause thou hast glad for to be
> Compared to the Land of Promise, Sion,
> Thou attainest my grace to stand in that degree
> Through this gracious Lady's supportacion,
> To be called in every realm and region
> The Holy Land, Our Lady's Dowry:
> Thus art thou named of old antiquity.
>
> And this is the cause, as it appeareth by likeliness,
> In thee is builded New Nazareth, a mansion
> To the honor of the heavenly Empress
> And of her most glorious Salutation,
> When Gabriel said at Old Nazareth, "Ave,"
> This Joy here daily remembered to be
>   [quoted from Gillett 1957:296–97].

The ballad goes on to narrate how Richeldis ordered her carpenters to construct a house with the exact measurements of the Holy House, measurements which she had obtained in her vision. (Eras-

177

mus, who visited the Walsingham facsimile not long before its destruction, noted that it was made of "wainscot.") Where to put the structure? Dew fell, covering the domain with white frost, except in two places of equal size, one of which was close to two wells believed to be holy. When the workmen tried to lay a foundation there on which to rest the structure, however, they were quite unable to make their work agree in measurement with the dimensions required. Richeldis remained all night in prayer, asking Our Lady to complete the work she had begun. In the morning the little house was found to have been moved to the other place, "two hundred feet and more away," and was set on a foundation made with a skill unknown to local craftsmen. The ballad explains that it was "Our blessed Lady" herself—with the help of "angels' hands"—who "areared this said house" and moved it to its new site.

Several motifs stand out here. The marking of the site by frost recalls the marking of the site of the Basilica of Santa Maria Maggiore in Rome by snow. Richeldis' visionary trip to the Holy Land is the structural inverse of the Virgin's bodily appearance, in Spain to St. James, which resulted in the foundation of the shrine of Our Lady of the Pillar. But the most remarkable parallel is with another famous replication shrine, the Holy House of Loreto in Italy.[3] (Both Loreto and Walsingham were reckoned among the twenty-four principal Marian shrines for the concelebration of Mass at the close of the Third Session of Vatican II, noted above, in chapter 4.)

The legend of Loreto relates that in 1291 Dalmatian shepherds found an odd-looking building in a field near Tersatto where no building had been before. It had an ancient altar, a Greek cross, and the statue of a lady. The local parish priest unhesitatingly declared that this was the Holy House of Nazareth, and that he had been told in a dream of its origin. Soon afterward, Nicolo Frangipane, the governor of Dalmatia, sent envoys to Nazareth who verified the story, saying that the Holy House was no longer at Nazareth, and that the dimensions of the little house at Tersatto agreed exactly with those of a foundation they could see beneath the Basilica of the

[3] There is a good account of this shrine in G. E. Philips, *Loreto and the Holy House* (1917).

Annunciation. The materials used in the little house were limestone, mortar, and cedar, the same as those used at Nazareth, and were unobtainable in that part of Dalmatia. After three and a half years, however, the Holy House took off again, this time turning up on the opposite side of the Adriatic in the middle of a wood called Lauretum (from which the present-day name Loreto is derived). It did not stay there long either, it is said, but moved when two brothers quarreled bitterly in its precincts, to a spot in the middle of the high road to Recanati. The famous Italian saint Nicholas of Tolentino, who had lamented the departure of the Holy House from Tersatto, was consoled by an apparition of Our Lady, telling him that the house was now near Recanati. From 1294 pilgrims began to converge on Loreto in huge crowds, and in the Jubilee year of 1300 the town was called the City of Mary, so great was the pilgrim throng.

The Walsingham cult is older than that of Loreto by about two centuries. Both refer to the Nazareth dwelling of the Holy Family, but only Loreto claims to have the original structure. Both legends have the motif of a sacred object's translation from one site to another. Both cults are centered, of course, on the "joyful mystery" (as it is termed in the Rosary) of the Annunciation, celebrated in the feast of March 25. Angelology plays a part in both devotions (as befits the Annunciation theme, with its apparition of Gabriel to Mary), for the transportation of the Holy House from Nazareth to Loreto and of its copy from one site to another at Walsingham were said to be "by angelic hands." Neither the materials nor the measurements of the English and Italian Holy Houses correspond, however. The Loreto structure, made of stone, is thirty-two feet long, thirteen feet wide, and eighteen feet high; the English St. Mary's Chapel, of wood, was considerably smaller, according to measurements made by William of Worcester in the latter part of the fifteenth century—twenty-three feet six inches long by twelve feet ten inches wide. Curiously enough, the Slipper Chapel, being twenty-eight feet six inches long, and twelve feet five inches wide, agrees more closely with the Holy House of Loreto's dimensions. Obsessively precise measurements of this kind abound in the pilgrimage literature.

Both Marian devotions, Loreto and Walsingham, express the medieval spirit, and repay closer scrutiny. Walsingham's sponsors essayed to build, if not Jerusalem, at least a token of Nazareth "in England's green and pleasant land." Loreto more literally represented the transplanting of an Eastern religion (Christianity) in European soil under Roman patronage. Indeed, Loreto is today one of the pope's "extraterritorial" state properties—like Castel Gandolfo, his summer residence. Both shrines, characteristically marginal or liminal to the major centers of political and ecclesiastical administration, conveyed the "far" quality of the Holy Land. They aptly stood for the "far" as against the "familiar," the pure as opposed to the impure, the sacred as against the mundane, communitas confronting social structure, with the Annunciation representing all new beginnings, and the long hard road to the shrine representing repentance for one's sins as householder and politician. The great shrines were like Christian Meccas. Both Loreto and Walsingham drew pilgrims from other lands; they functioned not merely at the national but also at the international level of Christianity. Like that of many other shrines, their history reveals an internal process of change from spontaneity to structure, though never with a total declension in communitas. (Indeed, as we have seen, structure may frame "flow," and flow, in turn, may sustain communitas.) That history also manifests the interaction between pilgrimage and context under changing economic and political conditions.

According to Ivor Dowse (1963:107), referring only to Anglican pilgrims, "as many as 100,000 people pass through Walsingham each year, many of them either privately or in an organized parish party." And at least as many today make the Catholic pilgrimage. But in the Middle Ages a much higher proportion of the population made the pilgrimage. There are many references to the Walsingham shrine and its pilgrims in the Paston Letters, for example.[4] The Marian cult grew exuberantly in England under Cistercian and Car-

---

[4] For example, when Margaret Paston's husband John fell ill about three years after their marriage, she wrote to him: "My mother promised another image of wax of the weight of you to Our Lady of Walsingham, and she sent four nobles to the four Orders of Friars at Norwich to pray for you, and I have promised to go on pilgrimage to Walsingham and to St. Leonard's [priory in Norwich] for you." Paston Letters, no. 36, quoted from J. Gairdner, ed., *Paston Letters* (1904).

melite tending, but it appears that the popularity of the Walsingham pilgrimage preceded the influence of these great religious orders. Many English kings visited Walsingham, including Henry III in 1241, Edward I (thirteen times), Edward II in 1315, Henry VI in 1455, Henry VII in 1487, and Henry VIII in 1513. The celebrated humanist Erasmus, who has left us both the best account of the shrine and the sharpest critique of the superstition and corruption he found there in its decadence, made a pilgrimage to Walsingham from Cambridge in 1511 in fulfillment of a vow, and left as his offering a set of Greek verses:

> . . . I poor bard
> Rich in goodwill, but poor in all beside,
> Bring thee my verse—nought have I else to bring—
> And beg, in quittal of this worthless gift,
> That greatest meed—a heart that feareth God,
> And free for aye from sin's foul tyranny
> [Calendar of Letters and Papers, Foreign
> and Domestic. Henry VIII no. 1188].

This was of course written before Erasmus began to turn against the pilgrimage idea.

Gillett (1957:301) cites evidence to show that by 1291, according to the *Taxatio* of Pope Nicholas IV, the priory of Walsingham then had possessions in eighty-six parishes in Norfolk alone. A great number of wills bequeathing money and property to the Holy House have also come to light. Royal and noble benefactors abound: the earls of Chester and Salisbury in Henry III's reign, and, after 1241, such illustrious personages as Isabel, countess of Arundel; Hubert de Burgh; Sir Robert and Sir William of Morley, marshals of Ireland; and many more. Foreigners were permitted to make the pilgrimage, even in time of war. "In 1361, Edward III granted £9 towards the expenses of John, Duke of Brittany, a prisoner of war, so that he might make the pilgrimage in suitable state. Already Edward II had given protection to Robert Bruce of Scotland, smitten with leprosy, for a similar pilgrimage. . . . There was a fixed scale of charges for pilgrims who visited Walsingham from Ghent, in Flanders, as the representatives of persons unable for various reasons to make the journey themselves" (Gillett 1957:301–2).

Nevertheless, it was the ordinary pilgrims who made the shrine the great center that it was. As Colin Stephenson has pointed out (*Walsingham Way* 1970:50), the multitudes of unidentified pilgrims, each of whom generally deposited a small coin in the Holy House, are the "real story of the rise of Walsingham." To bring them there, a network of roads, or "pilgrim's ways," was developed, lined with wayside shrines and other waystations. These included chapels for pilgrims to pray in at Hillborough, South Acre, West Acre, Lynn (later King's Lynn), Priors-Thorns, Stanhoe, Coston and many other places. The Slipper Chapel, mentioned previously, was the culmination of this chain, and the point from which the final ritualized approach to the Holy House was made. One etymological derivation of "Slipper," incidentally, is from "slype," which is the original name of this chapel of the pilgrimage saint Catherine and means "a covered passage" or "way-through"—a perfect metaphor for pilgrimage liminality. The main way-station from the continent of Europe was at Lynn, where those coming from the Low Countries landed. The cost of a pilgrimage to Walsingham from Ghent was put down as four livres. At Lynn was the strange red-brick octagonal tower, still standing, known as the Red Mount Chapel, containing an image known as Our Lady of the Red Mount, probably a facsimile of the one in the Holy House. Nowadays, on Marian feast days, particularly, of course, on the Feast of the Annunciation, a pilgrimage procession takes place from the Catholic church in Lynn (which has an exact replica of the Loreto Holy House, within which is a copy of the image of Our Lady of Walsingham), to the Red Mount Chapel. Such is the tenacity of ritual paradigms! Another well-defined route went from London to Newmarket, probably along the Icknield Way, the old Roman road, and thence via Brandon Bridge to the Green Way, or Walsingham Way, through Weeting, Hillborough Litcham and Barsham to Houghton and its Slipper Chapel. As in other pilgrimages, hospices gave shelter on the way. The Cluniac priory at Castleacre, for example, had a large guest house for Walsingham pilgrims. Another pilgrim way came from the east, through Norwich and Attleborough, where the Bec Hospital (a hospice) was founded with thirteen beds for poor pilgrims. Another route from the north crossed the Wash near Long Sutton, and went through Lynn, passing the priories of Flitcham, Rudham, and Cokesford, which would have also dispensed hospitality.

In Walsingham itself there was no lack of accommodation for the poorer pilgrims in the later Middle Ages. The names of some of the inns have come down to us: the Crowned Lion, the Dove, the Moon and Star, the Saracen's Head, The White Horse, the Swan and Bull, the Ram, and the Angel, and many others. But these were not numerous enough, apparently. Gillett notes (1957:308): "In 1431, according to John Amundesham, four inns were burnt down. 'Through what cause,' he wrote, 'no mortal knew, except that it might be for revenge for the excessive charges which the persons living in those inns had exacted from the pilgrims for their victuals.' "

We have mentioned in earlier chapters the frequent association between pilgrimage centers and markets. This was also the case at Walsingham in its prime. Today, the Friday Market Place is a reminder that in 1226, King Henry III, on pilgrimage, granted the priory the right to hold the weekly market in Walsingham.

The Walsingham pilgrimage seems to have been a going concern for many years, perhaps a century, before the rise of the cult of St. Thomas à Becket at Canterbury. Chaucer's poetic genius has immortalized the Canterbury pilgrimage, but the same kinds of pilgrims that he described must have taken the Walsingham way, too. J. J. Jusserand, in his classic study *English Wayfaring Life in the Middle Ages* (1891:349–50), presents both sides of the pilgrimage coin. First he gives us yet another illustration of the normative communitas characterizing pilgrim relationships; then he shows how wealth and power so corrupted the pilgrimage process in the later Middle Ages that Henry VIII's commissioners were provided with plenty of solid justification for their plundering of the great shrines. Jusserand allows that the majority of pilgrims were "sincere and in good faith."

They had made a vow and came to fulfil it. With such dispositions, the knight who found a pilgrim like himself upon his road must have been less inclined than ever to treat him with scorn; besides, if the distances were great between class and class at this period, familiarities were still greater. The distance has indeed diminished at

the present day, and familiarity also, as though in compensation.
. . . Arrived at the end of the journey, all prayed; prayed with fervour in the humblest posture. The soul was filled with religious emotion when from the end of the majestic alley formed by the great pillars of the church, through the coloured twilight of the nave, the heart divined, rather than the eye saw, the mysterious object of veneration for which such a distance had been traversed at the cost of such fatigue. Though the practical man galloping up to bargain with the saint for the favour of god, though the emissary sent to make offering in the name of his master might keep a dry and clear eye, tears course down the cheeks of the poor and simple in heart [pp. 349–50].

On the other hand, Jusserand goes on, pilgrims were undoubtedly "a very mingled race. . . . No reader of Chaucer needs to be reminded that the talk on the road was not always limited to edifying subjects, and that pilgrims themselves, even allowing the greater number to have been sincere and devout people, were not all of them vessels of election." From our own experience as members of a mixed band of Irish and American pilgrims who flew, under the aegis of Joe Doyle's Tours, from Dublin to Rome and Lourdes in the summer of 1972, we can confirm that what Jusserand said about unedifying talk still holds good. Walter Starkie, an indefatigable pilgrim toting his guitar along the trail, pointed out to us that in the Middle Ages the pilgrim ways to Compostela were lined as often with bordellos as with shrines.

Jusserand continues:

Some (pilgrims) went like gypsies to a fair, to gather money; some went for the pleasures of the journey and the merriments of the road; so that reformers and satirists, seeing only the abuse and not the good that might come along with it, began to raise a cry which became louder and louder until it was something like a storm at the time of the Reformation. Whom did Langland see on Palmer's Way, near Walsingham? Those same false hermits we have already met by the highroads and at the corner of bridges, and in what objectionable company did he find them!

> Hermits in a heap with hooked staves
> Went to Walsingham and their wenches after;
> Great loobies ["louts; great, clumsy fellows"] and long
>   that loth were to work,

184

Clothed them in copes to be known from others,
And made themselves hermits their ease to have
[*Piers Plowman*, Skeat's Edition, Text C, pass.
i. 1. 51; quoted from Jusserand 1891:350–51].

It was the wealth of Walsingham in the early sixteenth century
which aroused the sarcastic ire of Erasmus. He had gone there on
pilgrimage himself, as we have seen, and had written pious Greek
verses on his experience. Later he turned to satire in his colloquy
on pilgrimage, published in 1526, just before the destruction of the
shrine. Two friends, Menedemus and Ogygyus, meet and discuss
the latter's recent visits to Compostela and Walsingham, "the most
holy name in all England. . . . the towne is almost susteynyd by
the resort of pylgrymes." Ogygyus goes on to describe the abundance of gold, silver, and precious stones offered to the miracle-
working image of Our Lady, the marvels worked at the two holy
wells, the miracle of the knight who escaped from his foes on horseback through a low narrow gate in the wall enclosing the priory,
and the crystal phial alleged to contain some of the Virgin's milk.
The skeptical Menedemus assails images, relics, and pilgrimages as
worthless, and concludes by saying that he has enough to do with
his "stations of Rome." On being asked by Ogygyus, "Of Rome,
that dyd neuer see Rome?" Menedemus answers that he goes his
stations at home.

I go into the parler, and I see what the chaat lyuyng of my dough-
ters; agyne frome thense I go in to my shope, I beholde what my
servauntes, bothe men and women, be doynge. From thense into
the kytchyn, lokynge abowt, it ther nede any of my cownsell; frome
thense hyther and thyther, obseruynge howe my chylderne be oc-
cupyed, what my wyffe dothe, beynge carefull that euery thynge be
in ordre: these be statyons of Rome.[5]

The "Protestant ethic" clearly casts its shadow before in this dia-
logue. A virtuous life is better led in one's own household and secular vocation than by gadding off on pilgrimage and seeking saints'

[5] "A Dialoge or communication of two persons, deuysyd and set forthe in the laten
tonge, by the noble and famose clarke, Desiderius Erasmus, intituled ye pylgremage
of pure deuotyon. Newly translatyd into Englishe," London, 1540 16°; quoted by Jusserand 1891:353–54.

intercessions on one's behalf. Symbol-vehicles are condemned as idols, and iconoclasm is tacitly recommended. But the portrait Erasmus gives us as a model, of a sober-suited omnipresent busybody eavesdropping on the affairs of his household, is singularly without charm. Communitas seems to be thrown out, along with the penitential journeys and the shrines.

Erasmus's views were consistent with those of Henry VIII in his later years. Henry, however, also coveted the wealth of the Austin canons. The last prior of Walsingham, Richard Vowell, sought by concessions to placate Thomas Cromwell, Henry's "enforcer," evidently not understanding that Cromwell was determined at all costs to close down all religious houses and seize their wealth for the Crown, not forgetting the Crown's faithful servants. Vowell even got the Augustinian community to sign a document acknowledging the Royal Supremacy in 1534. Even as they were signing it, information was being garnered for the *Valor Ecclesiasticus,* a survey of the wealth of the English Church. The commissioners were guided by certain "Articles of Enquiry," which were clearly influenced by Erasmus's arguments. Not only did they seek to inventorize the jewels, ornaments, and plate; they also contained questions with a singularly modern, positivist ring:

(4) What were the main relics and how were they esteemed?
(5) What have they to show that the relics were genuine?
(6) In how many places were relics exposed and were people pestered to make offerings to them?
(7) Why were the relics shown in several places and not in one place?
(10) What was the greatest miracle claimed to have been worked by Our Lady or by the relics and what proof was there of these things?
(11) If the fact was well proved what proof is there that it could not have been worked by natural means?
(12) If that was proved, why could it not have proceeded directly from God and why should it be attributed to Our Lady or, if so, why to the particular image of Our Lady in that house?
(17) What proof they took of miracles claimed by pilgrims and whether they were accepted on the parties' own report or whether witnesses and depositions were taken?
(18) Whether Our Lady's milk was liquid?
[quoted from Stephenson 1970:60–61.]

The love of money evidently sharpened skepticism, for the valuables of Walsingham were soon sequestrated. In 1537 it was alleged by Henry's spies and informers that a rebellion against the threat of dissolution was being planned at the shrine. This report coincided with the so-called Pilgrimage of Grace in the north, a rebellion of the common people in protest against the suppression of the smaller monasteries, which, whatever their faults, had continued to provide work and welfare services. The upshot was that a Walsingham layman, George Gysborough, and the subprior, Nicholas Mileham, were hung, drawn, beheaded, and quartered in a field at Walsingham, still known as Martyrs' Field (Stephenson 1970:64). The following year the image of Our Lady of Walsingham was burnt in the courtyard of Cromwell's house in Chelsea, and the priory was dissolved. Vowell, whom some suspect of having informed against Mileham, was pensioned off, became a vicar of the Church of England, and later married.

Loreto, too, had its ebb and flow in the stream of history (Gillett 1949:vol.1,pp.37–43). Like Walsingham, it received homage from many famous people—prelates, kings, doctors of the church, and saints. Forty-seven popes knelt there as popes; others, who went as cardinals, later became popes. As at Walsingham, immense sums of money and quantities of treasure were lavished on the shrine. A huge outer basilica was erected around the Holy House. Millions of pilgrims visited it from all over Europe and beyond for centuries. Then in 1797, the commissaries of the French Directory seized the sanctuary, and carried off its treasures (as they had done elsewhere in Italy, taking revered religious objects and esthetic masterpieces) to Paris, where they were exhibited as curiosities. These treasures included the ancient statue of Our Lady of Loreto, which was made of cedarwood from Lebanon, and was apparently of Jewish-Egyptian origin. Napoleon Bonaparte, making one of his intermittent overtures to the Catholic Church, restored the figure to Pope Pius VII, after a period of exposition and veneration in the Cathedral of Notre-Dame in Paris. Thus Loreto (from which the Litany of Loreto, often sung at the office of Benediction, takes its name) suffered less from iconoclasm and covetousness than Walsingham.

In the High Middle Ages, pilgrimage to national and international shrines was, pragmatically, as much a pillar of Christendom as the hajj was, theologically, for Islam. Bernard Lewis's remarks, in the *Encyclopedia of Islam* (1966), on the social, cultural, and economic effects of the hajj in medieval Islam, *mutatis mutandis*, have relevance for the study of Christian pilgrimage. Islam made of Mecca a mandalalike center of normative communitas (a center topographically represented by the Black Stone at the Kaaba), and thus transformed liminality into its opposite. Islam is ideally conceived as a vast communitas of cobelievers. In Lewis's words (p. 37):

> The needs of the pilgrimage—the commands of the faith reinforcing the requirements of government and commerce—help to maintain an adequate network of communications between the far-flung Muslim lands; the experience of the pilgrimage gives rise to a rich literature of travel, bringing information about distant places, and a heightened awareness of belonging to a larger whole. This awareness is reinforced by participation in the common rituals and ceremonies of the pilgrimage in Mecca and Medina, and the communion with fellow-Muslims of other lands and peoples. The physical mobility of important groups of people entails a measure of social and cultural mobility, and a corresponding evolution of institutions.

Lewis goes on to contrast the unity of the Islamic world with the stratified, hierarchic society, with its intense local traditions, which characterizes the comparatively small area of Western Christendom.

> The Islamic world has its local traditions, often very vigorous; but there is a degree of unity in the civilization of the cities—in values, standards and social customs—that is without parallel in the medieval west. "The Franks," says Rashid al-Din, "speak twenty-five languages, and no people understands the language of any other." It was a natural comment for a Muslim, accustomed to the linguistic unity of the Muslim world, with two or three languages serving not only as the media of a narrow clerical class, like Latin in Western Europe, but as the effective means of universal communication, supplanting local languages and dialects at all but the lowest levels. The pilgrimage was not the only factor making for cultural unity and social mobility in the Islamic world—but it was certainly an important one, perhaps the most important.

It is certainly true that Islam tended to emphasize the pilgrimage to Mecca as a unifying and centralizing institution more than Christianity ever did for any of its pilgrimages. We wonder, however, whether similar integrative effects may not be brought about in polycentric as well as monocentric pilgrimage systems. Indeed, many medieval accounts show that pilgrims from all Christian territories visited such shrines as the Roman basilicas, Loreto, Walsingham, Chartres, Einsiedeln in Switzerland, Hal in Flanders, Le Puy in France, Canterbury, Compostela, Zaragoza, Montserrat, Rocamadour, Aachen, Cologne, and so forth. The crisscrossing of pilgrimage ways formed by these devotions of international repute must have had bonding effects on the entire sociocultural system of Christendem. Finally, our major criticism of Lewis's position is that he seems not to have taken folk Islam into account. In practice, pilgrimage journeys to marabouts' tombs in North Africa, for example, are as frequent as journeys to Christian saints' shrines in southern Europe.

Nevertheless, that the Roman Church's official vew of the relationship between communitas and social structure differed substantially from Islam's is reflected in its tolerance of pilgrimage polycentrism. The model of pre-Christian Roman imperial government lay to hand. This regarded the widest system under one authority as both hierarchical and segmentary in character, not as a homogeneous communitas. According to the Roman theory of ecclesiastical government: "The Church, as a perfect society, has supreme authority over her subjects, legislative, judicial, and executive, in all matters pertaining to her spiritual end. The supreme authority over the universal Church belongs by divine institution to the pope individually, and to the bishops collectively (in oecumenical council) in union with the pope. Bishops have authority in their own territories [segmentation] dependently on the pope [hierarchy]. The pope in the government of the universal Church is assisted by cardinals, either as a body (the Sacred College), or distributed in the Roman Congregations, Tribunals, and Offices. In microcosm, the bishop in his diocese is assisted by the cathedral chapter, officials of the diocesan curia, and rectors of parishes" (A Catholic Dictionary, ed. D. Atwater, s.v. "Government").

It can be seen that this structure assigns a high degree of administrative authority to the diocese. In fact, it is the bishop who is responsible for initiating inquiries into the apparitions, visions, and miracles which set the pilgrim stream on the move. A bishop can make or break an incipient pilgrimage. His power derives from the doctrine that the bishops are the successors of the apostles collectively, as the pope is of St. Peter in particular. Once chosen, they are not delegates of the Holy See (the see of Rome), but exercise their powers by virtue of their own office. They are responsible to the pope for the affairs of their own dioceses, however, and the pope can elect, translate, and even depose them. Yet, in practice, few popes interfere in the internal affairs of the dioceses. This allows for the growth of many local customs—lending some credence to Lewis's contrast between the West's patchwork and Islam's uniformity. Nonetheless, all the local variations are subtended beneath the governmental umbrella of Rome, and the pope and his delegates in Rome have always been alert to the possibility that variation might become deviation. In general, the Church has consciously aimed at *unity in diversity*, rather than at a uniformity which, it postulates, would be only external in effect and would cramp the genius of particular peoples and nations. Where it does insist on uniformity is in its defined system of faith and morals, which it holds to be true and necessarily the same always and everywhere. We have argued that these opposites coincide in the polar structure of dominant religious symbols, with theological uniformity at one pole and a vast range of local diversities at the other on the exegetical, operational, and positional levels of meaning (that is, what symbol users say about symbols, how they act toward them, and how they arrange them in relation to one another).

Another force counteracting local centripetalism in the Catholic system is the shared repertoire of nonverbal symbol-vehicles, essentially its visual, iconographic grammar and vocabulary, by means of which a rich variety of iconic forms may be generated in accordance with a few basic rules, all of which constitute a common language for millions of people otherwise divided linguistically and culturally. Catholic iconography and theology have the same underlying ideational structure, also expressed in other cognitive and sensory codes, such as mystical and devotional literature, liturgical forms, canon law, church music, and the form of the pilgrimage process itself. Central to this structure is the root paradigm of Christ's Passion and Resurrection, followed by the pentecostal birth of the Church.

Thus while Islam places communitas, *umma*, at the center of its unity, medieval Christendom and modern Catholicism place the structuring of diversity according to uniform principles in that central position. These ideal paradigms have paradoxical consequences in each case. The essence of spontaneous communitas is its temporal transience—the "wind that bloweth where it listeth." Yet Muhammad's declaration of the hajj as a duty incumbent on all Muslims is a formulation precluding both spontaneity and brevity, since long preparation, practical and spiritual, is required for this great journey, often overseas. The Catholic Church, on the other hand, has always been a little cautious about admitting any manifestation of communitas as a foundation for unity—except in the Gospel episode of Pentecost itself, when, in the brief spontaneity of the spirit, many became one though speaking various tongues. Communitas has often been seen as something to be brought under control, a charisma to be routinized, a grace to be thankful for, perhaps, but not part of the regular running of things, the business of the Church, as Arklike it floats through the choppy ages. But the pilgrimage process, when seen from the perspective of a given shrine's history, often begins with extraordinary manifestations or charisms, which are soon recognized as being for the good of others, not merely for their first recipients, and lead to an influx of pilgrims to the place where the manifestations are popularly believed to have occurred. Now the Church, unlike Islam (or, indeed, Judaism before the destruction of the Temple), does not generally require its believers to make any pilgrimage at all, much less one to a single holy place. Though many Christian lay persons have gone to Rome on pilgrimage from early times, Rome's official importance as a center of pilgrimage unity is based on the higher clergy's obligation to journey *ad limina apostolorum* ("to the thresholds of the apostles"). Every archbishop and bishop-in-ordinary (that is, diocesan bishop) must pay an official visit, in person if possible, to the tombs of the apostles Peter and Paul and to their living representative, the pope, once every five years from European localities, and once every ten, from more distant parts of the world. Each visitor must deliver a report of his diocese, according to a fixed syllabus of detailed questions about the spiritual state and observance of the clergy and the laity there and the wider intellectual, social, political, and economic contexts, with relevant statistics. Rome can be seen, once more, as a center of governmental structure. Structure, not communitas, is made central to this pilgrimage obligation; the continuity of canon law with imperial Roman law serves admirably. But one result of structuring the center is that communitas breaks out, like solar coronas, all over the peripheries, in spontaneously engendered pilgrimages, crackling with charisms. Because they are peripheral, responsibility for their legitimization is placed squarely in the lap of bishops. That is why we shall find, when we come to examine the genesis of modern pilgrimages such as Joaseiro (in northeastern Brazil), Notre-Dame-de-la-Salette, Lourdes, Knock, Beauraing, Banneux, and Garabandal, that the first obstacle to their acceptance is the local bishop and his commissions of inquiry, whose preliminary structuring is in his hands. The Church has always been a deft integrator, and bishops have, on the whole, tried to channel popular enthusiasm in orthodox directions—in other words, to effect a kind of social sublimation—rather than to quash it. But the bishop goes into all the circumstances of a reputed apparition or miracle, estimating the probity of witnesses, being watchful for contradictions in testimony, and assessing the theological implications of the alleged vision, to decide whether it would be more prudent to turn a blind eye to a popular *fait accompli* and give official approval to the nascent pilgrimage, or to condemn it out of hand.

The thriving medieval pilgrimages had the effect of bonding together—however transiently—at a certain level of social life, large numbers of men and women who, because of feudal localization and rural decentralization of socioeconomic relationships, would otherwise never have come into contact. Jusserand made this point well in his *English Wayfaring Life in the Middle Ages*, where he describes the role of itinerants (both lay and religious), among whom pilgrims are paramount, in serving as "a true link between the human groups of various districts" (p. 31). Local miracles drew pilgrims from everywhere, bringing news and ideas. Jusserand even touches upon the potential for revolution in the pilgrimage process (a potential we mentioned in our chapter on Mexican pilgrimage), when he writes that pilgrims and other nomads "brought to the men attached to the soil news of their brethren in the neighboring province, of their condition of misery or happiness, who were pitied or envied accordingly, and were remembered as brothers or friends to call upon in the day of revolt" (p. 31). Both civil and ecclesiastical authorities recognized the dangers inherent in holy nomadism. Jusserand notes that in fourteenth-century England "everyone . . . was obliged to furnish himself with true letters of travel or passports, in order to move from one country to another" (p. 269). This was partly to prevent serfs or villeins, weary of being attached to the soil, and to an exacting lord, from setting out, "under colour of going far on a pilgrimage," never to return. English pilgrims needed passports to cross the sea. These "licenses," or "special leave of the king," could be obtained only at certain fixed ports; that is, London, Sandwich, Dover, Southampton, Plymouth, Dartmouth, Bristol, Yarmouth, Boston, Kingston-upon-Hull, Newcastle-upon-Tyne, and the ports of the coast opposite to Ireland (p.362).

The Church, too, began to control pilgrimage as the Middle Ages wore on, especially as its penitential system, rooted in the sacrament of Penance, became more clearly defined and organized. When this system became authoritatively and legally structured, pilgrimages were themselves regarded as adequate punishment for certain crimes (thus the four murderers of St. Thomas à Becket, according to tradition, made the pilgrimage to Jerusalem to atone for their crime). "The hardships of the journey, the penitential garb worn, the mendicity it entailed, made a pilgrimage a real and effective penance" (Jarrett 1911:85). The granting of plenary indulgences to sinners for devotions made at certain great shrines stimulated pilgrimage and gave the Church greater control over the shrines. Placing pilgrim shrines under the custody of one of the religious orders or, in some cases, of specially delegated secular clergy, served the same end.

P. A. Sigal has admirably summarized the literature on the relationship between indulgences, penances, and civil penalties, in his *Marcheurs de Dieu: Pèlerinages et Pèlerins au Moyen Âge* (1974:12–25), and we draw upon his summary for the discussion that follows. An indulgence, as we have noted, is a remission of the temporal or purgatorial punishment due for a sin after the sinner's guilt has been absolved in the sacrament of penance. Undoubtedly, illness was thought of in the Middle Ages, as it is among Catholic peasants today, as a temporal punishment, and the healing of illness was seen as an indicator of "remission of sin." Hence pilgrimage to a holy shrine where a plenary indulgence might be obtained was regarded as a journey to a source of healing, as a therapeutic trip. Illness was more than a medical problem, it was a moral problem; pilgrimage shrines were, and are, the doctors of the poor. Sigal has traced the history of the practice of indulgences, demonstrating that it was not until the bull of Pope Urban II, in 1095, which accorded to Crusaders the full remission of all temporal punishment due them, that the notion of the plenary indulgence, as distinct from partial indulgences, became established. From that moment, the annexation of indulgences to selected shrines occurred more frequently, while the conditions necessary to obtain them grew easier. Clearly, the Crusaders' indulgence provided the model for less bellicose pilgrimages. When the Holy Places of Palestine were wrested by the Muslims from the Christians, the Roman Jubilee replaced the Crusade as the major source of plenary indulgences. When Pope Boniface VIII promulgated the jubilee of 1300, granting a plenary indulgence to all who made the pilgrimage to the shrines of Rome, he was, in effect, replacing Jerusalem with Rome as the spiritual center of Christianity. Other pilgrimage shrines were soon granted such indulgences: Canterbury, for its fourth jubilee, in 1370; Notre-Dame du Puy, for its jubilees of 1407, 1418, and 1429 (when Good Friday fell on March 25, the Feast of the Annunciation); and Compostela in 1435. With the multiplication of indulgences and jubilees, at more and more pilgrimage centers, pilgrimage grew at once more popular and less devout.

Pilgrimage as a form of penance had been known as far back as the Celtic and Anglo-Saxon monastic period and was then exported to the Continent by Irish missionaries. It followed then to Neustria and Austrasia in Frankish territory, to the Rhineland and northern Italy. Unlike earlier Christian forms, this monastically-spread penance was not public but private, and could be undertaken as often as one had sinned—whereas the ancient form could be performed only once. Penance was required for a whole tariff of faults, which were listed in the widely used penitentials, rule books cataloguing the penances appropriate to various sins. Temporal punishments included fasts, fines, exile, and condemnation to wander in a hostile, foreign land. In the ninth century, however, such exile was given a goal: penitents could travel to places renowned for their possession of saints' relics and tombs, for it was already well established doctrinally that saints were the best intercessors for the remission of one's sins. Sigal believes that the initiative probably came from the pilgrims themselves and was then enshrined in canonical legislation. In the Carolingian period, legislation clearly distinguished public penance from private penitence. By the beginning of the thirteenth century, three forms of penance coexisted: (1) solemn public penance, which was imposed by the bishop, and retained many features of the ancient Christian type; this was imposed for particularly scandalous crimes committed by the laity; (2) less serious public penance; this included the penitential pilgrimage, which any parish priest might impose, for the less severe sins of the laity and for particularly heinous crimes of the clergy which could not be dealt with under the rubric of solemn penance; and (3) private penance for hidden sins of any kind.

Penitential pilgrimage, as time went by, was increasingly incorporated into the system of solemn public penance. Later still, particularly in the Low Countries, perhaps because the documentation is richer there (p. 21), pilgrimage became a civil penalty, applied to a wide range of delicts, against the public weal, against persons, and against property. Data from the Low Countries reveal that some pilgrimages were more regularly recommended as penitential journeys for criminals than others. Sigal shows that from the thirteenth to the fifteenth century more than twenty towns imposed, on condemned criminals, penitential pilgrimages to the shrines of James of Compostela and Our Lady of Rocamadour; fifteen designated Saint-Larme in Vendôme and Heutes Saint-Josse in Normandy;

fourteen, St. Peter's and St. Paul's in Rome; thirteen, St. Nicholas of Bari; twelve, St. Martin of Tours; eleven, The Three Kings in Cologne; and so forth, down to five towns for each of the following: Notre-Dame in Bois-le-Duc, Notre-Dame in Hal, Notre-Dame in Cambrai, Saint-Maur-des-Fossés, Notre-Dame du Puy, Sainte-Croix in Strumberg, St. Francis at Assisi, Notre-Dame in Basel, Notre-Dame of Einsiedeln, and Notre-Dame in Riga.[6] What astonished us, as we read this list, was that most of these shrines continue to attract pilgrims today. Though many of the shrines are at a considerable distance from the Low Countries, it is obvious that we are dealing here with a case not of removing "bad lots" as far as possible from home but of the popularity of pan-European centers. These factors of persistence and distance provide further proof, if proof is needed, of the grooves worn in space and time by "flow" and "communitas."

Conceptual and institutional structuration of penitential pilgrimage prepared the way for the demise of the pilgrimage system in its high medieval form, for it no longer represented communitas, social antistructure. Even at the folk level, pilgrimage became encrusted with customs denying its original spirit. Religious "conmen" like Chaucer's Pardoner sold indulgences and relics by the bagful. The Crusades opened Europe to a spate of relics from the Holy Land, with much reduplication—St. John the Baptist's head, countless phials of Virgin's milk, parts of her girdle and veil, portions of her hair, and enough pieces of the "true Cross," as Erasmus acidly observed, to build a ship. A notion grew up, in fact, to account for the proliferation of reputed fragments of the Cross: it was said that the holy wood had a miraculous power of self-reproduction and could never be diminished, however much it was distributed.[7] (St. Cyril,

[6] Sigal drew on the following sources for his account of pilgrimages in the Low Countries: E. van Cauvenburgh, *Les pèlerinages expiatoires et judiciaires dans le droit communal de la Belgique au Moyen Âge* (1922); F. L. Ganshof, "Pèlerinages expiatoires flamands à Saint-Gilles pendant le XIVᵉ siècle" (1966:391–407); L. du Vallon, "Les pèlerinages expiatoires et judiciaries de Belgique aux sanctuares de Provence au Moyen Âge" (1935); and idem, "Les pèlerinages expiatoires et judiciaires de Belgique à Rocamadour au Moyen Âge" (1937).

[7] J. A. MacCulloch, *Medieval Faith and Fable* (1932:140): "Paulinus (Epistle 31) says that part of the cross of Jerusalem gave off fragments without diminishing. . . . The Nails of the Cross had the same power of reproducing themselves."

patriarch of Jerusalem, likened the holy wood to the five small loaves with which five thousand people were supplied.) Shrines and waystations competed for the attention of pilgrims in the display of sensational relics: one example was a portion of the manna with which God had fed the Israelites! There was, indeed, a surplus of signifiers, of visible and tangible symbol-vehicles, amounting to an inflation of the symbolic currency—dare one say, of generalized "ludic" media? A parallel might perhaps be drawn with the symbolic gold and silver paper money traditionally burned in rites of ancestor veneration or of deity worship in Chinese communities. This overemphasis on signifiers at the expense of meaning led to the attribution of magic power to relics, paintings, and images; they became fetishes operating by principles of sympathetic and contagious magic, rather than serving as vehicles of religious and ethical ideas. The laws of magic overruled the moral action of free will. Pilgrimage became a part of the structured social field of interacting feudal states and ecclesiastical institutions, and functioned to maintain it. Protected by ecclesiastical and political authorities, pilgrimage became worldly and fashionable. According to Sidney Heath (1911:33), "the scrip and the staff were as frequently assumed for the purpose of committing new sins as for the performance of penance for old ones." Assignations were made in the "leafy bowers" by holy wells or in the "dimly lighted cathedral." Adultery was said to be common in shrines in Lombardy, France, and England. Other abuses were rife.

Proscribed criminals or hunted debtors helped to fill the ranks of devout pilgrims. If a priest, the pilgrim drew his full stipend, providing that his absence did not exceed a term of three years. If a layman, he was excused the payment of all taxes. The property of all pilgrims was secured from confiscation and injury while on pilgrimage, nor could they be arrested and/or cast in any civil court. Their sanctity was universally respected, for once the sacred cross was sewn upon his garment and he had received the blessing of the Church, the pilgrim was above all law except the ecclesiastical. He was protected by St. Peter and the pope [Heath 1911:25].

But in one major respect pilgrimage could never be trivial, never become mere tourism. This was with reference to those major scourges (mentioned earlier here in connection with the Mexican pilgrimages) against which human action was powerless—drought, famine, plague, and blight (see Stephenson 1970:42). These were regarded, with abundant Biblical testimony, as signs of God's wrath at human sinfulness and rebellion against divine law. Severe penance on a mass scale was necessary to atone for mass delinquency. Pilgrimage was one form such penance took. In the overorganized waning years of the Middle Ages, confraternities proliferated for the systematic practice of self-inflicted bodily austerity[8] (the Penitentes of New Mexico were one modern survival of this practice). The insanitary conditions of the towns and the low level of personal hygiene were partly responsible for the many outbreaks of pestilence. Colin Stephenson (1970:41–42) gives us a case-study of how the Black Death affected Walsingham. This scourge, which first appeared in England in 1348, hit Norfolk and the eastern counties particularly hard. "Whole villages were depopulated and left to fall into ruins. Not far from Walsingham in the middle of a field can be seen the ruined tower of Egmere Church, which is all that remains of a village which was wiped out by the plague. . . . Men turned to religion for comfort and protection. The monasteries were hardest hit, in some cases they never recovered and it was the greatest cause of their decline. . . . It is not surprising to find the plague breaking out at [Walsingham] shrine, because the upsurge of religious fervour must have sent even greater crowds along the pilgrim way."

Pilgrimage in this case functioned similarly to those African communal rituals which are brought into operation to cope with collective disasters, over and above the fortunes and interests of specific segments of the tribal community. Response to plague and famine provides additional proof of the high degree of assimilation of pilgrimage into the social structural order, enabling us to speak of "pilgrimage systems" as well as "pilgrimage process." We have

---

[8] Sigal (1974:18) writes: "From the sixth and ninth centuries the abuses and disadvantages of penitential pilgrimage began to be denounced. These reservations became sharper in the middle of the thirteenth and beginning of the fourteenth century. At this time there developed another practice, flagellation, which attained its first primacy in 1260." Flagellation remained a familiar practice well into the eighteenth century.

argued in a previous chapter that Marian devotion is peculiarly adapted to the role of protecting communities from such scourges. In patrilineal, patrimonial, and patriarchal social systems, attachments through women (not merely the maternal bond alone) come to stand for the seamless unity of the whole community, its *prima materia*, so to speak—as against the association of paternity and, by extension, masculinity, with property, law, the delimitation and demarcation of rights and duties, the rules of succession to high office; that is, parceling out and division of all kinds, "pattern" against "matter." Thus Mary is purity, totality, protection against law, who pleads with her divine Son to show sinners mercy rather than punish them according to their just deserts. Mary is a sanctuary, a refuge, a source of remedies. Marian shrines share in these qualities of their patroness. They have often been destroyed, their images have been burnt; but sooner or later they have revived, while nearly all the shrines of lesser saints have remained neglected after their shattering by reformative or revolutionary iconoclasts. We have seen already how Walsingham revived. Here are some further instances: The image of Our Lady of Chartres was burnt during the French Revolution in 1793 (there is a legend that the burners all went mad), but a new figure was made by the Parisian sculptor Fontenelle, replicating it in the smallest details, and was enthroned in 1857; since then many national pilgrimages have visited it (Gillett 1949·61) When French troops arrived at Einsiedeln, the great Swiss shrine, in 1798, the Benedictine monks, custodians of the shrine, fled with the statue of the Virgin to the valley of Alp Thal. When the French demanded its surrender, a man named Placid Keller, disguised as a peddler, smuggled it away to a convent near Bludenz, passing right through the French lines, and selling merchandise as he went. In 1803 it was restored to the Abbey of St. Meinrad at Einsiedeln. According to Gillett (p. 68), Einsiedeln is today once more a major pilgrimage center. "More than a quarter of a million confessions are made there each year, . . . pilgrims flock from all the surrounding countries and a rule has been made that those who come from the furthest places should be shrived first. It can be gathered that this leads at times to some amusing arguments. There are some fifty hotels within a few minutes' walk." The shrine of Our Lady of Montserrat, near Barcelona, was sacked by Napoleon, suppressed in 1835, and restored in 1842; in 1936–38, during the Spanish Civil War, twenty-three monks of the custodian Benedictine congregation were shot to death. Yet the Moreneta, the "Little Dark Lady" (a title by which the Mexican Virgin of Guadalupe is also called), only three feet high and blackened with age and the soot of centuries of votive candles, has survived all these troubles. (Today there are on the mountain eight or nine giant hospices for pilgrims, hospitals and dispensaries run by the monks, and shops as well; Gillett, p. 76.) The shrine of Our Lady in Le Puy occupies the ancient cathedral in the chief town of the department of Haute-Loire in south-central France. Le Puy was once a center of ancient Celtic worship and pilgrimage (reputedly, a Druid altar, a monolith reminiscent of Stonehenge, once stood on Mont Anis, and was replaced in Roman times by Jupiter's temple). For centuries Le Puy was the greatest Marian shrine in France. Even after the Reformation it remained a center for Spanish, Portuguese, Italian, and French pilgrims, three hundred thousand of whom are alleged to have visited it in 1622. But during the French Revolution, troops swept into the cathedral and turned it into a Temple of Reason. The image of the Madonna was treated like the queen of France, dragged to her trial in a manure cart, and from there, in the same tumbrel used for Royalist victims, to the square, where it was burned with other ecclesiastical objects. As early as 1802, however, a local artist was commissioned to make a likeness of the immolated image, and the pilgrimage was revived. (A. Chanal, *Le Puy en Velay* 1942a: passim). Oddly enough, Lourdes, once the fief of Le Puy, has now surpassed it as a pilgrimage center, though Le Puy boasts the curious, grandiose statue, fifty-three feet tall, of Our Lady, cast of metal taken from 213 cannons taken from Russia at Sebastopol in the Crimean War. This stands atop the rock of Corneille, near where the druidic altar and the Jovian center once drew pilgrims from afar. In Le Puy we have a magnificent instance of how archaic pilgrimage centers graft new pilgrimages onto old, like scions on stocks. Communitas persists through dramatic religious and theological changes. Le Puy suggests an *axis mundi*, perched as it is on a huge lump of volcanic rock rising, like the hub of a wheel, in the center of a prosperous plain surrounded by mountains—the reader may recall that St. Patrick's Purgatory in Ireland, originally centered on a cave, is set in the middle of a lake surrounded by mountains, a sort of "structural inverse" of Le Puy, save for their similar mountain periphery. Both great shrines are also liminal—set apart from major administrative centers.

Many other famous medieval Marian shrines in France, Belgium, and Luxembourg were damaged or destroyed during the French Revolution: Rocamadour (once ranked almost equal with Rome, Jerusalem, and Compostela), Avioth in the Meuse region, Luxembourg, Notre-Dame de Fourvière in Lyons. Reopened in 1805 after the Revolution, Notre-Dame de Fourvière was saved from destruction by Napoleon, who, before the battle of Waterloo, fortified the hillside on which the chapel is situated. He is reputed to have said of the church: "My mother brought me here as a child to pray. Please take this offering and say several masses for my soul" (Gillett 1949:120).

One could multiply many times the examples of destruction and later revival of medieval Marian shrines. In Britain, Henry VIII's commissioners, Oliver Cromwell's Roundheads, and the Scottish Covenanters were the major iconoclasts. In Europe, the Hussites (who stormed the great Polish shrine of Częstochowa in the 1430s), the Huguenots, and the French Revolutionaries were the principal image breakers. But the pattern of medieval pilgrimage, in its ideal paradigmatic form, was exported to the colonies of the Catholic European nations, especially in the late fifteenth and early sixteenth centuries.

Though much of Northern Europe was erased from the pilgrimage scene, the medieval mode of Catholic pilgrimage was given a new lease on life in the overseas empires of Spain, Portugal, and France. Just as in European countries in the Middle Ages there was a tendency to arrange pilgrim shrines in a hierarchy of catchment areas of varying size, so also in the new Catholic realms—Mexico, Brazil, Venezuela, Uruguay, Bolivia, Chile, French Canada, Peru, the Philippines, Argentina, and so on—a similar pattern developed. Foremost among the shrines of the major pilgrimage systems are those dedicated to the Mother of God (as we noted earlier, this reverses the situation in India, where the majority of shrines to the mother goddess are at the subregional and local levels). Sometimes these correspond to important indigenous cultural and linguistic areas: in Mexico, for example, Our Lady of Ocotlán's catchment area is essentially the former Tlaxcalan-speaking region; Our Lady of Zapopan, whose tiny image is made, in Tarascan fashion, of *pasta de Michoacán,* is not only patroness of the medieval-style city of Guadalajara but also protectress of the Indian and mestizo people of Jalisco state; Our Lady of Ízamal (see plates 12 and 13) was for centuries the focus of the prime pilgrimage cultus of the Yucatecan Maya peoples. There are other important regional shrines—to Our Lady of San Juan de los Lagos (also in Jalisco), and to Our Lady of Solitude at Oaxaca. All are subordinate in fame and catchment scope to the cultus of the Virgin of Guadalupe, whose shrine originated in the first encounter between the Spanish conquistadors and the most powerful Indian state, the Aztec empire, in the heart of Mexico. Beneath these regional Marian shrines are innumerable minor ones, to which pilgrimage may mean hardly more than a walk across a hill, or the crossing of a nearby river, to the next village. But the system ensures the constant crisscrossing of pilgrimage ways, as in medieval Europe. As we have noted in the chapter on Mexico, several of the Marian shrines in the New World, like many in medieval Europe, are built on the site of pagan pilgrimage centers, and the routes of pilgrimage themselves sometimes have pagan antecedents.

Here, then, is yet another case of religious succession and pilgrimage stratification. Communitas persists through religious and theological change; but it requires terms and norms to give it frame, focus, and a flow pattern. While one religion prevails, social and cultural structures seem immutable. But structures, and the symbols which manifest them, do break up and crumble. What often persists is communitas, no longer normative or ideological, but waiting to be given new form by a new religion.

CHAPTER SIX

Apparitions, Messages, and Miracles:
Postindustrial Marian Pilgrimage

MARIAN PILGRIMAGES and images have had a dramatic resurgence in the nineteenth and early twentieth centuries.

In the Middle Ages, Mary as Theotokos, holding or even nursing her Divine Son, received much iconic representation. Marian devotion formed part of a vast system of beliefs and rituals. Early in the nineteenth century, though, the emphasis began to shift to Mary herself, as an autonomous figure who takes initiatives on behalf of mankind, often intervening in the midst of the economic and political crises characteristic of industrialized mass society.

As we have pointed out earlier (see chapter 4), the cultus of the Virgin Mary—and, *a fortiori*, Marian pilgrimage—depended on the doctrine of the communion of saints, expressed in the second clause of the ninth article in the received text of the Apostles' Creed. The Catholic interpretation of this doctrine, as we have seen, posits a spiritual solidarity linking "the faithful on earth, the souls in purgatory, and the saints in heaven in the organic unity of the same mystical body under Christ its head, and in a constant interchange of supernatural offices" (Sollier 1911:171). This view differs radically from the Protestant interpretation of the same clause of the Creed by emphasizing the continuing, active relationship between the living and the dead. True, in 1519 Luther argued that "the communion of saints" (and not the papacy) constituted the Church (*Werke* II, 1884:190). Later writers, however, have taken the phrase to mean an aggregate of persons having a community of faith and ties of Christian sympathy, but in no way organized or interdependent as members of the same visible body. Rejecting the doctrine of purgatory, and asserting that intercession by the saints would detract from Christ's mediatorship, the Protestant view tends to limit the communion of saints to the living and does not look favorably on the possibility of supernatural intervention by deceased saints. For the average Catholic, on the other hand, theological grounds do exist for admitting that possibility. In Catholic teaching, the good dead, but not the damned, may and do (as official reports of numerous devotions attest), communicate with the living, through apparitions, visions, dreams, and the like, and intercede with God to work miracles on behalf of the living. They do not communicate through mediums or diviners, as in animism or modern spiritualism, however, since they are not thought, officially at least, to haunt the fringes of the world of the living, the "middle earth," or to be semimaterial entities. The "good dead" are either saints in heaven or on their way to being saints through the fiery cleansing of purgatory. One's known and named ancestors are not capable of inhabiting shrines or ancestral tablets. For Catholics, prayer by the living to the saints in heaven, to intercede on their behalf with God, is also a mode of communication between members of the Church Militant and the Church Triumphant. Anyone who has lived in a society with a strong ancestral cult, as in tribal Africa, or China before the revolution, will find nothing unusual about this way of thinking. It is easy to comprehend "that corporate circulation of spiritual blessings through members of the same family, that domesticity and saintly citizenship which lie at the core of the Catholic communion of saints" (Sollier 1911:174). There is one important difference: while membership in an ancestral cult is "ascribed"—that is, dependent on ties of real or fictitious kinship (usually, lineal kinship)—membership in the communion of saints is "acquired," or "achieved," by faith, works, and submission to ecclesiastical rule. Nevertheless, the familial, domestic metaphor is highly appropriate to the Catholic concept of the communion of saints, and terms such as father, son, mother, daughter, brother, sister, spouse, are freely applied within that corporate body to created persons both living and dead, as well as to the uncreated Persons, the Father and Son of the Trinity. The Holy Spirit, moreover, personalizes the circulation of communitas through the entire corporate body.

The invisibility and intangibility of the spiritual and supernatural order obviously create problems regarding communication between incarnate and discarnate members of the Church. How does one know, how can one feel sure, that one's prayer has been heard by God or a saint? And how does one know where a preternatural event has originated? These problems always arise when one posits the possibility of interaction between a visible and an invisible domain. If people pray for some benefit or for deliverance from calamity, and the desired consequences ensue, the earlier prayer is readily regarded as cause and the later good fortune as effect. But the "favors," as they are often called, are not sufficient proof that direct supernatural communication or intervention has occurred. There is still plenty of room for a natural explanation. Pilgrimages often begin when a considerable number of people are satisfied that a "sign" of supernatural intervention in human affairs has indeed been given at a particular place in a particular way. The sign must clearly be of a supernatural sort, whether it be an apparition witnessed by several people at once (as at Knock in Ireland or Fátima in Portugal) or a miraculous cure. Catholics have always held that the supernatural is not a theoretically derived conception, but a positive fact, which can be known only as a result of initiatives taken by beings or powers from beyond the sensory "veil." It is manifested through revelation, miracles, prophecies, and apparitions. The Catholic Church considers itself a living body, perpetuated from biblical times on, through postscriptural and postapostolic history; since the generative biblical era was full of revelations and miracles, the possibility remains that similar phenomena may occur today. Indeed, a mark of the true Church is that it is electrically charged, so to speak, with the potential of miracle. Miracles did not cease at the death of the last apostle. The doctrine of the communion of saints posits that Jesus, who became man and had a human soul, his mother Mary, the apostles, and all the saints, whether canonized or not, are still, in some sense and at certain times, quasi-materially "present," and can manifest themselves to men and women like ourselves and mediate in various ways between the spiritual and material orders. The scenes of such manifestations are thought to be gaps in the curtain, tears in the veil, separating the two orders. If, for example, Our Lady appeared in the grotto of Massabielle near Lourdes, the popular assumption is that petitions offered there stand a better chance of being heard and answered than at home. It is not merely that making the long journey of pilgrimage is deemed more worthy than leading a decent life in one's village; more important, the place of revelation continues to "vibrate" with supernatural efficacy. This is not just magical thinking, for it refers to the theological doctrine, ethical in nature, that salvation, or "justification" (the passage from a state of sin to one of sanctifying grace or "justice"), is linked to the communion of saints, the reciprocal action of soul on soul in a corporate circulation of blessings—a view clearly opposed to the Protestant notion of justification through faith alone, which is essentially individualistic. Catholic thought supposes that there is actual merit to be had from interaction with one's "even-Christians," in the mode of good will.

We mention these elementary theological conceptions because they have for centuries been the stock-in-trade of the persons who go on Christian pilgrimages. When these ideas decline or are abolished, the pilgrimages tend to decline also, as they did in the seventeenth and eighteenth centuries in Catholic Europe. If one does not hold the doctrine of the communion of saints in the Catholic sense, one can no longer believe that one's spiritual and material welfare may be promoted in a particular place by the intercession of a saint—no longer thought of as one's brother or sister in a family spanning the ages.

The cults of regional and local pilgrimage saints have been steadily on the decline for almost a century in Europe. This deemphasis of pilgrimage saints may be partly due, as William A. Christian, Jr., has suggested (*Person and God in a Spanish Valley* 1972:48,181–82), to a major change in the relationship between a traditional image of a saint and a specific territory, a sociogeographical region. Saints' shrines mark "critical points in the ecosystem—contact points with other worlds." In the past, they also "marked off boundaries between village and village . . . cultivated and uncultivated land." Some of these shrines, as the result of various circumstances, came to be regarded as holier than others, their saints as more efficacious intercessors than others; in this way regional devotions were born, drawing pilgrims from a wide catchment area containing many parishes. William Christian argues that mobility and the mass media have broken down boundaries, that industrialization has led to the migration of labor and the reallocation of resources in the rural areas; non-Catholic schemes for living have had wide circulation, and the rise in the standard of living has made people loath to undergo such hardships as pilgrimage journeys, while natural means are at hand to procure benefits previously thought to be beyond the power and means of peasants and urban workers. Forces in the Catholic Church itself, such as the Catholic Action movement (which involves the laity in the planning and management of church affairs and in proselytizing) and the major reforms promulgated by the Second Vatican Council, have contributed to bringing localized Catholic communities into regular contact with other worlds, ideas, life-styles.

One result of all this has been to undermine the influence of saints' images as *genii loci*, territorial demideities bound up ceremonially with the seasonal reproductive cycle, through feasts celebrated at critical points in the agricultural year. There are, of course, many exceptions to William Christian's generalization. The major saints—for example, St. James in Spain, St. Patrick in Ireland, and St. Anne in French Canada—whose status as dominant symbols of religious nationalism were firmly fixed earlier, have not suffered so much from the attritional processes accompanying industrialism. The year 1971, in which July 25, the day of St. James, fell on a Sunday, became a holy year for all Spain; more than three million pilgrims passed through the ancient cathedral shrine of Santiago de Compostela that year, and on the patronal feast day, members of

207

the national cabinet participated in daylong activities, centering on the cathedral, to culminate the special holy-year program. As for St. Patrick in Ireland, let us supplement what we have already said about the Purgatory, by citing the *Connaught Telegraph* of August 3, 1972, with reference to the other major Patrician pilgrimage, the hard climb to the summit of the Reek, as the mountain Croagh Patrick is sometimes called, where the saint is believed to have fasted and meditated for forty days before beginning his definitive mission to convert Ireland.

Prayers for peace throughout all Ireland were offered at Masses on the summit of Croagh Patrick on Sunday when about 40,000 people—many in their bare feet—made the annual national pilgrimage. Dry shale, after the recent fine weather, squally showers that fell from dawn, and a slippery descent, made the pilgrimage this year particularly hazardous on the three-and-a-half mile climb of the 2,510 ft. mountain. . . . There were 15 accident victims, and six cases were detained at the Co. Mayo Hospital, Castlebar. All were carried down on stretchers by the Knights of Malta.

May we say, parenthetically, that meteorological hazards are no new thing on Croagh Patrick. The *Chronicon Scotorum* recorded, at the year 1106, that Na Longain, bishop of Ardpatrick, was struck by lightning and killed; and, at 1113, the "Four Masters" note that a thunderbolt fell on the Reek on the eve of St. Patrick's festival and killed thirty of those "engaged on the summit in fasting and prayer" (quoted from D'Alton 1928:321).

But Christian is right about what he calls the "deemphasis" of local saints' shrines, especially minor pilgrimage shrines. This is certainly happening in Mexico, where we have seen the images of village and barrio patron saints frequently consigned to the sacristy, even to the lumber room. The mobility of mass society, with the permanent loss of many young people to the urban areas, undermines the efficacy and coherence of localized norms and value-systems. These factors have not influenced Marian devotion in the same way, however. The nineteenth century and the first half of the twentieth have constituted what has been called, in Catholic circles, the Age of Mary (though the Second Vatican Council, which tended to deemphasize Mariology, possibly for ecumenical reasons, has had the effect of discouraging excessive Marian zeal in very recent years). Some of the most popular Marian pilgrimages originated in this period. All of them began with a vision in which Mary delivered an important message. Unlike the messages characteristic of the medieval "shepherds' cycle" discussed earlier, in which the Virgin instructed the individual visionary to found a shrine to her, the message of the modern visions is a general call to all humankind to repent and be saved. A considerable populist literature, often chiliastic in tone, has developed in connection with apparitional pilgrimages. The Virgin's message is identified with lower-middle-class interests, and both big business and international socialism are condemned as major causes of humankind's sins, the sins we are called upon to repent. Whereas medieval Marian pilgrimages are seldom known to have begun as the immediate consequence of a vision (the foundation narratives have a mythical quality and seem to have arisen long after the pilgrimages were operant), the postindustrial pilgrimages clearly owe their origin to particular visionary or apparitional experiences.

In *The Sun Her Mantle,* an influential study of the postindustrial pilgrimage phenomenon, John Beevers cites (p. 5) two texts as prophetically interconnected and centrally related. The first of these texts is the verse which we have already quoted from the Apocalypse ("And now, in heaven, a great portent appeared; a woman that wore the sun for her mantle, with the moon under her feet, and a crown of stars above her head"). The second is a statement by Pope Pius XII, from his *Evangeli Praecones* (1951): "The human race is today involved in a supreme crisis, which will end in its salvation by Christ, or in its dire destruction." Beevers links the modern appearances of the Virgin (often cloaked in the imagery of the apocalyptic vision with the "supreme crisis" referred to by Pius XII. "From 1830 to 1933, the Blessed Virgin . . . appeared at nine places in Europe: at five in France, one in Ireland, one in Portugal and two in Belgium. At two of these places, she appeared only once. At the others she made several appearances. At all but one, she spoke, sometimes many sentences. . . . On our response to her messages may depend our temporal and eternal future" (Beevers, pp. 9–10). This tendency to regard Mary as a sibyl is often depreciated by

209

theologians, who insist that nothing can be added to the deposit of faith, the body of revealed truths and principles of conduct given by Christ to the apostles, to be preserved by them and their successors. Visions cannot add to, or even embellish, the deposit of faith; if genuine, and not spurious or of diabolic origin, they can only enhance devotion to, and perhaps understanding of, the truths there contained. The Church obviously has a strong interest in strengthening and periodically revivifying faith in its basic doctrines and tenets. As abstractions, these have scant attractive power, except for intellectuals. But if these concepts are associated with a vision in all its social circumstances—for instance, the appearance of the Queen of Heaven to a poor peasant girl—the impoverished masses, the damned of the earth but blessed of heaven, can easily identify with such a figure. Theological abstractions are fleshed out with historical circumstances through a clearly perceived imagery, and eventually through a pilgrimage process involving the faithful in a reenactment of the generating vision. The problem of the Church is to assess whether the circumstances of the vision can form an appropriate symbol-vehicle for doctrines valid for all human generations, everywhere and always. Where there is too great a disparity—bordering, on the grotesque, ridiculous, or improbable—between the alleged vision and the deposit of faith, the Church, working through its corporate scrutinizing mechanisms rejects the vision as not of God, and nips the devotion in the bud. (Nevertheless, some alleged miracles, such as the Host's reputedly turning to blood at Joaseiro in Brazil, have given rise to pilgrimage devotions by popular fiat, despite ecclesiastical censure.)

It is possible that the Catholic Church has been motivated to support (or, at any rate, not to oppose) such visions, because they give emotional expression to doctrines under fire from scientific and rational criticism. Marian doctrines, by patristic and subsequent tradition, hinge on the notion of Mary as the new Eve, redeeming mankind from the original sin of the first Eve. The new Eve entails a first Eve; Mary and Eve are structurally interconnected. Modern evolutionary theories, however, have claimed the prestige of science, in an age of mounting technological achievement, to argue against the notion that a special creative act of God brought humanity's first parents, Adam and Eve, onto the terrestrial scene. Lamarck and Étienne Geoffroy Saint-Hilaire had proposed evolutionary theories before Darwin—Lamarck, in 1809, in fact. The miracle of Lourdes preceded the publication of *The Origin of Species* (1859) by one year, but the evolutionist issues had been raised at least half a century before that. The Church must have recognized that if, in the view of the masses, Mary truly lived, then Adam and the first Eve would have lived, too, and man would be seen as more than just a nodal point on the wavering line of biotic evolution, indeed as the "express image and likeness of God," qualitatively distinct from the animal kingdom. If theological argument could not prevail among the faithful, against the evolutionists, then popular movements, rooted in and stimulated by corporeal visions, and associated with a plethora of miraculous cures, could convince the people that biblical times were not dead, that they continued through the Church. An urgent, though sometimes muted, polemical tone pervades the arguments supporting devotions founded on corporeal visions, a tone deriving from the conflict between expanding, humanist atheism and major religion, the latter magnificently organized and philosophically entrenched, fighting for its life in a cultural equivalent of Darwin's "survival of the fittest"—in a contest between cultural "pseudo-species," to use Erik Erikson's controversial term.

Yet the redoubtable conservative Cardinal Alfredo Ottaviani, regarded as an archfoe by the proponents of Catholic reform, wrote an article in the Vatican newspaper *Osservatore Romano*, in 1951, cautioning Catholics about accepting visions too credulously. "Even the most accredited visions cannot furnish us with new elements of life or doctrine, but only with new motives for fervor. True religion abides essentially, not only in the conscience, but in the love of God and the consequent love of our neighbor." "New motives for fervor" indeed proliferated in Marian visions, miracles, and devotions. Though "feudal and idyllic relations," in the words of the *Communist Manifesto* (1848), were ending, and with them many of the regional and district saints' devotions, a generalized, universal mother, "heart of the heartless world," the Mother of God, was available to the dispossessed, uprooted masses of Catholic Europe;

according to immemorial pilgrimage tradition, she had many times manifested herself to the poor and despised. France of the post-Napoleonic era might well be thought of as a peculiarly appropriate soil for the seeds of Marian devotion. Exhaustion and depression at the failure of the emperor's campaigns; the growth of industrialism and bureaucracy; the emergence of a proletariat, lumpen proletariat, and petite bourgeoisie, in distinctive forms; the overt failure of rationalism and the Goddess of Reason, all provided auspicious conditions for mass receptivity to allegations of the ingress of supernatural power into a flawed natural scene. Collective salvation was longed for, by whatever means, traditional or unconventional.

Foremost among the Marian pilgrimages in France which arose from apparitions occurring in the post-Napoleonic era are (in chronological order, according to the date of their generative apparitions) the following: *La Salette* (on September 19, 1846, two children, Mélanie Mathieu Calvat and Maximin Giraud, had a vision of the Virgin); *Lourdes* (the Virgin appeared to Bernadette Soubirous eighteen times between February 11 and July 16, 1858); *Pontmain*, in Mayenne (on January 17, 1871, the Virgin predicted the speedy end of the Franco-Prussian War)[1]; *Pellevoisin*, in the department of Indre (February 13 to December 8, 1876, the Virgin appeared to a maidservant, Estelle Faguette, and told her, among other things, that she could no longer restrain her son, and that "France will suffer much"—which later commentators have taken to apply to the two world wars).

Beevers cites a fifth major set of Marion apparitions occurring in France in this period; that is, the series of visions experienced by St. Catherine Labouré. Those visions generated the widespread cultus of the Miraculous Medal. Although St. Catherine Labouré's visions occurred between July, 1830, and September, 1831, and therefore antedated the others in our list, we do not include them there, since, unlike the pilgrimage devotions, the cultus of the Miraculous Medal—which has come to be associated with a number of organizations, such as the Archconfraternity of the Holy and Im-

---

[1] R. Laurentin and A. Durand have compiled a collection of 111 documents (selected from more than a thousand) relating to the apparition and sanctuary of Pontmain, entitled *Pontmain: Histoire authentique, documents* (1970).

maculate Heart of Mary, the Association of Children of Mary, and the Legion of Mary, as well as the Association of the Miraculous Medal itself—has no prime locus, but is diffused throughout the Catholic world. Unlike the visionaries of the pilgrimage devotions, moreover, Catherine Labouré was a religious, a Daughter of Charity (like other French visionaries, though, she was of rustic origin and just barely literate). Some medieval pilgrimages (for example, that to Aylesford in Kent, which originated in a vision of the Virgin Mary experienced by a Carmelite prior, St. Simon Stock) owed their beginning to the dream or vision of a religious, but, even in the Middle Ages, the laity, particularly the poor, played a fundamental role in determining where, when, and how pilgrimages would develop. This tendency continued, both in modern Europe and in the colonial areas. We have already noted the role of Indians in the genesis of the Mexican pilgrimage devotions of Guadalupe, Ocotlán, and Los Remedios; there were many more. In other Latin American countries the same trend prevailed. The regular connection between Mary, the laity, the poor, and the colonized, in the rapid development of pilgrimages from visions and apparitions of the corporeal type, and from related miracles, points to the hidden, nonhierarchical domain of the Church, with its stress on the power of the weak, on communitas and liminal phenomena, on the rare and unprecedented, as against the regular, ordained, and normative.

In the post-Tridentine period, the visions (sometimes imaginative or intellectual rather than corporeal) of religious have often given rise to generalized devotions, rather than pilgrimages. The cultus of the Sacred Heart of Jesus (which was revitalized by the Visitation nuns following the revelations of Margaret Mary Alocoque, a member of the order, in the latter part of the seventeenth century) and the early nineteenth-century Miraculous Medal devotion, mentioned earlier, are two important examples. Nearly every parish has a devotion of this kind (or did have, before Vatican II), often formalized in a sodality or fraternity. Such devotions attempt to purify, and render more virtuous, life in a familiar, structured place, rather than to seek initiatory renovation through a journey to a far shrine—one where the Mother of God is believed to have appeared to a humble lay person, short-circuiting all the customary ecclesiastical connections. We have argued that the dominant symbols of the Church are multivocal, deriving their cognitive meaning from generalized, universalized theology and ethics, and their orectic or emotional-volitional charge from their particular, local geography and history. The generalized devotion, sponsored by religious orders and, ultimately, by the secular hierarchy of the structured Church, lays initial stress on the normative pole, though it builds up meaning at the orectic pole through proselytization by the local sodalities. The pilgrimage devotion, generated by particular lay persons in specific localities, strikes a sympathetic chord throughout the Church, not only among members of the same class as the visionary but among those of a higher class as well, since Catholic ideology values the lowly and the weak. Here the ever-present drive to semantic polarization expresses itself in the accretion of normative meaning to the deeply localized symbol-vehicle.

LA SALETTE

About the same time that Catherine Labouré experienced her visions of the Virgin, two children were born in the little town of Corps (then having 1,300 inhabitants), thirty miles south of Grenoble. These were the visionaries of La Salette, today an important pilgrimage center in France.[2] They were a girl, Mélanie Mathieu Calvat (born November 7, 1831), and a boy, Maximin Giraud (born August 7, 1835). Her father worked in a lumberyard and was desperately poor; Maximin's was a wheelwright and a drunkard, whose second wife, Maximin's stepmother, behaved to the child like the wicked prototypes in fairy tales, denying him food and love. Maximin lived by his wits, was illiterate, had no religious education to speak of, and could do little in life but take cattle to pasture. Maximin and Mélanie had known one another for only two days, when, on September 19, 1846, they joined forces to drive two small herds of cows up the mountain pastures to a stream near Corps, about five thousand feet above sea level. After lunching on

[2] Our account of La Salette is based on the admirable summary by Beevers (1953:23–109) of the copious La Salette literature.

rye bread and sour local cheese, the two cowherds fell asleep by the so-called Little Spring for an hour, an unusual circumstance. When they woke, they found that their eight cows were missing. They crossed the stream and eventually found the herd, but they had left their food satchels at the Little Spring. Returning to fetch them, the children saw a dazzling globe of light revolving over the stones surrounding the spring. They crossed themselves and prayed, for fear that they had encountered the devil. Then the globe began to swirl and appeared to boil, growing in size until it was about five feet in diameter. Slowly it opened. Within its shifting splendor of fiery color, Mélanie and Maximin could see the seated figure of a woman, with elbows on knees and face in hands. The children thought of attacking her with their cattle sticks. But the Lady then stood, removed her hands from her face, folded her arms across her breast, and in a low, musical voice told them to advance and hear the news she had to give. Her dress and ornament, as the children later described it, contained many traditional motifs of Christian iconography. On a chain around her neck she wore a crucifix, with a hammer represented on its left arm and a pair of pincers on the right (well known as Instruments of the Passion). She seemed also to wear a crown, from whose base, encircled with roses, sprang shafts of light. Her whole figure seemed transparent, composed of crystalline light, ringed in an almost blinding light, with a softer outer aureole that almost encompassed the children. An important detail, affecting the symbolism and interpretation of the vision ever since (see, for example, Léon Bloy's *Celle Qui Pleure*, 1906), is that the Lady wept throughout the encounter. (It has often been noted that September 19, 1846, was an Ember Day, a special day of penitence in the Catholic calendar, and, before Piux X's reform of the Roman breviary, was also the eve of the Feast of the Seven Sorrows of the Virgin Mary.)

Though Mélanie and Maximin continued for years to elaborate on their first account in many matters of detail, that early account concerned the Lady's warning that, unless the people repented their prevailing religious apathy, she could no longer prevent the "heavy and powerful arm" of her Son from falling on the world. She then predicted that the potato crop would go on rotting until Christmas, that pests would devour the wheat, that the nuts would be grub-ridden, the grapes would rot, and the little children under seven would die of the palsy. Mélanie, who almost always spoke in the local patois, did not understand the term *pommes de terre*, which the Lady had at first used for "potatoes" (the cowherds thought that all *pommes* grew on trees). But when the Lady began to speak of the harvest, she apparently switched into fluent patois and continued in it till the end of her message.

She asked the children if they said their prayers well. When they replied, "Hardly at all," she urged them to say an Our Father and a Hail Mary every night and morning. She then stated that only a few elderly women went to Mass any more, and that if others attended, when they had nothing else to do, they went only to jeer at religion. "And in Lent," she continued, "they go to the butchers as if they were dogs [instead of fasting]."

She then asked the children if they had ever seen spoilt wheat. When they said they had not, she reminded Maximin that a man in the nearby hamlet of Coin had once shown him and his father some ears of wheat that crumbled into dust when they were rubbed on the back of his hands; on the way home, Maximin's father had given him a bit of bread and said, "Here, my child, you can still eat bread this year, but if things go on like this, we don't know who will eat it next year."

"Right you are, Madame," Maximin replied. "I didn't remember it at first, but I do now."

Finally, the Lady said in French, "Well, my children, spread my message among all my people." She then moved past Mélanie, across the stream and up the side of the valley, "as though she hung above the ground and someone were pushing her," Maximin later said. At the top of the slope, she rose into the air, hung there for about half a minute, looked very sadly toward the southeast, in the direction of Italy, then seemed to "melt" into a globe of light like the one in which she had come; and the globe soon faded into "the light of common day."

The message seems simple enough: repent, pray, and attend Mass. But the prophecy of potato and wheat blights and infant deaths excited attention. The usual sequence of events followed the children's return to Corps. Family and friends, and later the parish priest, heard the tale; they were skeptical, at first, then became convinced. Finally, the aged bishop of Grenoble, Philibert de Bruillard, set up two commissions, one of cathedral canons, the other of professors of the Grand Séminaire, to take testimony and gather evidence. They reported to him in mid-December, 1846, that they were quite favorably impressed by the children's testimony, and their "simplicity and unshakable artlessness," but they nevertheless concluded that "there are certain things which arouse some caution about the truth of the Lady's words."

Later, in the summer of 1847, the bishop appointed two members of the faculty of the Grand Séminaire—Canon Rousselot, professor of theology, and Canon Orcel, the superior—to make a thorough investigation of the whole affair. Not only did these men interview the children separately and thoroughly, they also collected evidence from the local peasants that there were many extraordinary cures as a result of either the intercession of Our Lady of La Salette (the name of the mountain from which the Little Spring ran) or the use of water from the spring. The people also alleged that, since the apparition, the spring had flowed there uninterruptedly, though it was formerly dried up for most of the year.

By mid-October the bishop had established another commission of sixteen members, presided over by himself, to consider the canons' report and question the children further, first separately and then together. Twenty cases of healing were considered, and objections to the truth of the story were raised and probed. In the final session, on December 13, 1847, the majority of the commission approved the validity of the apparition. Yet the bishop then thought it "not prudent" to allow his clergy to accompany the faithful on the ever-growing pilgrimages to the mountain. He also authorized Canon Rousselot to publish on the happening at La Salette, reporting on the commission's findings. But four years passed before the bishop, in an episcopal letter of November 16, 1851, informed the six hundred or so churches of the diocese of Grenoble that "the apparition of the Blessed Virgin to two shepherds, on September 19, 1848, on a mountain in the Alps in the parish of La Salette, bears in itself all the marks of truth, and that the faithful are justified in believing without question in its truth." He then authorized the cult of Our Lady of La Salette. He sent a copy of the letter to the Sacred Congregation of Rites at Rome; the prefect of the Congregation, with characteristic caution, spoke of "the praiseworthy thoroughness" of the years of investigation, and declared that "all was in order." Thus the devotion had received both diocesan and provincial approval.

Almost at once, in the secular world, the storm broke. In the post-Voltairian age, all phenomena proclaimed to be of preternatural origin immediately came under sharp critical scrutiny. It was to be expected, therefore, that scientists, skeptics, and freethinkers would question the La Salette apparition and the alleged miracles of healing at the new pilgrimage center. But the most serious opposition to the devotion came from within the Church itself. First, there was the "incident of Ars" in 1850, involving Jean Baptiste Marie Vianney, the celebrated Curé d'Ars, a living legend for his holiness and for his ability to "discern souls" in confession. This nineteenth-century exemplar of Catholic sanctity (he himself became a goal of pilgrimage in his lifetime, attracting more than a hundred thousand pilgrims to the undistinguished village of which he was parish priest, and was finally canonized by the Church in 1925) declared that Maximin, the reputed boy visionary, had told him that "he had not seen the Blessed Virgin." The bishop of Grenoble, then on the point of authorizing the cult, tried to get the curé to modify his statement, but the curé replied:

I had great faith in Our Lady of La Salette: I blessed and distributed many medals and pictures representing the happening; and I gave away fragments of the stone on which the Blessed Virgin sat and always had one of these fragments on me. I even put one in a reliquary. I think, Monseigneur, that few of the priests in your diocese have done as much for La Salette as I have. When the lad told me that he had not seen the Blessed Virgin, I was tired for a couple of days. But after all, Monseigneur, the wound is not so serious, and if La Salette is the work of God it will not be destroyed by men [quoted from Beevers 1953:62].

Men, and churchmen at that, did make a major attempt to destroy the devotion, however. The principal detractors were the Abbé Cartellier, curé of the St. Joseph parish in Grenoble; and the Abbé Déléon, curé of Villeurbanne, a parish quite close to Lyons but in the diocese of Grenoble. No love was lost between Déléon and the elderly bishop, who, at the end of January, 1852, laid an interdict on Déléon, forbidding him to perform his priestly functions, on the ground that his private sex life gave scandal. In August of that year, Déléon published, under the pseudonymn Donnadieu, a book entitled *La Salette—Fallavaux* [La Salette—valley of lies]. At the end of the year, the bishop announced his resignation, since he was very old and ailing. When the pope invited him to name his successor, he chose the Abbé Ginoulhiac, then vicar-general of Aix. Déléon now produced a sequel: *La Salette—Fallavaux, Part II*. When the new bishop was installed in May, 1853, he tried to make peace in the diocese by offering to remove the interdict on Déléon, provided that the maverick priest would turn out the women he was living with, withdraw his books on La Salette, and write a personal letter of apology to the retired bishop. Déléon accepted these conditions, and the ban was removed. Nevertheless, it was not long before he returned to his onslaught on La Salette with a new book, *La Salette devant le Pape* (1854), backing up Cartellier. Déléon alleged, among other matters, that the new bishop of Grenoble had been offered the see on the sole condition that he support his predecessor's position on La Salette. (This allegation was strongly denied by both bishops, and by other high ecclesiastics, including a cardinal archbishop.) Déléon's main accusation, however, was that the Lady seen by the children was, in reality, a certain Mlle Constance de La Merlière, a wealthy and charitable middle-aged woman who lived at St. Marcellin, between Valence and Grenoble. According to Déléon, she had set off by coach, in September, 1846, on a pilgrimage to the shrine of Notre-Dame du Laus in the department of Hautes-Alpes,[3] and had carried with her, in a hatbox, just such gar-

---

[3] The shrine of Notre-Dame du Laus was founded on the site where, according to *The Catholic Encyclopedia* (1909: s.v. "Gap, Diocese of"), the Blessed Virgin appeared "an incalculable number of times," over a period of fifty-four years (1664–1718), to a shepherdess, the venerable Benoîte Rencurel. Interestingly, the pilgrimage is a late instance of the "shepherds' cycle" type, rather than a forerunner of the modern "visionary" pilgrimage. Gillette (1949:161–68), drawing on the shrine's literature and Spencer Northcote's *Celebrated Sanctuaries of the Madonna* (1868), notes that Benoîte

ments as the children had seen on the Lady of their vision. Déléon claimed that Mlle de La Merlière had left the coach clad in these garments, met the children, started to speak to them in French, and changed to the local patois when she saw that they did not understand her. After their conversation, she had seen a low cloud approach, walked toward it, and then hurried away under its cover. Later, some sisters at the convent of Le Laus had allegedly seen her dressed in the same attire. There had been no apparition, Déléon charged; rather, a harmless hoax by an eccentric and pious woman had escalated into a major new Marian cultus. Déléon's narrative was most circumstantial, full of names and dates. Unfortunately, inquiry disclosed that the abbé himself had resorted to fraud! Witnesses came forward to testify that on September 19, 1846, Mlle de La Merlière was at St. Marcellin, seventy-five miles from La Salette. And many other details in Déléon's account did not tally with documented facts: for example, he had stated that Mlle de La Merlière's coachman was named Fortin; but the owner of the coach service between Valence and Grenoble declared that Fortin did not enter his service until 1849, three years after he was said to have driven Mlle de La Merlière to Le Laus. This lady, moreover, was short and fat, neither luminous nor transparent, like the Lady in the alleged vision.

These arguments and counterarguments give a notion of the rhetoric and polemical style of mid-nineteenth-century controversies over apparitions and miracles and their role in the inception of pilgrimage devotions. It is tempting to analyze the Salette controversy, from the point of view of political anthropology, as a "social drama" or an "extended case history" (see V. Turner 1974: ch. 1). Historians have unearthed enough salient data to make this possible. Evidently, factions existed among the clergy of the Grenoble diocese, and they mobilized external support from higher officials

---

spoke not only with the Virgin but also with St. Maurice, who showed her a healing spring; and that she once saw the Lady with a child. Though her conversations took place in the mountain pastures, she was told to instruct the people to rebuild and enlarge a ruined wayside chapel in the hamlet of Le Laus. Pilgrims each fetched a stone from a nearby quarry to do this. Despite initial opposition from the Embrun diocesan chapter, the pilgrimage throve. Oil from the lamp on the Virgin's shrine allegedly cures the sick.

of the Church. As so often happens, however, people "voted with their feet," quite literally, whatever the clergy said or did, and the pilgrimage established itself, with the usual array of "cures" and spiritual and material "favors," and the rapid creation of pilgrim ways and facilities.

In 1851, before the detractors Cartellier and Déléon published their books, Pope Pius IX had officially declared that the faithful might accept the veracity of the apparition at La Salette. He took this step after having received letters in which Mélanie and Maximin recorded the "secrets" of La Salette—words the Lady had allegedly spoken to each individually, without the other's having heard what was said. The pope had promised the children not to reveal the details, for they had made a similar promise to the Lady. Later, he told the superior of the Missionaries of Our Lady of La Salette, an order founded at the shrine: "So you want to know the secrets of La Salette? Well, here they are: unless you repent, you will all perish."

What is interesting about La Salette is that it seemed to set the apocalyptic tone for the latter-day Marian pilgrimages. The notion of a "secret" communication is found again in the Fátima and Garabandal cultuses. The overt message contains a call to repentance— and sometimes a threat, if the people do not respond. The threat is either of local calamities (such as the potato and wheat blights foretold at La Salette) or of a widespread disaster. At Pellevoisin, for example, in the archdiocese of Bourges, the Virgin is said to have appeared to the housemaid Estelle Faguette, and told her sadly: "As for France, what have I not done for her? She still refuses to pay heed. Very well, I can no longer restrain my Son. France will suffer much" (Banron 1938; Gillett 1949: 288–39). The theme of penance is prominent, too, in the message Our Lady of Lourdes gave to Bernadette, and in that of Fátima, where three children, cousins aged ten, nine, and seven, were shown a vision of Hell, after which the Virgin told them: "You have just seen Hell, wherein are cast the souls of poor sinners. To save them, the Lord wishes to establish in the world devotion to my Immaculate Heart. If people do as I tell you, many souls will be saved, and there will be peace. The War [First World War] will end. But if people do not stop offending the

Lord, another worse than this will start during the next pontificate."

As we noted earlier, a considerable populist literature has developed from apocalyptic Marianism. Seldom dealt with by theologians or intellectuals, this literature is highly influential among segments of the Catholic laity all over the world. The "messages" of La Salette, Pontmain, Beauraing, and other places of pilgrimage recognized by the Vatican are not the worst with regard to prophecies and admonitions. The messages accompanying the alleged visions at Garabandal in Spain, the grotto of Ulzio in Italy (near the French border), Palmar de Troya in Spain (near Seville), and many other places in France, Portugal, Venezuela, and elsewhere, are colorful and violent to an extreme, accompanied by quite ferocious denunciations of the Aggiornamento and other recent developments in the Catholic Church. These "messages," particularly marked since the Second World War, are reminiscent of the doomsday writings of Jehovah's Witnesses and other millenarian movements; they are published and discussed weekly in such periodicals and reviews as *Michael* (formerly *Vers Demain*) in Rougement, Quebec, Canada, and *Maria Messajera* in Spain (Zaragoza).

These frenetic outpourings are totally different in quality from the Marian message of Lourdes. Though it also stressed penance, the Virgin's message at Lourdes had a simple, down-to-earth tone, like that of the Virgin of Guadalupe. But a fundamental difference derives from the nature of the visionaries. Neither Maximin Giraud nor Mélanie Calvat was a prepossessing individual—though, from the theological viewpoint this need not be a stumbling-block, given the truths uttered by Balaam's ass! The spirit moveth where it listeth, whatever the quality of its vessel or instrument. Many who knew Maximin shared the opinion of Abbé Félix Dupanloup, who questioned the boy in 1848 (when Maximin was thirteen years old): "I have seen many children during my life, but I have seen few, if indeed any, who have made such an unpleasing impression on me. . . . The way he fidgets is really extraordinary. His character is peculiar. It has a kind of uncouth flippancy, a violent instability and something insufferably queer about it . . . . I had the greatest difficulty in preventing very serious suspicions from mastering

222

me." Of Mélanie, the abbé said: "The girl seemed just as unpleasant in her own way. But she gives a better impression than the boy. According to what people say, the eighteen months she has spent with the nuns at Corps have improved her a little. Nevertheless, she seemed to me peevish and sulky, and silent because of her stupidity" (quoted from Beevers 1953:50–51).

Dupanloup, who later became famous as bishop of Orléans, eventually joined the camp of those who believed that precisely because the children were so displeasing their testimony had to be taken seriously—that is, because their description of the Lady and her words differed so sharply from their habitual outlook, they could not have invented it. The adult careers of Mélanie and Maximin were not particularly edifying either. When it seemed likely that La Salette was going to attain international prominence as a pilgrimage center, the visionaries were taken in charge by the Church authorities, and received some support from the bishop of Grenoble and, later, from the pope. They were given a rather severe education at the convent of Corps, under the eagle eye of the Sisters of Providence. There they learned to read and write fluently in French, a skill which Mélanie was to put to embarrassing use. Maximin rebelled against convent restrictions more than once: his trip to the Curé d'Ars, for example, was made without permission. After a longish career as a drifter, he did a six-month spell as a papal guard. But, being fond of more than a glass or two of wine, he became involved with a wine merchant and "hustler," who persuaded him to join in selling, at high prices, an herb-flavored liqueur called Salettine, with his name on the label. When people were scandalized at this attempt to cash in on his holy vision, he replied: "I only did it to earn my living by the sweat of my brow" (Beevers 1953:97). Unfortunately, he was duped by his partner, who soon disappeared, leaving Maximin with a heap of debts—a tribute to his naiveté if not his innocence. On his deathbed, in 1875, Maximin called on God to be his judge that he had never lied about the apparition of La Salette, and he took several sips of water from the "miraculous spring" in order to swallow the Host during his last communion.

Mélanie provides an even more striking and hardly less interesting contrast to Bernadette Soubirous, as we shall see. Though both were shepherdesses, speaking the local patois, and both entered religious orders after making known that they had seen a vision of, and received a message from, a beautiful lady who appeared and disappeared in a miraculous fashion, the resemblance there ends. After making a series of attempts to be admitted to religious orders, Mélanie was finally permitted to take the Carmelite habit in a convent at Darlington in England. Before that, it appears, her head was turned by the adulation the people accorded her. She had become the center of a cult at Corenc, just outside Grenoble, where she had gone as a postulant after leaving the convent school at Corps. She used to tell tales of her life as a cowherd to a throng of admiring postulants and novices. One tale related how she had led packs and herds of wild animals through the woods in religious processions, chanting God's praises, the cross being carried by a wolf. The bishop of Grenoble visited the convent, rebuked her for her conceits and fantasies, and refused to let her make her profession as a nun. She then had a wild three weeks in the convent of the Daughters of Charity at Vienne, where she "refused to eat for nearly forty-eight hours, screaming until a crowd gathered outside the convent, and [she] tried to bite the Reverend Mother" (Beevers 1953:84–85). She obviously disrelished the style of the Sisters, who "before anything," according to their Rule, "strive for uniformity with the other Sisters and conceal everything which is in any way singular and peculiar to themselves." I will not detail the complex events which finally led to her profession as an English Carmelite, but this was only the beginning of Mélanie's career as a sibyl and prophetess. As an English Carmelite, she no longer considered herself under the canonical jurisdiction of the bishop of Grenoble, and she delivered herself of a stream of apocalyptic writings. The earliest of these, in the form of letters to the curé of her old parish, Corps, set the tone for later Catholic apocalyptic literature far more emphatically than the children's original account of the message of Our Lady of La Salette. Her utterances now became definitely anticlerical. She alleges that the Virgin told her: "Today and every day I am crucified by those who know Me [sic], by many priests. They imagine they see, but it is not by my light, but by the light of the devil. Formerly, priests and nuns were the pillars of my Church, but today the pillars have fallen. Calamities are going to rain upon the world and then cries and groans will rise up to Me, but for a time I shall be as if dead" (Beevers 1953:87).

Mélanie later became homesick for France. She did not stay with any religious order for very long. For a time she was with the Sisters of Our Lady of Compassion at Marseilles. From 1867 to 1884, she lived quietly in Castellammare in Italy with her friend Sister Marie, teaching French for board and lodging, and receiving occasional sums of money from the then thriving Missionaries of Our Lady of Salette. But she had a book brewing, and in 1879 she brought out *L'Apparition de la très sainte Vierge sur la montagne de la Salette*, bearing the imprimatur of Monseigneur Zola, bishop of Lecce (in southern Italy). In this book, Mélanie professed to deliver the full text of the "secret" given her by the Virgin. It was full of apocalyptic material. She claimed that the Blessed Virgin had commanded her to found a new order, the Order of the Mother of God; both men and women were to belong to it, and would be known as the "Apostles of the Last Days" (Beevers 1953:92). She further declared that in six or seven years, St. Michael, the warrior archangel, would succeed the archangel Gabriel in the government of the world. Mélanie did not initiate this genre, which derives from well-known biblical prototypes (particularly the Books of Daniel and Revelation) and the powerful millenarian tradition of the Middle Ages, but she gave it a strong impetus among the struggling lower-middle-class Catholics of southern Europe and the New World, people of almost pathological respectability, crushed between big business and the organized working class. Her end was sad. Beevers, who believes in the authenticity of Mélanie's and Maximin's first vision, writes (pp. 94–95):

There is almost unbearable pathos in the picture of the ageing woman, clothed in black, with a heavy, almost sullen face, wandering about France and Italy, her mind filled with bloody images of universal carnage, of falling mountains, gulfs of fire, and the evil splendour of anti-Christ and his legions riding in triumph across the world. Her life was almost without friends and one darkened by the conviction that spies and enemies surrounded her; materially it was one of penury and spiritually, one shot through with delusions. Old and defeated she returned to die (December 15, 1904) in the southern Italy she loved, to the hot little town of Altamura, decaying in the sun, far from the cool mountain meadow where, nearly sixty years before, her fresh young eyes had been dazzled by the radiant glory of the Mother of God.[4]

LOURDES

Of the visionaries whose revelations have generated pilgrimages and have been approved by the Church, only a few have been canonized.[5] Bernadette Soubirous is possibly the best known of these; her visions stand at the beginning of more than a century of pilgrimage to the grotto of Massabielle. Since Bernadette's visions and their religious, social, and symbolic consequences have been widely dealt with in the modern media, we shall be brief,[6] merely pointing up some decisive contrasts between La Salette and Lourdes, and between Mélanie and Bernadette. At Lourdes, she whom Bernadette called the Lady spoke only eleven times in the course of eighteen apparitions (between February 11 and July 16, 1858). All of her statements were single sentences; several were requests to Bernadette to undertake some simple action before a crowd, as for instance: "Go drink at the spring and wash yourself in it"; "Go eat that plant which you will find there"; "Go kiss the ground as penance for sinners." Such penitential exercises and personal humiliations are often regarded in the Judeo-Christian tradition as tests of faith and marks of saintly election. Bernadette was hard put to it to find the "spring" that the Lady had mentioned. She had to dig in the muddy sand of the grotto to open up the spring, and thus started the celebrated source of the miraculous "Lourdes water,"

---

[4] However, Mélanie still has her clerical defenders. As recently as 1973, Hyacinthe Guilhot published *La vraie Mélanie de La Salette*, citing (p. 17) R. P. André Triclot that Mélanie "certainly practised the virtues perfectly" and especially lived the "eighth beatitude: that of the persecuted—probably the most difficult."

[5] Benoîte Rencurel, for example, of Le Laus fame, was only declared venerable by Pope Pius IX in 1871.

[6] There is an immense literature on Lourdes, both polemical and devotional. One of the fullest accounts of the apparitions and subsequent events is J. B. Estrade, *Les apparitions de Lourdes* (1899).

which later developed into a flow of 32,000 gallons a day. Some of the water is piped into baths housed in a separate building where the pilgrims bathe; and many cures are attributed to its efficacy. Bernadette's washing and drinking provided the model for subsequent pilgrim behavior.

Other messages from Our Lady of Lourdes called for universal penance. Bernadette, like other Marian visionaries before her (Juan Diego, for example, who spoke with the Virgin of Guadalupe), was commanded "to tell the priests to have a chapel built here," for the Lady wished people "to come here in procession"—which they have done, of course, to the number of many millions. In her final message, theological in character, the Lady declared: "I am the Immaculate Conception." The date was only three years after Pius IX had proclaimed the dogma of the Immaculate Conception, the dogma that Mary was, in the first instant of her conception, preserved from the stain of original sin; that she was, in theological language, conceived immaculate. For the masses, the apparition seemed to confirm the dogma, by giving it a concrete embodiment, although, according to Catholic thought, this was not needed, since the proclamation by the pope *ex cathedra* is believed to be "perfect in its own order." Many critics of Pius IX's actions have hinted that these apparitions of the Immaculate Conception, which pointedly upheld his dogma, came at a suspiciously convenient moment. For the pope had it in mind, some time in the future, to proclaim another dogma, that of papal infallibility. The apparitions of Lourdes seemed to prove his case. Whatever the cause, Bernadette did announce the Lady's declaration on March 25, the Feast of the Annunciation, one of the three most ancient Marian feasts of the universal church.

The events and symbols connected with the Lourdes apparitions, whether influenced by clerical prompting or not, have a highly orthodox flavor, as contrasted with the heterodox, apocalyptic messages to Mélanie. Lourdes is not divinatory. The apparitions of Lourdes simply reinforce traditional doctrines; they add nothing to the "deposit of faith," though amateur Catholic exegesis delights in finding portents in apparitions, as we have seen. Some clerical exegetes have found a symmetry in the events comparable to that in a

Lévi-Straussian analysis of myth—perhaps it is to be expected that a French Mary would work in a French fashion! For example, one commentator, Joseph Deery (1958:41–42), finds "a harmonious arrangement in the eighteen apparitions." In the first and second, as in the seventeenth and eighteenth, no words were spoken; "a silent establishment of contact was balanced by a silent breaking-off of contact." In the third apparition, the Lady spoke her first words; in the sixteenth, or third-last, her final words. In between were twelve apparitions (distributed equally over two weeks), manifesting her wishes: prayer (February 19–23); penance (the general demand, on February 24, was followed by specific instructions for exercises of penance, February 25–March 1); a chapel and pilgrimages, whereby her desire for prayer and penance might be fully realized (March 2–4). Thus we have three silent, twelve spoken, and three more silent apparitional communications, the numerical factors being the sacred numbers three (representing the Trinity) and four (the four Evangelists, the four Last Things—Death, Judgment, Heaven, and Hell—and the like). Deery also notes that the messages concerning prayer and penance were conveyed, appropriately, in the Lenten season. Further, Thursday was an important day in the series: "It was on a Thursday that Our Lady first revealed herself, that she requested Bernadette to return for a fortnight, that the miraculous spring was discovered in the course of the ninth apparition, that the fortnight ended, and that proclamation of her name was made" (p. 42). Deery points out that Thursday, the day of the Last Supper, has been traditionally designated by the Church for honoring the sacrament of the Eucharist, and states that Lourdes has become the world's greatest center of devotion to the Eucharist. Many of the miracles at Lourdes are reported to have occurred during the short service called the Benediction of the Blessed Sacrament, in which a bishop or priest blesses the long line of the sick, most of them in wheelchairs, by making the sign of the cross above them with the consecrated Host displayed in a monstrance.

The orthodox character of the Lourdes apparitions and their interpretation, as contrasted with Mélanie's fearful message, was matched by the paradigmatic sanctity, in Catholic terms, of Bernadette herself. Not that she was docile and serene, but she had a charism of goodness, a singular human warmth, in no way denying her earthy peasant frankness, or even occasional roughness of tongue.

Once Bernadette was taken to a dress shop and was asked to describe the kind of dress material the Lady of her vision wore. The dressmaker showed her a fine piece of Lyonnaise silk. Bernadette replied: "Nothing like it."

"But, Mam'selle, this is the whitest and silkiest fabric in the city."

"That only shows," retorted Bernadette, "that the Blessed Virgin did not have her dress made by you!" (Gillett 1949:204).

Bernadette did not enter St. Gildas, the motherhouse of the Sisters of Charity and Christian Instruction of Nevers, until six years had passed after her final vision. There, despite intense homesickness and serious illness, she remained until her death, on April 16, 1879, in her thirty-sixth year, the twelfth year of her religious profession. There are numerous stories of her phlegmatic, indeed heroic, endurance of suffering. She did not lose her sense of humor—another quality distinguishing her from Mélanie. Two years before her death, when she was suffering from a severe tubercular condition in her right knee, she said to another nun: "Pray for me when I am dead, because people will say, that 'little saint' doesn't need prayers, and I shall be left grilling in Purgatory."

Like Mélanie, Bernadette was entrusted with a secret; but, unlike Mélanie, she never divulged it, not even to the pope. Bernadette was asked by the bishop's commission: "Would you tell your secrets to the pope?"

She replied: "The Blessed Virgin told me to tell no one. The pope is someone."

"Yes. But the pope has the authority of Jesus Christ."

"The pope has authority on earth," answered Bernadette. "The Blessed Virgin is in heaven." She refused to discuss the matter further and never raised it again herself.

The quality of her life as well as her visions led eventually to Bernadette's canonization on December 8, 1933, the Feast of the Nativity of the Blessed Virgin Mary. Lourdes, unlike La Salette, has become an authentic, international devotion within the Catholic

Church. Immense crowds take part in the rituals of the grotto and in the processions at the sanctuary. They speak all the languages of Europe, and many of Asia and Africa. The number of pilgrims continues to climb steadily. In 1950, nearly 1,600,000 persons visited the shrine. In 1958, the centenary of the apparitions, more than 5,000,000 came. In 1970, there were 3,100,000. In 1972, the year of our visit, 3,500,000 attended. The literature produced at the shrine is without apocalyptic overtones. *Lourdes: Journal de la Grotte,* the weekly paper, confines itself, quite unpretentiously, to information about different parties of pilgrims (gypsies, Australians from Melbourne, Limburg Hollanders, Barcelonans, to take a random count from two issues); historical articles on the shrine; an occasional sermon; and practical information about the shrine, the town of Lourdes, and the surrounding districts.

In Lourdes there is a sense of living communitas, whether in the great singing processions by torchlight or in the agreeable little cafés of the back streets, where tourists and pilgrims gaily sip their wine and coffee. Something of Bernadette has tinctured the entire social milieu—a cheerful simplicity, a great depth of communion.

CHAPTER SEVEN

Conclusions

❧❦❧

OUR STUDY of the Marian pilgrimage type and of selected Catholic pilgrimages in Western Europe and the New World suggests some tentative conclusions. We have seen, for example, that pilgrimage should be regarded not merely as an ideal model but as an institution with a history. Each pilgrimage, of any length, is vulnerable to the history of its period and must come to terms with shifts of political geography. Pilgrimage is more responsive to social change and popular moods than liturgical ritual, fixed by rubric.

Pilgrimage systems are more "liminoid" (open, optational, not conceptualized as religious routine) than "liminal" (belonging to the mid-stage in a religious processual structure consisting of rites of separation, limen or margin, and reaggregation—as discussed by Arnold van Gennep). Liminal phenomena are embodied in the collaborative "work" of a tribal or early agrarian society's annual ecological and social structural round, and are obligatory for all. Liminoid phenomena, though present in the simpler societies, prevail in societies of greater scale and complexity, and tend to be generated by the voluntary activity of individuals during their free time. The universal religions, addressed to the salvation of individuals, with a stress on individual choice, establish favorable conditions for the development of liminoid phenomena and processes in the total culture. Liminal features persist, however, in the liturgical structures of the universal religions, and, indeed, in many secular institutions. But the developing, secular leisure domain becomes crowded with liminoid genres such as the fine arts, the folk arts, and critiques of social structure, as well as apologies for it. The voluntaristic character of pilgrimage in the formative centuries of the historical religions places it within the liminoid camp, but the "archaic" category (for example, Ocotlán, Le Puy, St. Patrick's Purgatory) bears clear traces of an antecedent liminality.

More important, when a religious system becomes tightly structured and organized, and closely articulated with nonreligious structures, political, legal, and economic, its pilgrimages tend to revert from the liminoid to the liminal or "pseudo-liminal"; that is, they "regress" from voluntaristic processes to become pseudo-tribal initiatory institutions, stressing relics, ritualistic acts, and the "miraculous" properties of wells, trees, places where saints stood or rested, and other concrete objects associated with holy individuals. In our view, this is what happened with Catholic pilgrimage in the High Middle Ages.

The earliest Catholic pilgrimages, to Jerusalem and Rome, were liminoid; that is, they were made voluntarily, by truly devout pilgrims—for example, St. Sylvia or Aetheria of Aquitaine, Holy Paula, St. Willibald, St. Adamnan, and St. David of Wales. The desire to go on pilgrimage is itself a charism, a special gift of faith. As Christianity developed, pilgrimages became integrated with the total system. In the High Middle Ages, especially when the Church became strongly structured, pilgrimage was incorporated into its penitential system, and was even prescribed as a punishment for secular crimes. Institutionalization, even in the mode of rational bureaucratization, paradoxically reverts to tribalization. The corporations of complex societies replicate morphological features of tribal corporate groups: initiation into such corporations, as well as movement to higher grades within them, is comparable to a tribal rite of passage. But Catholic pilgrimage in the High Middle Ages became an extension, as it were, of the sacrament of penance, an institutionalized means of keeping everyone's moral state under ecclesiastical control.

Specific historical factors expedited pilgrimage structuration. When Islam closed off the Holy Places of Palestine to almost all Christian pilgrims, and occupied the North African coast and much of Spain, the Mediterranean, says Jacques Pirenne, ceased to be *mare nostrum*, our (Roman) sea; and the center of gravity of Christendom shifted to France, Germany, and northern Europe. Charlemagne's western empire, forced from the Mediterranean into continental Europe, became polarized against Islam, which for a time virtually controlled the southern Mediterranean. In the struggle, parallel developments occurred in the two great opposed systems. It was roughly in Charlemagne's time that Santiago de Compostela in Galicia began its career as a pilgrimage shrine, and it has been called, both by Christian and by Muslim medieval commentators, "the Christian Mecca." The pilgrimage complex of the Holy Land, made up of sites traditionally connected with the life, teaching, and death of Jesus, was in effect transferred piecemeal to Europe in the form of shrines dedicated to different aspects of Jesus and Mary and often reputed to be of miraculous or apparitional origin. The result was pilgrimage polycentrism, in a multilingual Europe. In other words, many shrines were founded, in many linguistic and cultural regions, as though to compensate for the lost compact shrine cluster in Palestine, where Jesus' life and death had been mapped on a limited cultural space. This multiplication of shrines in Europe in time became subject to great abuses—competition among shrines for pilgrims and relics, the multiplication of relics to the point of absurdity, the growth of an indifferent attitude toward holy doctrines, and so forth.

Polycentrism had an important, but much neglected, impact on future economic and political, as well as religious, developments. A multitude of pilgrim routes converge on a great shrine, each route lined with sacred way stations (chapels, abbeys, shrines, etc.) and such service institutions as hospices, hospitals, inns, markets, and taverns. The major shrines exert a magnetic effect on the whole communications and transportation system, charging with sacredness many of its features, and fostering the construction of sacred and secular edifices to serve the needs of the human stream passing through it. Pilgrimage centers in fact generate a socioeconomic "field"; they have a kind of social "entelechy." It may be that they have played at least as important a role in the growth of cities, marketing systems, and roads, as "pure" economic and political factors have. Otto von Simson (*The Gothic Cathedral*, pp. 6–7) argues this case persuasively: "The religious impulse was so all-pervading an element of medieval life that even the entire economic structure depended upon it. Almost static otherwise, the economy received from religious customs and experiences the impulse it needed for its growth." Simson cites the growth of Chartres, Canterbury, Toledo, and Compostela, all pilgrimage centers, to support his view. If the Protestant ethic—with its stress on diligence, thrift, virtue, and fair-dealing in one's secular vocation, and its belief that one's place in the world is a God-given sign of faith or election—was, indeed, as Max Weber thought, a precondition (a necessary if not sufficient cause) of capitalism, then the "pilgrimage ethic," with its emphasis on "holy travel" and the benefits flowing from such travel, may very well have helped to create the communications networks that later made mercantile and industrial capitalism a viable national and international system. At the very least, Jusserand's point, that pilgrimage was the main type of mobility in the locally fixated feudal system of landholding and production, is well taken. It may not be too fanciful even to see medieval pilgrimage as a prototype, under different socioeconomic conditions, of more egalitarian, voluntaristic, contractual types of secular social relationships, as a ludic and liminoid preenactment of significant later modalities in the work domain.

MARIAN PILGRIMAGE AND ICONICITY

Marian pilgrimages, in particular, throw into high relief the problems involved in iconicity, the material representation of religious ideas. Iconic symbols, though stylized in varying degree, clearly link signifier and signified in some way: the signifier may be a metaphor for the signified; may be an attempt to portray the meaning literally, as in a picture of the Assumption for example, or there may be other connections, sometimes metonymic, of association or genealogy, between them. Each type of iconic symbol exemplifies Thomas Aquinas' dictum that men "apprehend intelligibles through sensibles."

This raises the question of iconophily versus iconophobia (the sentiment of which iconoclasm is the behavioral expression) and aniconism (indifference to icons). Beyond all other types of Christian representation, Marian icons excite the greatest devotion from iconophiles, and the greatest hostility and hate from iconophobes. Doubtless Freud would have had a word for this divided state. Indeed, the violent dichotomy between these two classes of believers seems to illustrate, on a societal scale, the schizoid mentality distinguishing—in Melanie Klein's analysis—between "the good breast," which gives nurturance, and "the bad breast," which does not come when the infant needs it.

In tribal and simple agrarian societies, iconicity and iconoclasm coexist in many rituals (notably those of initiations) as different phases or moments of a single ritual process. The Bemba of Zambia, for example, make large, elaborate clay figures which are revealed and explained to the novice during female puberty rites; the figures are totally destroyed the following day, despite the patient work put into them. Examples could be multiplied: Navajo sand paintings, elaborately colored designs full of cosmological meaning, are created for use in curative and other ceremonies, and then are swiftly destroyed; the same is true of the skillfully designed symbolic earth moldings in the circumcision rites for boys of the Yao tribes in southern Malawi. The guiding notion here seems to be that the cosmos can be seen and ritually represented as plural and complex; it is also very simple and deep, nondualistic perhaps, and always exceeds any representation of it. Its secret powers are, moreover, invisible. By destroying the elaborate signifiers made to represent the plural nature of things, one indicates "there is that of which we cannot speak," a pure nonduality.

In the development of the great historical religions, iconophily has become attached to certain theological positions, iconoclasm to others. They are no longer moments in a single process, but antithetical, consciously defended stances, sometimes indeed the fun-

235

damental postulates of great opposed institutions. Marianism has become almost the epitome of iconicity, even iconophily, in Christian ritual practice, while contra-Marianism is the most extreme form of iconoclasm. This issue is perhaps the one which most deeply divides Catholics from Protestants. One underlying cause may be the pervasive evaluation of woman, in the Western tradition, as the dominant symbol of the sensorily perceptible. Woman is seen not merely as *a* vehicle, or *a* vessel, but as vehiclehood, vesseldom. From this structural perspective, she is the essence of *signifying*, while man, or maleness, is the essence of the *signified*. The eternal feminine is the orectic *signifiant;* the eternal masculine is the cognitive and normative *signifié*. Woman is form, man is meaning. This is sexism indeed. Christian churches and sects that reject icons and other signifiers may be asserting the male principle, the spermatic Logos, the "Spirit that giveth life," the principle of individuation, and so on, at the expense of the female principle of a visible Church, a communion of saints (of which Mary is the most perfect representative and representation), and of all collective vehicles and vessels. Puritanic critiques of the flesh (as in Milton's epic) may have a similar basis. In the High Middle Ages, Marian representations portrayed mother and son in balance and unity. Then followed several centuries of iconoclasm. In the recent period, new Marian pilgrimage shrines have been founded, associated with visions indicating a tension between mother and son: the mother holds back the son's punishing arm, and yet she upbraids mankind for forgetting religious faith, and promises disasters on earth and hell in eternity if there is not widespread repentance. The recent trend may be one index of a resurgent "female" principle, after centuries of "male" iconoclasm, technical progress, bureaucratization, the conquest by reason and force of all natural vehicles. May we not trace, in the history of Marian pilgrimage, woman's progress from almost anonymous and faceless nurturant vehiclehood to an individuated, liberated femaleness, seen through the "masculine" eyes of Western culture as both nemesis and the coming of a new age?

One might say that by eliminating the icons most indicative of Christianity's lapse into pseudotribal liminality, iconoclasm cleared the way for a modern era characterized by the multiplication of liminoid genres—especially the arts and literature. The new postindustrial pilgrimages, as well as the revived and modernized traditional pilgrimages, are all liminoid. They are, in their way, critiques (or metasocial commentaries, as Clifford Geertz might say), in the true liminoid style, of the main social processes of our time. As such, they resonate with the present-day counterculture, whose communes recall the pilgrimages of earlier iconoclasts like the Pilgrim Fathers, the Mormons, and the African Wapostori, who journeyed away from "unholy" places to dwell permanently in a holy place of their own making.

It may be, too, that iconophily fled, during the Renaissance, to the secular domains of art and literature, where its first glories held more than a memory of its sacred origins. Certainly in England, only a few decades after the venerable Marian images of Walsingham and Ipswich had been burnt by Thomas Cromwell, the great Elizabethan dramatists were dedicating their richly symbolic, metaphorical verse plays to Gloriana or Oriana, the Virgin Queen on earth. The migration of signifiers from the sacred to the humanistic spheres lies beyond the scope of this book. But in our own time we see, once more, a tendency to *re*sacralize symbols by way of depth psychology, consciousness-raising techniques, and liturgiological experiments. Here, too, the study of pilgrimage symbols has its part to play, as does the study of pilgrimage *as* a symbol. Pilgrimage has long stood for voluntaristic mobility in a rooted system. In a destabilized system, life has become one long pilgrimage, without map or sacred goal.

PILGRIMAGE STRATIFICATION

S. H. Bhardwaj made a most significant contribution to "comparative peregrinology" when he advanced the view that pilgrimages can be arranged in strata, each involving its own type of religiosity, style of veneration, symbolic emphases, and appeal to certain groups of individuals. In his *Hindu Places of Pilgrimage in India* (1973), drawing on data obtained (through questionnaires) from 5,454 pilgrims at twelve sacred places in Himachal Pradesh and the

Himalayan districts of Uttar Pradesh, he suggests (p. 146) that Hindu pilgrimage sites may be viewed as "a system of nodes at different levels": (1) Pan-Hindu, (2) supraregional, (3) regional, (4a) subregional (high), (4b) subregional (low), and (5) local. "The nodes at the highest levels can throw light on those aspects of Hinduism which integrate the Hindu population of diverse cultural regions of India. The nodes at lowest levels may point out the immense diversity within Hinduism and the local basis of integration." To simplify Bhardwaj's rich data and complex argument rather drastically: Pilgrims to high-level shrines exhibit a "merit pattern" of religiosity and are the least likely to seek material benefits. Often the sites are distant shrines at which "an event of supreme religious significance may be happening," and the pilgrims tend to be persons of high caste and "relative affluence" (p. 169). Pilgrims to low-level (usually nearby) shrines generally seek "the place of a specific deity, at a climactic religious occasion, and with a tangible purpose" (p. 171). Such pilgrims often belong to either the cultivating castes or the untouchables (p. 172).

At the highest level the religiously oriented elite, by making pilgrimages to famous shrines eulogized in the traditional Sanskritic literature, maintains the vitality of a pan-Indian Hindu holy space. . . . At the lower levels of religious circulation both the materialistic elements of Hinduism and its regional or subregional folk elements find expression. The gods and goddesses no longer remain philosophical abstractions; instead man begins to "use" them as instruments for tangible purposes. It is also within the framework of this religious circulation that elements of the "little tradition" may become parts of the "great tradition"—a local goddess may be transformed to Durga, or a local male deity may eventually become Siva [Bhardwaj, pp. 173–74].

In *Dramas, Fields, and Metaphors* (V. Turner 1974a), the chapter entitled "Pilgrimages as Social Processes"[1] suggests (p. 209) that pilgrimage centers can be arranged in order of importance, in relation to the size of their catchment areas; that is, the areas from which they draw their pilgrims. Pilgrimages are regarded as strat-

---

[1] A paper first presented at the Department of Anthropology, Washington University, St. Louis, in February, 1971, under the title, "The Center Out There: Pilgrims' Goal," later published in the journal *History of Religions* (1973).

ified, as in the system of Bhardwaj. Christian pilgrimages are stratified into four major levels: (1) international (for example, Jerusalem,
Rome, Lourdes, Guadalupe in Mexico); (2) national (for example,
San Juan de los Lagos in Mexico, St. Anne de Beaupré in Canada,
Our Lady of Czestochowa in Poland, Our Lady of Knock in Ireland,
Our Lady of the Pillar in Spain); (3) regional (for example, Our Lady
of Ocotlán for Tlaxcala state in Mexico; and (4) intervillage (for example, the "valley shrines" described by William Christian
1972:61–78). Though these strata are roughly comparable to the
levels observed by Bhardwaj in India, some major differences may
be noted in the patterns of worship at the various levels. Christian
pilgrims seem to frequent the high-level (national and international) shrines quite as much for "favors" (including miraculous
cures) as for purely devotional reasons corresponding to Bhardwaj's
"merit pattern." In contrast, the deepest personal piety may be
expressed in private devotions at a domestic shrine dedicated to
one of the many aspects of Jesus or Mary. Another feature distinguishing the Christian pilgrimage system from the Hindu is the
pervasiveness of the supreme maternal prototype, the Virgin Mary.
She is venerated at every shrine level and in generalized devotional
cults, whereas Hindu mother deities tend to be worshiped primarily at the local level (Bhardwaj 1973:92). These differences may
perhaps be correlated with the caste principle in Hindu ritual as
against the dogma of the Incarnation in Christianity. Mary as Theotokos was the means by which the divine Logos, the Second Person
of the Trinity, was "given flesh," in an Incarnation intended for the
salvation of all men equally and simultaneously. It is not here a
matter of gradual karmic ascent from lower to higher in successive
incarnations, through the performance of caste duties. Part of one's
caste duty would be to honor the local deity traditionally associated
with one's caste. Members of higher castes tend to frequent the
upper-level shrines of the major deities, particularly Shiva and
Vishnu (Bhardwaj 1973:93).

Nevertheless, broad similarities of social structure may be de-
tected in the two major pilgrimage systems. Local-level pilgrimage
shrines in both Hinduism and Christianity fall at the "liminal" end
of the spectrum; high-level shrines at the more "liminoid" end—

even though, as we noted earlier, the penitential system of the medieval Church came more to "reliminalize" many major pilgrimages.

Perhaps the most fruitful way of viewing the matter is to postulate that pilgrimage shrines become stratified fairly soon in the history of a major salvation religion. The problem then becomes one of discovering which of the levels is paramount at a given time and place, and why—rather than of postulating a succession of ideal pilgrimage "types," each of which monopolizes an "age." As we have seen, the Catholic Church has often been perfectly conscious of this phenomenon, and has sought to maintain the various levels in some sort of balanced relationship by distributing honors—such as papal coronation of devotional images, designation of the shrine as a minor basilica, beatification or canonization of a local visionary—among pilgrimage shrines in degrees commensurate with their current popularity, political importance, and doctrinal significance. It will probably be impossible ever to discover the details of the decision-making processes involved here—unless the Vatican sessions of the Congregation of Rites were to disclose their minutes!

It is clear, however, that major societal change often affects the preponderance of shrines at a given level. The Industrial Revolution has led to depopulation of the countryside, mass migration to the rapidly growing cities, communal labor in factories, and an ever-finer division of labor; to the growth of trade unions, managerial associations, and political parties based on socioeconomic class; to mass transportation and communication; to the segregation of an individual's roles as parent, citizen, breadwinner, householder, political participant, religious group member, sportsman, and so on (each role being played, for the most part, with a different set of people); to a sharp cleavage between work and leisure; to increased literacy and a host of other consequences. One result has been an erosion of village and intervillage corporateness. Although one may still find, as we have in Mexico and Ireland, local parishes arrayed behind their religious banners in processions at low-level pilgrimage centers, the most characteristic modern pilgrimage is blended with tourism, and involves a major journey, usually by modern means of transportation, to a national or international shrine.

CONCLUSIONS

Both for individuals and for groups, some form of deliberate travel to a far place intimately associated with the deepest, most cherished, axiomatic values of the traveler seems to be a "cultural universal." If it is not religiously sanctioned, counseled, or encouraged, it will take other forms. In the United States, for example, the bicentennial year 1976, celebrating the birth of the United States, was a sort of secular jubilee, with millions of travelers visiting the scenes of military and legislative triumphs and tragedies in the liberation struggle against British rule. And every year, millions visit national parks and forests (the precincts of "Old Faithful" in Yellowstone Park irresistibly recall the cultural landscape of a major religious shrine), mostly, no doubt, for recreational reasons, but partly to renew love of land and country, as expressed by "secular psalms" like "America the Beautiful."

The pilgrimage impulse may take an overtly political form, as in the visit made by millions of Russians annually to Lenin's tomb in the Kremlin. It may be present even among those Protestant denominations regarding it with least favor. We have in mind the revivalist camp meetings of rural America: instead of a pilgrimage by the faithful to a distant holy place, a holy person or preacher comes to a familiar place, where it is not a visual symbol, an image, that is efficacious for salvation or healing, but an auditory symbol, the word of Holy Writ. Significantly, however, the meetings are held not in the midst of a town or village but in a campsite in the countryside, a little apart from a number of villages or homesteads. In *Dramas, Fields, and Metaphors*, we have already noted that the holiest pilgrimage shrines in several major religions tend to be located on the periphery of cities, towns, or other well-demarcated territorial units. Peripherality here represents liminality and communitas, as against sociocultural structure. Catholic and Protestant faithful alike seek retreat from quotidian preoccupations and sins by making a pilgrimage movement of some kind, a step *per agros*, "through the fields," to the shrine or preacher bringing them renewal of faith and heart.

APPENDIX A

Notes on Processual Symbolic Analysis

THE TERM *processual symbolic analysis* has been employed by Charles Keyes (1976) to describe the mode of analysis followed by Victor Turner and others dealing with symbols and ritual. It refers to the interpretation of symbols operating as dynamic systems of signifiers (the outward forms), their meanings, and changing modes of signification, in the context of temporal sociocultural processes (V. Turner 1975c:149). The focus of study is meaningful performance, rather than underlying competence; thus the definitions assigned to certain terms here are not quite the same as those assigned in the study of the structure of cognition. This disparity particularly affects the terms "sign" and "symbol," defined below (see also Keyes 1976:1).

Ritual. Formal behavior prescribed for occasions not given over to technological routine that have reference to beliefs in mystical beings or powers (V. Turner 1967a:19). The unity of a given ritual is a dramatic unity. Observation of the rubrics of the ritual is deemed essential, for only by staying within the channels, marked out by custom, through which the collective action should flow (*ritus*

243

derives from an Indo-European Base, RI, meaning "flow"), will the peace and harmony typically promised to ritual participants finally be achieved (V. Turner 1968a:269).

Ritual is a "transformative performance revealing major classifications, categories, and contradictions of cultural processes" (Grimes 1976:16). "It is not a bastion of social conservatism whose symbols merely condense cherished cultural values. Rather it holds the generating source of culture and structure" (see below). "Hence, ritual is by definition associated with social transitions, while ceremony is linked with social states" (ibid., p. 24). Performances of ritual are distinct phases in the social process, whereby groups adjust to internal changes and adapt to their external environment (V. Turner 1967a:20).

Ritual System. In the simpler preindustrial societies a ritual system is the articulated, institutionalized complex of ritual actions, objects, events, words, and the like, employed under circumstances specified for communication with the invisible powers regarded as the origin and purpose of all effects, particularly of prosperity or adversity.

Ritual systems in posttribal industrial societies, from an anthropological point of view, may be defined to include not only the enactment of all the rites contained in the liturgical books of a given universal religion but also the rites transmitted, often by oral means, in paraliturgical folk traditions.

Since ritual is itself an orchestration of many different kinds of performance and is expressed in terms of all the five senses, we may suppose that underlying any ritual system there is not merely a single syntax and vocabulary but several "generative grammars." How these "grammars" produce articulated "surface structures" (the actual observable rites) is a function of the relationship between the "grammatical" rules and the contemporary sociocultural situation. Ritual genius consists in the deftness with which officiants relate the interconnected grammars and vocabularies to the immediate circumstances of the worshiping community.

Ritual symbol. The smallest unit of ritual behavior, whether associated with an object, activity, relationship, word, gesture, or spatial arrangement in a ritual situation (V. Turner 1967a:19). It is a factor influencing social action, associated with collective ends and means, whether explicitly formulated or not (V. Turner 1968a:269).

A *symbol* is distinguished from a *sign* by both the multiplicity of its meanings and the nature of its signification. In symbols there is some kind of likeness (either metaphoric or metonymic) between the thing signified and its meaning; signs need bear no such likeness (V. Turner 1975c:150–51). Signs are almost always organized in "closed" systems; while symbols, particularly dominant symbols, are themselves semantically "open." The symbol's meaning is not absolutely fixed. New meanings may be added by collective fiat to old symbol vehicles. Moreover, individuals may add personal meaning to a symbol's public meaning, either by utilizing one or another of its standardized modes of association, to bring new concepts within its semantic orbit, or by including it in a complex of purely private fantasies. Initially private "construction" of this kind may become part of public hermeneutic or standardized interpretation if the exegete has sufficient power, authority, or prestige to make his view stick (ibid., p. 154).

Signans (also called the *signifier*). The sensorily perceptible vehicle or outward form which carries a meaning.

Signatum (also called the *signified, designatum, significatum, signifié*). The meaning, sense, designation, denotation, or connotation associated with a signans in a given culture or religion.

Dominant symbol (also called *core, key, master, focal, pivotal,* or *central symbol*; ibid., p. 152). Dominant symbols appear in many different ritual contexts, sometimes presiding over the whole procedure, sometimes over particular phases. Their meaning is highly constant and consistent throughout the total symbolic system. (A good example is the image of the Virgin of Guadalupe.) They possess considerable autonomy with regard to the aims of the rituals in which they appear. Precisely because of these properties, dominant symbols are readily analyzable in a cultural frame of reference. They may be regarded as "eternal objects," objects not actually of infinite duration but to which the category of time is not applicable. They are the relatively fixed points in both the social and the cultural structure (see below), and indeed constitute points of junction between these two kinds of structure (V. Turner 1967a:31–32). Each dominant symbol may be said to represent a crystallization of the flow pattern of the rituals over which it presides (V. Turner 1968a:80).

Instrumental symbols. Their use depends on the ostensible purpose of a particular ritual. These symbols must be interpreted in terms of their wider context; that is, in terms of the total system of symbols in a given ritual (V. Turner 1967a:32). Examples are candles and the act of kneeling.

Meanings of dominant symbols. In any given instance of a symbol's use, there are at least three orders of reference: (1) the *manifest* meaning, of which the subject is fully conscious, and which is related to the explicit aims of the ritual; (2) the *latent* meaning, of which the subject is only marginally, but may later become fully, aware, and which is related to other ritual and pragmatic contexts of social action; and (3) the *hidden* meaning, of which the subject is completely unconscious, and which is related to infantile (and possibly prenatal) experiences shared with most other human beings (V. Turner 1968a:81).

PROPERTIES OF DOMINANT SYMBOLS

1. *Multivocality, polysemy, or condensation* (see Edward Sapir 1935:492–93). A single dominant symbol may stand for many things, and allows for the economic representation of key aspects of a whole system of culture and belief. Each dominant symbol has a fan, or spectrum, of referents, which are interlinked by a simple mode of association; the very simplicity of the outward form of a dominant symbol enables it to interconnect a wide variety of signata. Different meanings may become paramount at different times (V. Turner 1967a:50–52).

2. *Unification of disparate signata.* The disparate signata of a dominant symbol are interconnected by virtue of their analogous qualities or by association in fact or thought (ibid., pp. 28–29). Of course, "analogy" and "association" are themselves culture-specific.

3. *Polarization of meaning.* Dominant symbols possess two clearly distinguishable poles of meaning. At the *ideological pole,* is found a cluster of signata referring to components of the moral and social orders, to principles of social organization, to kinds of corporate grouping, and to the norms and values inherent in structured relationships. At the *sensory* (or *orectic*) *pole,* the signata are usually natural and physiological phenomena and processes. Here meaning is closely related to the outward form of the symbol. At the sensory pole are concentrated those signata that may be expected to arouse desires and feelings; they are gross, in that they take no account of detail or of the precise qualities of emotion, for dominant symbols have broad social meanings. Sensory signata are also gross in that they are frankly, even flagrantly, physiological, and thus have links with the unconscious. They represent items of universal experience (ibid.).

The unity of these two poles in one symbolic object gives the dominant symbol its transforming power. For it brings the ethical, jural norms of society into close contact with strong emotional stimuli. During a ritual performance, with its social excitement and its direct physiological stimuli, a dominant symbol effects an interchange of qualities between its poles of meaning. Norms and values become saturated with emotion, while gross and basic emotions become ennobled through contact with social values (ibid., p. 30). The symbols are felt to possess ritual efficacy; that is, they are believed to be charged with power from unknown sources, and to be capable of acting on persons and groups in such a way as to change them for the better (ibid., p. 54).

Interpretation of meaning in a symbol. Interpretation is possible at three levels of meaning:

1. *Exegetic meaning* is supplied by indigenous interpretation, given by those inside the ritual system. At the exegetic level, the symbol has four categories of meaning, from the sensory (orectic) pole, which constitute points of departure for analogy and association: (a) Nominal—the name of the symbol, which may be heavily charged with meaning; (b) Substantial—the physical and biological characteristics of the symbol; (c) Artifactual—the symbol as a product of human fashioning or an object of culture (V. Turner

1968a:82–83); (d) Historical—the origins and subsequent history, often dramatic or moving, of the symbol.

2. *Operational meaning* is derived from the use made of the symbol, the social composition of the groups performing the ritual, the affective quality of the ritual, and so on.

3. *Positional meaning* is the relationship of the symbol to other symbols in the total ritual system, for in any given ritual only a few of the meanings of a polysemous symbol may be stressed (V. Turner 1967a:50–51). The latent, and, to a certain extent, hidden meanings of a dominant symbol in one context may be discovered by using exegetic reports on the significance of the same symbol in different ritual contexts. (In a given ritual, certain meanings of a dominant symbol may be manifest, while others are latent.) This method may be used where the juxtaposition of certain symbols defies indigenous explanation (V. Turner 1968a:81).

Root paradigm. A higher-order concept than symbols, root paradigms are certain consciously recognized (though not consciously grasped) cultural models for behavior that exist in the heads of the main actors in a social drama, whether in a small group or on the stage of history (V. Turner 1974a:64). (A prime example of a root paradigm is the Way of the Cross.) They represent the goals of man as a species, where they prevail over particular interests—the general good over the individual welfare. They are, as it were, the cultural transliterations of genetic codes; that is, they represent the species life raised to the more complex and symbolic organizational level of culture, and are concerned with fundamental assumptions underlying the human societal bond, with preconditions of communitas (ibid., pp. 67–68).

Root paradigms are shown in behavior which appears to be freely chosen but resolves at length into a total pattern. They go beyond the cognitive, and even the moral, to the existential domain, and in so doing become clothed with allusiveness, implicitness, and metaphor. They reach down to the irreducible life stances of individuals, passing beneath conscious prehension to a fiduciary hold on what the individual senses to be axiomatic values, matters literally of life and death. Root paradigms emerge at life crises, whether of groups or individuals, whether institutionalized or compelled by un-foreseen events. One cannot escape their presence or their conse-quences (ibid., p. 64). In cultures deeply influenced by Christian beliefs and practices, for example, the *via crucis*–Resurrection para-digm seems to have affected the behavior of a number of major his-torical figures (ibid., pp. 60–155).

THE PROCESSUAL
FORM OF RITUAL

Rite of passage. An important category of ritual, which Arnold van Gennep first isolated and named (1908), rites of passage are the transitional rituals accompanying changes of place, state, social po-sition, and age in a culture. They have a basically tripartite proces-sual structure, consisting of three phases: separation, margin or limen, and reaggregation. The first phase detaches the ritual sub-jects from their old places in society; the last installs them, inwardly transformed and outwardly changed, in a new place in society.

Liminality (from Lat. *limen*, a threshold.) The state and process of mid-transition in a rite of passage. During the liminal period, the characteristics of the *liminars* (the ritual subjects in this phase) are ambiguous, for they pass through a cultural realm that has few or none of the attributes of the past or coming state. Liminars are be-twixt and between. The liminal state has frequently been likened to death; to being in the womb; to invisibility, darkness, bisexuality, and the wilderness (V. Turner 1969:94–96). Liminars are stripped of status and authority, removed from a social structure maintained and sanctioned by power and force, and leveled to a homogeneous social state through discipline and ordeal. Their secular power-lessness may be compensated for by a sacred power, however—the power of the weak, derived on the one hand from the resurgence of nature when structural power is removed, and on the other from the reception of sacred knowledge. Much of what has been bound by social structure is liberated, notably the sense of comradeship and communion, or communitas; while much of what has been dispersed over the many domains of culture and social structure is now bound, or cathected, in the complex semantic systems of pivotal, multivocal symbols and myths, numinous systems which achieve great conjunctive power (V. Turner 1974a:259). In this no-place and no-time that resists classification, the major classifications and categories of culture emerge within the integuments of myth, symbol, and ritual (ibid.). The category of liminality is useful in understanding such cultural phenomena as subjugated autochthons, small nations, holy mendicants, good Samaritans, millenarian movements, "dharma bums," matrilaterality in patrilineal systems, patrilaterality in matrilineal systems, monastic orders, and many more (V. Turner 1969:125).

Transience (also expressed as "nomadism," "movement"). Arch-metaphor for that which lies outside structure or between structures, or is a dissolvent of structure. Transience is exemplified by the liminal religious man who has renounced world and home, moving from village to village—the pilgrim, or the hero of the "quest" tales, who goes on a long journey to seek his identity outside structure (V. Turner 1974a:182,285).

Communitas, or social antistructure. A relational quality of full unmediated communication, even communion, between definite and determinate identities, which arises spontaneously in all kinds of groups, situations, and circumstances (V. Turner 1978). It is a liminal phenomenon which combines the qualities of lowliness, sacredness, homogeneity, and comradeship. The distinction between structure and communitas is not the same as that between secular and sacred; communitas is an essential and generic human bond (V. Turner 1969:96,97).

The bonds of communitas are undifferentiated, egalitarian, direct, extant, nonrational, existential, I-Thou (in Buber's sense). Communitas is spontaneous, immediate, concrete, not abstract. It is part of the "serious life." It does not merge identities; it liberates them from conformity to general norms, though this is necessarily a transient condition if society is to continue to operate in an orderly fashion (V. Turner 1974a:274). It is the *fons et origo* of all structures and at the same time their critique. As Jean-Paul Sartre said (1969:57), structures are created by activity which has no structure but suffers its results as structure. Communitas strains toward universalism and openness, it is a spring of pure possibility. It may be regarded by the guardians of structure as dangerous and may be hedged around with taboos, and associated with ideas of purity and pollution (V. Turner 1974a:202). For it is richly charged with affects, mainly pleasurable. It has something magical about it. Those who experience communitas have a feeling of endless power (V. Turner 1969:139).

Communitas is a fact of everyone's experience, yet it has almost never been regarded as a reputable or coherent object of study by social scientists. It is, however, central to religion, literature, drama, and art, and its traces may be found deeply engraven in law, ethics, kinship, and even economics (V. Turner 1974a:231). In the works of prophets and artists we may catch glimpses of the unused evolutionary potential of communitas, a potential not yet externalized and fixed in structure (V. Turner 1969:128).

Location of communitas in society. Communitas breaks into society through the interstices of structure, in liminality (as discussed above); at the edges of structure, in marginality; and from beneath structure, in inferiority. Liminality, marginality, and inferiority frequently generate myths, symbols, rituals, philosophical systems, and works of art (V. Turner 1969:128).

Marginality. A category whose individuals (marginals) often look to their group of origin, the so-called inferior group (see below), for communitas; and to the more prestigious group in which they mainly live, for their structural position. They may become critics of the structure from the perspective of communitas; many writers, artists, and philosophers are marginals (V. Turner 1974a:233).

Inferiority. A value-bearing category that refers to the powers of the weak, countervailing against structural power, fostering continuity, creating the sentiment of the wholeness of the total community, positing the model of an undifferentiated whole whose units are total human beings. The powers of the weak are often assigned in hierarchic and stratified societies to females, the poor, autochthons, and outcasts (ibid., pp. 152, 234).

APPENDIX A

TYPES OF COMMUNITAS

1. Spontaneous, existential communitas: "the wind which bloweth where it listeth," which defies deliberate cognitive and volitional construction. At the pole opposite to spontaneous communitas is social structure (V. Turner 1978).

2. Normative communitas: the attempt to capture and preserve spontaneous communitas in a system of ethical precepts and legal rules.

3. Ideological communitas: the formulation of remembered attributes of the communitas experience in the form of a utopian blueprint for the reform of society (1969:132).

Social structure. The patterned arrangements of role sets, status sets, and status sequences consciously recognized and regularly operative in a given society and closely bound up with legal and political norms and sanctions (V. Turner 1974a:20). The term "structure" is here used in the sense of the British school of anthropology. Lévi-Strauss and his disciples apply the term to cognitive, not social, phenomena.

Relationship between communitas and structure. Communitas and structure are indisseverably related in sociocultural processes. Some of their salient attributes may be contrasted as follows: communitas/structure; transition/state; totality/partiality; homogeneity/heterogeneity; equality/inequality; absence of property/property; absence of rank/distinctions of rank; simplicity/complexity; anonymity/systems of nomenclature; acceptance of pain and suffering/avoidance of pain and suffering. Emphasis on one provokes its contrary into cultural prominence. Mediation may follow, as new institutions are invented to reconcile these contrary processes and ideas (V. Turner 1969:106–7).

There may be a continuous cycle of communitas/structure/communitas, etc. For example, religious vision becomes sect, then church, then a prop for a dominant political system, until communitas resurges once more from the liminal spaces (V. Turner 1974a:293). These processes can coexist and modify one another continuously over time in the same ritual field (ibid., p. 282).

252

Ritual of role reversal. In hierarchical societies communitas is symbolically affirmed by periodic rituals in which the lowly and the mighty reverse social roles (ibid., p. 53).

Iconophiles, iconoclasts. Image lovers, image breakers. Iconophiles stress signans over signatum in relating them; iconoclasts regard signans as unnecessary, even obstructive. Iconophilic religions often develop complex and elaborate systems of ritual; symbols tend to be preeminently visual, and exegesis is bound up with the ritual round. Iconoclastic religions are associated with radical reform, and seek to purify "underlying meaning" by erasing the symbol vehicles, the iconic symbols, which appear to them to be "idols" interposed between individual believers and the truths enunciated by religious founders, truths which are no longer valued for themselves, but merely as the signata of iconic vehicles (V. Turner 1975c:155).

Liminoid, or *quasi-liminal.* Terms describing the many genres found in modern industrial leisure that have features resembling those of liminality. These genres are akin to the ritually liminal, but not identical with it. They often represent the dismembering of the liminal, for various components that are joined in liminal situations split off to pursue separate destinies as specialized genres—for example, theater, ballet, film, the novel, poetry, music, and art, both popular and classical in every case, and pilgrimage. These genres develop most characteristically outside the central economic and political processes, along their margins, on their interfaces, in their tacit dimensions. They are plural, fragmentary (from the point of view of the total inventory of liminoid thoughts, words, and deeds), experimental, idiosyncratic, quirky, subversive, utopian, and characteristically produced and consumed by identifiable individuals, in contrast to liminal phenomena (see V. Turner 1976), which are often anonymous or divine in origin.

Pilgrimage as a liminoid phenomenon. Pilgrimage has some of the liminal phase attributes in passage rites: release from mundane structure; homogenization of status; simplicity of dress and behavior; communitas, both on the journey, and as a characteristic of the goal, which is itself a source of communitas, healing, and renewal;

ordeal; reflection on the meaning of religious and cultural core-values; ritualized reenactment of correspondences between a religious paradigm and shared human experiences; movement from a mundane center to a sacred periphery which suddenly, transiently, becomes central for the individual, an *axis mundi* of his faith; movement in general (as against stasis), symbolizing the uncapturability and temporal transience of communitas; individuality posed against the institutionalized milieu; and so forth. But since it is voluntary, not an obligatory social mechanism to mark the transition from one state or status to another within the mundane sphere, pilgrimage is liminoid rather than liminal (see above, pp. 34–35). Insofar as it is a rite of passage, an initiation, it succeeds the major initiation rites of puberty in tribal societies as the dominant historical form. It is, indeed, the ordered antistructure of patrimonial feudal systems (V. Turner 1974a:182).

Flow (M. Csikszentmihalyi's term, 1975a, 1975b). The merging of action and awareness, the crucial component of enjoyment. Flow is the holistic sensation present when we act with total involvement, a state in which action follows action according to an internal logic, with no apparent need for conscious intervention on our part. Flow is experienced in play and sport, in artistic performance and religious ritual. There is no dualism in flow. While an actor may be aware of what he is doing, he cannot be aware that he is aware, or the flow will be interrupted. Flow is made possible by a centering of attention on a limited stimulus field, by means of bracketing, framing, and often a set of rules. There is a loss of ego, the self becomes irrelevant. Flow is an inner state so enjoyable that people sometimes forsake a comfortable life for its sake (Csikszentmihalyi 1975b:11–38).

Symbols of flow and communitas. In flow and communitas, what is sought is unity, not the unity which represents a sum of fractions and is susceptible of division and subtraction, but an indivisible unity, "white," "pure," "primary," "seamless." This unity is expressed in such symbols as the basic generative and nurturant fluids semen and milk; and as running water, dawn, light, and whiteness. Homogeneity is sought, instead of heterogeneity. The members of the religious community are to be regarded, at least in rite and symbol, as a simple unit, not as a sum of segments or the ultimate product of some mode of division of labor. They are impregnated by unity, as it were, and purified from divisiveness and plurality. The impure and sinful is the sundered, the divided. The pure is the integer, the indivisible (V. Turner 1968b:517–18).

APPENDIX B

Chronology of Lough Derg Pilgrimage

c. 310	Death of St. Catherine of Alexandria.
c. 432	St. Patrick came to Ireland.
c. 445	According to tradition, St. Patrick founded the Purgatory.
c. 463	Death of St. Patrick.
c. 510	Pilgrimage of St. M'Nisse, the first recorded pilgrimage to Lough Derg.
c. 523	Death of St. Brigid.
c. 578	Death of St. Brendan, age 94.
c. 597	Death of St. Columcille.
c. 610	St. Dabheoc, patron of Lough Derg, flourished.
c. 635	St. Molaise (known also as St. Laserian), patron of Leighlin and Kildare, prepared Ireland for the Roman observance.
664	Synod of Whitby determined that the British Church would follow Roman centralization rather than Celtic decentralization.
c. 836	Plundered by the Danes.

1050	Pilgrimage of Harold, later king of England.
1130	Augustinian canons regular take charge of the holy places of Lough Derg.
1153	Pilgrimage of the Knight Owen, whose account spread the fame of Lough Derg on the Continent.
1169	Norman invasion of Ireland.
1353	Pilgrimage of George Chrissaphani, a Hungarian.
c. 1370	St. Patrick's Purgatory mentioned by Catherine of Siena in her letter to a monk who was refused permission to make the pilgrimage.
1397	Pilgrimage of Perrilleux, chamberlain of king of France.
1399	Murder of Raymond, Italian noble, at Lough Derg by Ugolino, his sister's lover. Raymond was doing penance for his own previous murder of his sister. According to legend, Raymond's ghost haunted Lough Derg.
1411	Pilgrimage of Mannini, a Florentine, and Rathold de Pasztho, a Hungarian noble.
1455	Dispute between Maguire, prior of Lough Derg, and Trianor, abbot of Armagh, over control of Lough Derg. Rome settled for Maguire.
1494	Dutch monk visited St. Patrick's Purgatory and made an unfavorable report to Rome.
1497	Pope Alexander VI closed the cave at Lough Derg as a result of the Dutch monk's report.
1503	Pope Pius III reopened the pilgrimage at the request of the archbishop of Armagh. Indulgences were granted.
1517	Visit of papal nuncio, who reported that for the past 400 years the names of all pilgrims had been recorded in a book.
1539	Dissolution of all monasteries under British crown.
1545	Beginning of the Council of Trent.
1546	First Protestant bishop of Clogher is appointed under Henry VIII.

1625   "Pilgrims so numerous, many had to return without making the pilgrimage rounds."

1631   Archbishop of Armagh assigned Lough Derg to the Franciscans.

1632   Structures destroyed by government order, under direction of the Protestant bishop of Clogher, but pilgrims came as usual.

1638   Henrietta Maria, queen of Charles I, petitioned Lord Deputy Wentworth to reopen the pilgrimage.

1649   Favorable report to Rome by papal nuncio.

1649–1650 Cromwell's campaign prepared the way for extensive Protestant settlement in Ulster.

1680   Again demolished by the government. Estate surrounding Station Island conveyed to Charles Leslie, a Protestant landowner, lord of Leslie Castle in Monaghan.

1689   "Patriot Parliament" followed by Williamite War. Defeat of James Stuart at Boyne.

1691–1778 Penal era: Catholics excluded from Parliament and legal profession; denied schools, and religious and civil rights.

1693   Excavation to discover ancient cave by Lodoricus Phynus, a Frenchman.

1700   Annual number of pilgrims about 5,000.

1704   Queen Anne forbids the pilgrimage.

1730   Pilgrimage of O'Carolan, "last of the bards."

1780   Penitential cave closed for the last time; St. Patrick's Church built by Father Truagh, first prior from the diocesan clergy.

1800–1824 Annual number of pilgrims averages 10,000.

1824   On one occasion, pilgrims in the "prison chapel" numbered 1,100.

1829   Catholic Emancipation Act.

1834   Pilgrims numbered 19,000 that year.

1844   Annual number of pilgrims averaged 15,000.

258

1845	Great Famine began.
1846	Highest recorded number of pilgrims: 30,000 for the year; 1,300 in one day.
1846–1870	Decline of pilgrimage, owing to the famine.
1870	Plenary indulgence granted by the pope.
1879	Visit by two archbishops and two bishops.
1880	New hospice was begun (now the men's hospice).
1882	Marble statue of the Virgin was erected.
1891	Statues of SS. Patrick and Joseph were erected.
1912	Ladies' hospice completed. Typhoid outbreak.
1913	Visit of Cardinal Logue.
1914–1918	World War I.
1916	Easter Rebellion.
1916	Pilgrims numbered 10,584, the largest annual total since the famine years.
1917	Sir John Leslie withdrew his claim to proprietary rights over Station Island, which reverted to church ownership.
1918	Pilgrims numbered 12,420.
1919	Pilgrims numbered 14,287.
1919 1922	Ireland's struggle for independence.
1929	Depression.
1931	New Church of St. Patrick consecrated as basilica by cardinal, papal nuncio, and eight bishops.
1933	Annual number of pilgrims averaged 15,000.
1939–1945	Second World War.
1949	Ireland became a republic.
1960	All of Lough Derg and its islands were ceded to the bishop of Clogher by Shane Leslie.
1962–1965	Vatican II.
1968	Start of conflict in Northern Ireland.
1971	Annual number of pilgrims, from June 1 to August 15, estimated at 15,000 per year.

Bibliography

Adam, R. 1934. *Histoire de son pèlerinage*. Sedan, France: Balan.

Albareda, D. Anselmo M. 1946. *Historia de Montserrat*. Montserrat, Spain.

Albe, E. (1861–?). 1966. "Notes et documents sur Roc-Amadour," *Revue Religieuse de Cahors*.

—— 1923. *Notre-Dame de Roc-Amadour*. Paris: Loto-uzey.

Alcedo, Antonio de (1736–1812). *Diccionario geográfico de las Indias Occidentales o America*. Reprinted 1967. Madrid: Atlas.

Almond, Richard. 1974. *The Healing Community: Dynamics of the Therapeutic Milieu*. Stanford, Stanford University Press.

Apocrypha Syriaca: The Protevangelium Jacobi and Transitus Mariae, with texts from the Septuagint, the Corân, the Peshitta, and from a Syriac Hymn in a Syro-Arabic palimpsest of the Fifth and Other Centuries. Manuscript no. 2241:14. 1902. Ed. and tr. Agnes Smith Lewis. London: C. J. Clay and Sons.

Aradi, Zsolt. 1954. *Shrines to Our Lady around the World*. New York: Farrar, Straus, and Young.

Arroyo, Hector. 1971. "Naucalpan y su santuario de los Remedios." *Tierra de Emmedio: Revista del Seminario Diocesano de Tlalnepantla*, 10, January and February.

Attwater, Donald, ed. 1958. *A Catholic Dictionary*. 3d ed. New York: Macmillan.

Babcock, Barbara, ed. 1978. *The Reversible World*. Ithaca, N.Y.: Cornell University Press.

Banron, P. 1938. *Notice sur Notre-Dame de Pellevoisin*. Lyons, France: St. Eucher.

Barth, Fredrik. 1975. *Ritual and Knowledge among the Baktaman of New Guinea*. New Haven: Yale University Press.

Bede, the Venerable. A.D. 700(?). *A History of the English Church and People*, tr. Leo Sherley-Price. Baltimore: Penguin Books, 1955.

Beevers, John. 1953. *The Sun Her Mantle*. Dublin: Browne and Nolan.

Behrens, Helen. 1966. *The Virgin and the Serpent God*. Mexico City: Progresso.

Bergoénd, Bernardo. 1967. *La Nacionalidad Mexicana y la Virgen de Guadalupe*. Mexico City: Jus.

Bhardwaj, S. H. 1973. *Hindu Places of Pilgrimage in India*. Berkeley: University of California Press.

Bieler, Ludwig. 1960. "Topography of Lough Dearg." *The Irish Ecclesiastical Record*. March.

Bloy, Léon. 1907. "Celle qui pleure (Notre-Dame de la Salette)." In *Oeuvres*, ed. Jacques Petit, pp. 111–259. Reprinted, Paris: Mercvre de France, 1970.

—— 1947. *Pilgrim of the Absolute*. Selections by Raïssa Maritain; Introduction by Jacques Maritain. New York: Pantheon Books.

Bond, H. A. 1960. *The Walsingham Story through 900 Years*. Walsingham: Greenhoe Press.

Bonilla Luis. 1965. *Los peregrinos*. Madrid: Biblioteca Nueva.

Braden, Charles. 1930. *Religious Aspects of the Conquest of Mexico*. Durham, N.C.: Duke University Press.

Brown, Paul Alonzo. 1930. *The Development of the Legend of Thomas Becket*. Philadelphia: University of Pennsylvania Press.

Burton, Richard F. 1893. *Narrative of a Pilgrimage to Al Madinah and Meccah*. Memorial ed. 2 vols. New York: Dover, 1964.

Bushnell, John. 1958. "La Virgen de Guadalupe as Surrogate Mother in San Juan Atzingo." *American Anthropologist* 60:261–65.

Byrnes, Joseph F. 1975. "Pilgrimage at Chartres, from the Second Empire to the End of World War I." Paper prepared for the seminar on Comparative Symbology at the University of Chicago. Unpublished.

Callejo, Carlos. 1968. *El Monasterio de Guadalupe*. Madrid: Plus-Ultra.

Camarino, Angelo di. 1923. *Il Santuario di Loreto*. Pesaro.

Camelot, P. T. 1962. *Ephèse et Chalcédoine*. Vol. 2 of *Histoire des Conciles Oecuméniques*. Paris.

—— 1967. "The Council of Ephesus." *New Catholic Encyclopedia*. New York: McGraw-Hill.

Carey, F. P. 1939. *Lough Derg and Its Pilgrimage*. Dublin: *Irish Messenger* Office.

Casola, Pietro. *See* Newett, M. Margaret.

Cassidy, J. L. 1958. *Mexico: Land of Mary's Wonders.* Paterson, N.J.: St. Anthony's Guild.

Castro, Américo. 1954. *The Structure of Spanish History,* tr. Edmund I. King. Princeton: Princeton University Press.

Cauvenburgh, E. van. 1922. *Les pèlerinages expiatoires et judiciares dans le droit communal de la Belgique au Moyen Âge.* Louvain.

Cava, Ralph della. 1970. *Miracle at Joaseiro.* New York: Columbia University Press.

Chanal, André. 1942a. *Le Puy en Velay.* Le Puy: Jeanne d'Arc.

—— 1942b. *Cloître du Puy.* Le Puy: Jeanne d'Arc.

Christian, William A., Jr. 1972. *Person and God in a Spanish Valley.* New York and London: Seminar Press.

Clerval, Jules Alexandre. 1896. *Chartres: Its Cathedral and Monuments.* Reprinted, Chartres: Renier, 1926.

Colín, Mario. 1968. *Indice de documentos relativos a los pueblos del Estado de México,* in *Ramo de mercados del archivo general de la nación.* Vol. 1. Mexico City: Biblioteca Enciclopedica.

Cortés, Hernán. n.d. *Cartas de Relación.* Mexico City: Porura. 1960.

Courten, Sigismond de. 1938. *Notre-Dame des Ermites.* Einsiedeln: Benziger.

Coyne, William D. 1935. *Knock Shrine.* Galway: O'Gorman.

—— 1948. *Our Lady of Knock.* New York: Catholic Books.

—— 1953. *The Venerable Archdeacon Cavanagh.* Bridgemount, Ireland: Knock Shrine Society.

—— 1957. *Cnoc Mhuire in Picture and Story.* Dublin: Frederick Press.

Csikszentmihalyi, Mihaly. 1975a. "Play and Intrinsic Rewards." *Journal of Humanistic Psychology* 15:41–63.

—— 1975b. *Beyond Boredom and Anxiety: The Experience of Play in Work and Games.* San Francisco: Jossey-Bass.

Cuevas, Mariano. 1928. *Historia de la iglesia en México,* vol. 1. Reprinted Mexico City: Editorial Patria, 1946.

Curtayne, Alice. 1944. *Lough Derg: St. Patrick's Purgatory.* London: Burns, Oates and Washbourne.

Cushing, Richard Cardinal. n.d. *Mary.* Boston: Daughters of St. Paul.

D'Alton, Edward. 1928. *History of the Archdiocese of Tuam,* vol. 2. Dublin: Phoenix.

Deery, Joseph. 1958. *Our Lady of Lourdes.* Dublin: Browne and Nolan.

Delahaye, Hippolyte. 1933. *Les origines du culte des martyrs.* Brussels: Bollandistes.

Delaport, Yves. 1927. *Le Voile de Notre-Dame.* Chartres.

Demarest, Donald, and Taylor, Coley. 1956. *The Dark Virgin.* Freeport, Maine: published by Coley Taylor.

Deyrieux, L. 1943. *Notre-Dame de Fourvière.* Grenoble, France: Revue des Alpes.

Díaz del Castillo, Bernal. 1521. *The Discovery and Conquest of Mexico*, ed. Genaro García, tr. A. P. Maudslay. New York: Noonday Press, 1965.

Dickinson, J. C. 1956. *The Shrine of Our Lady of Walsingham*. Cambridge: Cambridge University Press.

Dingre, Gajanam. 1968. "A Study of a Temple Town and Its Priesthood" (Pandharpur). Unpublished Ph.D. Dissertation. University of Poona, Deccan College Post-Graduate and Research Institute.

Dowse, Ivor. 1963. *The Pilgrim Shrines of England*. London: Faith Press.

Duffy, Joseph. 1972. *Patrick in His Own Words*. Dublin: Veritas.

Du Vallon, Ludovic. 1928. *Documents nouveaux sur Rocamadour*. Marseilles.

—— 1935. "Les pèlerinages expiatoires et judiciares de Belgique aux sanctuaires de Provence au Moyen Âge." *Provincia: Bulletin de la Société Historique de Provence et de Marseille*, vol. 15.

—— 1937. "Les pèlerinages expiatoires et judiciares de Belgique à Rocamadour." *Bulletin trimestrial de la société des études littéraires, scientifiques et artistiques de Lot*, vol. 58.

Eliade, Mircea. 1971. *The Myth of the Eternal Return*. Princeton: Princeton University Press.

England's Nazareth: A History of the Holy Shrines of Our Lady of Walsingham. Published by the Guardians of the Shrine of Our Lady of Walsingham.

Erasmus, Desiderius. 1512. Great Britain, *Calendar of Letters and Papers, Foreign and Domestic*, Henry VIII.

—— 1540. *Ye Pylegremage of Pure Deuotyon*. Newly translatyd into Englishe. London(?): Press of John Byddele(?).

Estrade, Jean-Baptiste. 1899. *Les apparitions de Lourdes*. Tours: Maison Mame.

Fabri, Felix. *See* Palestine Pilgrims Text Society.

Felice, Philippe de. 1906. *L'Autre monde*. Paris: Champion.

Frankfort, Henri. 1954. *The Art and Architecture of the Ancient Orient*. Baltimore: Penguin Books.

Fuente, Vicente de la. 1879. *Vida de la Virgen Maria con la historia de su culto en España*, vol. 2. Barcelona.

Fuller, M. 1880. *Our Lady of Walsingham*. London: Kelly.

Gallery, J. I. 1960. *Mary vs. Lucifer*. Milwaukee: Brace.

Ganshof, F. L. 1966. "Pèlerinages expiatoires flamands à Saint-Gilles pendant le XIVᵉ siècle." *Annales du Midi* 78:391–407.

García, Genaro. 1909. *Historia incidental de Nuestra Señora de los Remedios*. Mexico City: Jus.

García Gutiérrez, Jesus. 1875. *Datos historicos sobre la Venerable Imagen de Nuestra Señora de Guadalupe de México*. 2d ed. Mexico City: Jus, 1940.

García Icazbalceta, Joaquin. 1947. *Don Fray Juan de Zumarraga*. 4 vols. Mexico City: Porrua.

Garibay, A. M. 1967. "Our Lady of Guadalupe." *New Catholic Encyclopedia*. New York: McGraw-Hill.

Geertz, Clifford. 1972. "Deep Play: Notes on the Balinese Cockfight." *Daedalus* 101:1–37.

—— 1972. "Religion as a Cultural System." In W. A. Lessa and E. Z. Vogt, eds., *Reader in Comparative Religion*, pp. 167–78. 3d ed. New York: Harper and Row.

Gennep, Arnold van. 1908. *The Rites of Passage*. New ed. London: Routledge and Kegan Paul, 1960.

Gibbons, Margaret. 1937. *The Ownership of Station Island, Lough Derg: With a Brief Historic Sketch of the Pilgrimage*. Dublin: James Duffy.

Gillett, H. M. 1946. *Walsingham*. London: Burns, Oates.

—— 1949. *Famous Shrines of Our Lady*, vol. 1. London: Samuel Walker.

—— 1953. *Famous Shrines of Our Lady*, vol. 2. London: Samuel Walker.

—— 1957. *Shrines of Our Lady in England and Wales*. London: Samuel Walker.

Goldkind, Victor. 1966. "Class Conflict and Cacique in Chan Kom." *Southwestern Journal of Anthropology* 22:325–45.

Gossen, Gary. 1972. "Temporal and Spatial Equivalents in Chamula Ritual Symbolism." In W. A. Lessa and E. Z. Vogt, eds., *Reader in Comparative Religion*, pp. 135–48. 3d ed. New York: Harper and Row.

Gray, Robert F. 1963. *The Sonjo of Tanganyika*. London: Oxford University Press.

Grimes, Ronald. 1976. "Ritual Studies: Two Models." *Religious Studies Review* 2, 4:13–25.

Gross, Daniel R. 1971. "Ritual and Conformity: A Religious Pilgrimage to Northeastern Brazil." *Ethnology* 10:132–39.

Hakluyt, Richard. 1589. *The Principall Navigations, Traffiques, and Discoveries of the English Nation*. Reprinted, New York: Dutton, 1926.

Hall, Donald. 1965. *English Mediaeval Pilgrimages*. London: Routledge and Kegan Paul.

Hamil, Hugh M., Jr. 1966. *The Hidalgo Revolt*. Gainesville: University of Florida Press.

Hanson, F. A. 1975. *Meaning in Culture*. London: Routledge and Kegan Paul.

Hardy, Philip Dixon. 1836. *The Holy Wells of Ireland*. London: Groombridge.

Heath, Sidney. 1911. *Pilgrim Life in the Middle Ages*. London: Fisher Unwin.

Henderson, Arthur E. 1967. *Canterbury Cathedral Then and Now*. London: Society for the Propagation of Christian Knowledge.

Hickey, D. F. 1967. "Dormition of the Virgin." *New Catholic Encyclopedia*. New York: McGraw-Hill.

Hobgood, John. 1970a. *Chalma: A Study in Directed Cultural Change*. Huixquilucan Project, Working Papers. Madison, Wisc.: Department of Anthropology, University of Wisconsin.

Hobgood, John. 1970b. *A Pilgrimage to Chalma*. Huixquilucan Project, Working Papers. Madison, Wisc.: Department of Anthropology, University of Wioconoin.

Houvet, Étienne. 1930. *Monographie de la Cathédrale de Chartres*. Chartres.

Huizinga, Johan. 1950. *Homo Ludens*. New York: Roy.

—— 1924. *The Waning of the Middle Ages*. Reprinted, New York: Doubleday, Anchor Books, 1956.

Hunt, Eva. 1976. *The Transformations of the Hummingbird*. Ithaca, N.Y.: Cornell University Press.

Jarrett, Bede. 1911. "Pilgrimages." *The Catholic Encyclopedia*, ed. C. Herbermann *et al*. New York: Appleton.

Juan Diego: Revista Guadalupano. Monthly. Cuernavaca. (Passim.)

Jugie, Martin. 1944. *La Mort et l'Assomption de la Sainte Vierge: Étude historico-doctrinale*. Vatican: Biblioteca Apostolica Vaticana.

Jusserand, J. J. 1891. *English Wayfaring Life in the Middle Ages (XIV Century)*, tr. Lucy Toulmin Smith. London: T. Fisher Unwin.

Keyes, Charles F. 1976. "Notes on the Language of Processual Symbolic Analysis." Unpublished synopsis of a course of lectures, Department of Anthropology, University of Washington.

King, Georgiana Goddard. 1920. *The Way of St. James*. 3 vols. London: Putnam.

Knock Shrine Annual. 1965. Bridgemount, Ireland: Knock Shrine Society.

—— 1973. Bridgemount, Ireland: Knock Shrine Society.

Laurentin, René. 1973a. "The Persistence of Popular Piety." In A. Greeley and G. Baum, eds., *The Persistence of Religion*. New York: Herder and Herder.

—— 1973b. *Lourdes: Documentation authentique*. Paris: Lethellieux.

—— and Durand, A. 1970. *Pontmain: Histoire authentique, documents*. Paris: Lethellieux.

Layral, J. T. 1912. *Défense de la tradition de St. Amadour*. Paris: Vie et Amat.

Lazo de la Vega, Fr. Luis. 1649. *Huei Tlamahuicoltica: El Gran Acontecimiento*. Mexico City: Carreno e hijo, 1926.

Le Braz, Anatole. 1906. *The Land of Pardons*, tr. Frances M. Gostling. London: Methuen.

Leclerc, C. 1907. "St. Anne of Beaupré." *The Catholic Encyclopedia*, ed. C. Herbermann *et al*. New York: Appleton.

Lee, G. 1910. "The Shrine of Guadalupe." *The Catholic Encyclopedia*, ed. C. Herbermann *et al*. New York: Appleton.

Leies, Herbert. 1964. *Mother for a New World*. Westminster, Md.: Newman Press.

Lemieux, Ernest. 1954. *Marie: Documents pontificaux sur La Très Sainte Vierge parus depuis un siècle, 1854–1954*. 2 vols. Quebec: Les Presses Universitaires Laval.

Leon-Portilla, Miguel, ed. 1972. *The Broken Spears: The Aztec Account of the*

Conquest of Mexico. Tr. from Nahuatl into Spanish by Angel Maria Gari-bayk; English tr. by Lysander Kemp. Boston: Beacon Press.

Leslie, Shane. 1917. *The Story of St. Patrick's Purgatory*. St. Louis and London: Herder.

—— 1932. *Saint Patrick's Purgatory*. London: Burns, Oates and Washbourne.

—— 1961. *Saint Patrick's Purgatory*. Monaghan, Ireland: At the Sign of the Three Candles.

Lewis, B. 1966. "Hadjdj." *Encyclopaedia of Islam*. Leiden: Brill.

—— 1976. "The Return of Islam." *Commentary* 61:39–49.

López Beltrán, Lauro. 1966. *La Protohistorica Guadalupe*. Mexico City: Jus.

Maas, A. J. 1912. "Virgin Mary, the Blessed." *The Catholic Encyclopedia*, ed. C. Herbermann *et al.* New York: Appleton.

MacCulloch, J. A. 1932. *Medieval Faith and Fable*. London: Harrap.

MacNeill, Máire. 1962. *The Festival of Lughnasa: A Study of the Survival of the Celtic Festival of the Beginning of Harvest*. London: Oxford University Press.

Madsen, William. 1960. *The Virgin's Children*. Austin: University of Texas Press.

—— 1967. "Religious Syncretism." In M. Nash, ed., *Handbook of Middle American Indians*, pp. 369–91. Austin: University of Texas Press.

Maquet, J. J. 1954. "The Kingdom of Ruanda." In *African Worlds*, ed. C. Daryll Forde, pp. 164–89. London: Oxford University Press for the International African Institute.

María Carreno, Alberto. 1950. *Don Fray Juan de Zumárraga*. Mexico City: Jus.

Marrus, Michael R. 1976. "Culture on the Move: Pilgrims and Pilgrims in Nineteenth-Century France." Paper read to Davis Center Seminar, Princeton University, January 16, 1976.

Martínez, Luis M. 1963. *El Poema del Tepeyac*. Collección Mariana, no. 28. Madrid: Ediciones Stvdivm.

Maza, Francisco de la. 1953. "El Guadalupanismo Mexicano." *México y lo Mexicano*, vol. 17. Mexico City: Porrua y Obregon.

Mexico City. Archivos de la Basilica de Santa María de Guadalupe. "Informaciones de 1666." Copy of the Original, October 27, 1751.

Migne, J. P., ed. 1850. *Encyclopédie théologique*, vols. 43, 44, on "Pilgrimage," passim. Paris: Ateliers Catholiques du Petit-Montrouge.

Myerhoff, Barbara. 1974. *Peyote Hunt: The Sacred Journey of the Huichol Indians*. Ithaca: Cornell University Press.

Neumann, Erich. 1955. *The Great Mother*, tr. Ralph Manheim. Princeton: Princeton University Press, 1972.

Newett, M. Margaret. 1907. *Canon Pietro Casola's Pilgrimage to Jerusalem; in the Year 1494*. Manchester: Manchester University Press.

Northcote, J. Spencer. 1868. *Celebrated Sanctuaries of the Madonna*. London: Longman Green.

Nutini, Hugo. 1970. "A Brief Theoretical Sketch of Syncretism and Acculturation." Unpublished manuscript. Department of Anthropology, University of Pittsburgh.

—— 1976. *Ritual Kinship: The Structural and Historical Development of the Compadrazgo System in Rural Tlaxcala, and Its Comparative and Ideological Implication for Latin America*. Pittsburgh: University of Pittsburgh Press.

O'Connor, D. 1903. *St. Patrick's Purgatory, Lough Derg*. Dublin: Duffy, Gill.

Oursel, Raymond. 1963. *Les pèlerins du Moyen Âge*. Paris: Fayard.

Pagani, Antonio. 1907. *Santa Casa di Loreto*. Rome: Desclee.

Palacio y Basave, L. del R. de. 1942. *Nuestra Señora de Zapopan*. Guadalajara, Jalisco: José Garibi Rivera.

—— 1950. *Breve Historia de Nuestra Señora de Zapopan*. Guadalajara, Jalisco: Basilica de Zapopan.

Palestine Pilgrims Text Society. Vol. 1. Eusebius. A.D. 337. *The Churches of Constantine*, tr. by John H. Bernard. London, 1891.

—— Vol. 1. A.D. 385. *Pilgrimage of St. Sylvia of Aquitania to the Holy Places*, tr. John H. Bernard. London, 1891.

—— Vol. 1. A.D. 754. *The Hodoeporicon of St. Willibald*, tr. Rev. Canon Brownlow. London, 1891.

—— Vol. 1. St. Jerome. A.D. 382–84. *Pilgrimage of the Holy Paula*, tr. A. Stewart. London, 1887.

—— Vol. 3. A.D. 670. *The Pilgrimage of Arculfus in the Holy Land*, tr. Rev. James Rose Macpherson. London, 1889.

—— Vol. 3. A.D. 876. *Itinerary of Bernard the Wise*, tr. H. Bernard. London, 1893.

—— Vol. 10. Felix Fabri. 1483. *The Book of the Wanderings of Brother Felix Fabri*, tr. A. Stewart. London, 1887–97.

Partin, Harry Baxter. 1967. "The Muslim Pilgrimage: Journey to the Center." Ph.D. Dissertation, University of Chicago Divinity School.

Paston Letters, The. 1422–1529. Ed. James Gairdner. Westminster: Constable, 1904.

Paul, J. and P. 1942. *Notre-Dame du Puy*. Le Puy: Jeanne d'Arc.

Pérez y Gomez, Antonio. 1965. *Dos Historias*. Valencia: Artes Gráficas Soler.

Perrin, Sainte-Marie. 1942. *La Basilique de Fourvière*. Lyons: Lescuyer.

Philibert, J. M. 1942. *Notre-Dame du Puy*. Le Puy: Jeanne d'Arc.

Philips, G. E. 1917. *Loreto and the Holy House*. London: R. T. Washbourne.

Pirenne, Jacques. 1959. *The Tides of History*, tr. L. Edwards. London: Allen and Unwin, 1963.

Popper, William. 1921. "Pilgrimage, Hebrew and Jewish." *Encyclopaedia of Religion and Ethics*, ed. James Hastings. New York: Scribner.

Prescott, W. H. 1891. *History of the Conquest of Mexico*. 3 vols. Philadelphia: David McKay.

BIBLIOGRAPHY

Quirk, Robert. 1971. *Mexico*. Englewood Cliffs, N.J.: Prentice-Hall.
Quiroz y Gutiérrez, Nicanor. 1940. *Historia de la Aparición de Nuestra Señora de Ocotlán*. Puebla: Mexico.
Ramos, Samuel. 1934. *Profile of Man and Culture in Mexico*. Reprinted, Austin: University of Texas Press, 1962.
Redfield, Robert. 1956. *Peasant Society and Culture*. Chicago: University of Chicago Press.
Ricard, Robert. 1966. *The Spiritual Conquest of Mexico*. Berkeley: University of California Press.
Richards, Audrey. 1956. *Chisungu*. London: Faber and Faber.
Ringholz, P. Odilo. 1904. *Histoire du Monastère de Einsiedeln*. Einsiedeln, Waldshut, and Cologne: Benziger.
Robertson-Smith, W. 1889. *The Religion of the Semites*. Reprinted, New York: Meridian Books, 1959.
Roure, Lucian. 1912. "Visions." *The Catholic Encyclopedia*, ed. C. Herbermann *et al.* New York: Appleton.
Roussel, Romain. 1954. *Les Pèlerinages à travers les siècles*. Paris: Payot.
Rupin, E. 1904. *Roc-Amadour: Étude historique et archéologique*. Paris: Baranger.
Ryan, John. 1972. *Irish Monasticism*. Shannon: Irish University Press.
Sahagún, Bernardino de. 1529. *Historia de las cosas de Nueva España*, vol. 3. Reprinted, Mexico City: Porrua, 1956.
Sanctuaires de la Vierge dans Luxembourg. 1943. Brochure Mariale, no. 9. Namur: Comité Marial.
Sapir, Edward. 1935. "Symbols." *Encyclopedia of the Social Sciences*. New York: Macmillan.
Sardo, Joaquin. 1810. *Relación historica y moral de la portentosa imagen del Sr. Jesucristo aparecida en una de las cuevas de S. Miguel de Chalma*. Mexico City: Casa de Arizpe.
Sartre, Jean-Paul. 1969. "Itinerary of a Thought." *New Left Review* 58.
Schlarman, Joseph H. L. 1951. *México: Tierra de volcanes*. Mexico City: Jus.
Schneider, David M. 1968. *American Kinship: A Cultural Account*. Englewood Cliffs, N.J.: Prentice-Hall.
Septien García, Carlos. 1940 (July). "Fifty Years of Guadalupan Pilgrimage." *La Voz Guadalupana: Mexicana Revista de Cultura*, p. 16. Monthly. Mexico City: Basilica of Guadalupe.
Sharbrough, Steven. 1975. "El Ciclo de los Pastores." *History of Religions at UCLA, Newsletter* 3:7–11.
Shields, J. A. 1971. *Guide to Lourdes*. Dublin: Gill.
Sigal, Pierre André. 1974. *Les Marcheurs de Dieu: Pèlerinages et Pèlerins au Moyen Âge*. Paris: Armand Colin.
Simson, Otto von. 1956. *The Gothic Cathedral: Origins of Gothic Architecture and the Medieval Concept of Order*. Reprinted, New York: Harper, 1967.
Solis, Miguel Flores. 1972. *Nuestra Señora de los Remedios*. Mexico City: Jus.

Sollier, J. F. 1911. "Communion of Saints." *The Catholic Encyclopedia*, ed. C. Herbermann *et al*. New York: Appleton.

Soustelle, Jacques. 1955. *Daily Life of the Aztecs*. Reprinted, Stanford: Stanford University Press, 1970.

Starkie, Walter. 1965. *The Road to Santiago*. Berkeley and Los Angeles: University of California Press.

Stephenson, Colin. 1970. *Walsingham Way*. London: Darton, Longman, and Todd.

Stone, J. S. 1927. *The Cult of Santiago*. New York: Longmans, Green.

Thompson, J. Eric. 1970. *The Rise and Fall of Maya Civilization*. 3d ed. Norman: University of Oklahoma Press.

Thurston, Herbert. 1912. "Virgin Mary." *The Catholic Encyclopedia*, ed. C. Herbermann *et al*. New York: Appleton.

—— 1912. "Santa Casa di Loreto." *The Catholic Encyclopedia*, ed. C. Herbermann *et al*. New York: Appleton.

—— 1925. *The Roman Jubilee: History and Ceremonial*. London: Sands.

Tibón, Gutierre, ed. 1956. *Diccionario Etimológico Comparado de Nombres Propios*. Mexico City: Union Tipografica Editorial Hispano Americana.

Tinkle, Lon. 1965. *Miracle in Mexico: The Story of Juan Diego*. New York: Hawthorn Books.

Tormo y Monzó, Elías. n.d. *Monasterio de Guadalupe*. Barcelona: Hijos de J. Thomas.

Tornel y Mendivil, Julián. 1849. *La aparición de Nuestra Señora de Guadalupe de México*, vol. 1. Orizava, México: José Ma. Naredo.

Turner, Frederick C. 1968. *The Dynamic of Mexican Nationalism*. Chapel Hill, N.C.: University of North Carolina Press.

Turner, Victor. 1957. *Schism and Continuity*. Manchester: Manchester University Press.

—— 1966. "Ritual Aspects of Conflict Control in African Micropolitics." In M. Swartz *et al*., eds., *Political Anthropology*, pp. 239–46. Chicago: Aldine.

—— 1967a. *The Forest of Symbols*. Ithaca, N.Y.: Cornell University Press.

—— 1967b. "Aspects of Saora Ritual and Shamanism: An Approach to the Data of Ritual." In A. L. Epstein, ed., *The Craft of Social Anthropology*, pp. 181–204. London: Tavistock.

—— 1968a. *The Drums of Affliction*. Oxford: Clarendon Press.

—— 1968b. "Myth and Symbol." *International Encyclopedia of the Social Sciences*, ed. D. Sills. New York: Macmillan.

—— 1968c. "The Waters of Life: Some Reflections on Zionist Water Symbolism." In J. Neusner, ed., *Religions in Antiquity: Essays in Memory of Erwin Goodenough*, pp. 506–20. Leiden: Brill.

—— 1969. *The Ritual Process*. Chicago: Aldine.

—— 1971. "Introduction." In R. Spencer, ed., *Forms of Symbolic Action*, pp. 3–25. Seattle: University of Washington Press.

—— 1973. "The Center Out There: Pilgrim's Goal." *History of Religions* 12:191–230.

—— 1974a. *Dramas, Fields, and Metaphors*. Ithaca, N.Y.: Cornell University Press.

—— 1974b. "Liminal to Liminoid, in Play, Flow, and Ritual: An Essay in Comparative Symbology." *Rice University Studies* 60:53–92.

—— 1974c. "Pilgrimage and Communitas." *Studia Missionalia* 23:305–27.

—— 1975a. *Revelation and Divination in Ndembu Ritual*. Ithaca, N.Y.: Cornell University Press.

—— 1975b. "Death and the Dead in the Pilgrimage Process." In Michael G. Whisson and Martin West, eds., *Religion and Social Change in Southern Africa: Anthropological Essays in Honour of Monica Wilson*, pp. 107–27. Cape Town: David Philip and Rex Collings.

—— 1975c. "Symbolic Studies." In B. Siegal *et al.*, eds., *Annual Review of Anthropology*, pp. 145–61. Palo Alto: Annual Reviews.

—— 1978. "Variations on a Theme of Liminality." In Sally Moore, ed., *Secular Ritual*, pp. 27–41. Leiden: Van Gorcum.

Ugarte, José Bravo. 1947. *Historia de México*, vol. 2. Mexico City: Jus.

Vaillant, G. C. 1953. *The Aztecs of Mexico*. Bungay, Suffolk: Penguin Books.

Velásquez, Primo Feliciano. 1931. *La aparición de Santa María de Guadalupe*. Mexico City: Imprenta Patricio Sanz.

Verrie, F. P. (Undated but post-1948.) *Los monumentos cardinales de España*. Vol. 9. Madrid.

Wallace, Anthony F. C. 1956. "Revitalization Movements." *American Anthropologist* 58:264–81.

Waterton, E. 1879. *Pietas Mariana Britannica*. London.

Watson, Simone. 1964. *The Cult of Our Lady of Guadalupe*. Collegeville, Minn.: The Liturgical Press.

Wensinck, A. J. 1966. "Hadjdj." *Encyclopaedia of Islam*, Leiden: Brill

Wilson, Monica. 1957. *Rituals of Kinship among the Nyakyusa*. London: Oxford University Press.

Wolf, Eric R. 1958. "The Virgin of Guadalupe: Mexican National Symbol." *Journal of American Folklore* 71:34–39.

Yogeshananda, Swami. 1973. *The Visions of Sri Rama krishna*. Madras: Sri Ramakrishna Math.

Index

Page references to the principal treatment of an entry are in boldface.

273